KENTUCKY'S LAND OF THE ARCHES

A descriptive guide of Kentucky's Red River Gorge in the Daniel Boone National Forest and Natural Bridge State Park.

By Robert H. Ruchhoft
Associate Professor Emeritus of History
The University College, University of Cincinnati

New Revised and Enlarged Edition
Thirteenth Printing

All photographs by the Author except where otherwise noted

P.O. Box 19161
Cincinnati, Ohio 45219

ACKNOWLEDGEMENTS TO FIRST EDITION

If this book fails in its purpose, I must accept the blame; but if it succeeds, on the other hand, I know the manuscript's information, organization and readability has been improved by the special knowledge and talents provided by the following individuals: To my University College Colleagues, Bill Bocklage, Harry Horner and Jackie Jones for reading the original manuscript and giving me their experienced judgment on content and style; to my fellow educator and outdoor enthusiast, John Watts who helped me in many areas, especially the Geology section; to Carl Clark and Clarence Henson who both have explored the vicinity of the Red River Gorge for over three decades and shared with me their encyclopedic knowledge of the area; to Steve Stacey and Dell Sasser, the former naturalists of Natural Bridge State Park, for the many hours they spent with me on and off the trails enriching my limited knowledge of plant and animal life of the area; to Don Fig and John Moore of the Staton Ranger Station of the U.S. Forest Service for aiding me with maps, trail measuring devices, official booklets on environmental statements and area management as well as answering hundreds of questions about the area in general; to Larry Meadows of the Red River Historical Society who kindly lent me many rare articles and documents which helped me greatly with the historical sections; to my wife, Nancy, the eagle eye of the misspelled word and the badly constructed sentence, who, while doing the difficult job of proofreading the galley sheets discovered a multitude of errors that had slipped by unnoticed in the earlier readings of the manuscript; and to Shirley Thorpe who took many of my crude and often vague sketches and turned them into understandable diagrams.

I want to give special thanks to Bruce and Myra Poundstone. Bruce has probably done more and worked harder than anyone I know to increase the enjoyment and understanding of the average visitor. He has enriched the knowledge of thousands of tourists during his weekend evening slide shows at Hemlock Lodge, often later arranging specific hikes and auto tours for special groups. I don't think he could have been as successful an ambassador in the vicinity of Natural Bridge for these many years without his wife, Myra. With her calm disposition and understanding of her husband, she has always given him the necessary support while he openly carried on an affair with his other great love—the Natural Bridge/Red River Gorge area.

Many a time I have asked Bruce about a particular spot that I couldn't locate or needed help in exploring and found him rearranging his schedule so he could personally accompany me to the desired location. Often my wife, Nancy, was able to accompany us because Myra Poundstone volunteered to babysit with our two young daughters during our absence. Such noble gestures for our benefit goes far beyond the call of duty and shows a warmth and desire to help others which is a tribute to these two rare human spirits.

(for new acknowledgements, see Preface to the Revised Edition.)

PREFACE TO THE REVISED EDITION

While taking a family vacation in the Great Smoky Mountain National Park some years before I began writing this book, I happened on a small, inexpensive guide to the trails of that marvelous hiking area. I was impressed with the author's ability to give good, easy to understand trail descriptions which left you with the feeling that you wanted to hike the trail. It also was balanced nicely between short, easy walks and more arduous treks. It gave me much food for thought and ideas that I later incorporated into the first writing of this book.

Several years later on a return trip to the Smokies, I discovered the same book was still selling well. I was disappointed to find that, although several of the trails had been rerouted or done away with, there had been no attempt to ever revise the book and it was badly out of date. When I completed this book, I vowed that if it continued to sell I would not let that happen. From the second printing on, minor changes were incorporated. But as time passed, I saw that a major revision was going to be necessary. Even though the book was still selling well, after eight years of publication and 12,000 copies sold, I felt uncomfortable about republishing a book that was now inaccurate and incomplete in many places. I therefore, let it go out of print and began this rewrite. I thought I could accomplish the task in six months. But, with the problems of completing and publishing a new book called BACKBACK LOOPS AND LONG DAY HIKES IN SOUTHERN OHIO, plus the many changes I found had to made in this volume, the task took a full two years. So, this revised edition is being published exactly ten years after the original printing, almost to the very month.

I think those of you that are familiar with the first edition will notice that I have learned much about improving such a volume through the ensuing years. Many things have changed in the Gorge during those ten years. The geologic features remain pretty much the same and will largely remain so during our short transitory visit to this planet. But there are many man-made changes. New trails, as well as reroutings, improvements, and name changes of old trails brought on not only much rewriting, but also required a substantial number of additional pages. New land acquisitions in key locations have opened up several exciting areas for hikers and sightseers that previously would have required trespassing.

And there are the human changes, too. The two very small children that can be seen under Natural Bridge on this book's picture cover are my own. Almost babies then, they are now young ladies busy pursuing their college careers. In reviewing the material of the first edition, I was reminded, over and over again, of the tremendous help Bruce Poundstone had been to me in bringing out that first printing. He was excited about this revision and probably would again have been tremendously helpful in bringing it to fruition. But a serious illness slowed him down and he died before I could finish this rewriting project. He will be missed by many of us.

Don Fig of the Stanton Ranger District again was as helpful as he had been for the first volume. His many years of experience in the Gorge has proved invaluable to me in this rewriting.

For several years the visitors to Natural Bridge State Park have enjoyed the knowledgeable presentations and expertise of its naturalist, Wilson Francis. He too has aided me many times in my research and helped me with many a knotty problem. These two men are the most knowledgeable public servants in the Gorge today and their help has aided me in turning out a book that I hope will continue to help visitors get the most out of a visit to this beautiful Kentucky area.

In the equally important activities of editing, word processing and many other details of transforming scribbled handwritten sheets to the printed pages of this book, I am deeply indebted to Mike and Linda Sears. Linda often did battle with me in trying to carve down my long winded sentences and, occasionally, won. She and her husband, Mike, were responsible for getting the entire book on computor disc, ready for the typesetter. They also assisted me in countless other ways, both at home and on the trail, speeding up the rewriting task by many months.

TABLE OF CONTENTS

MAPS

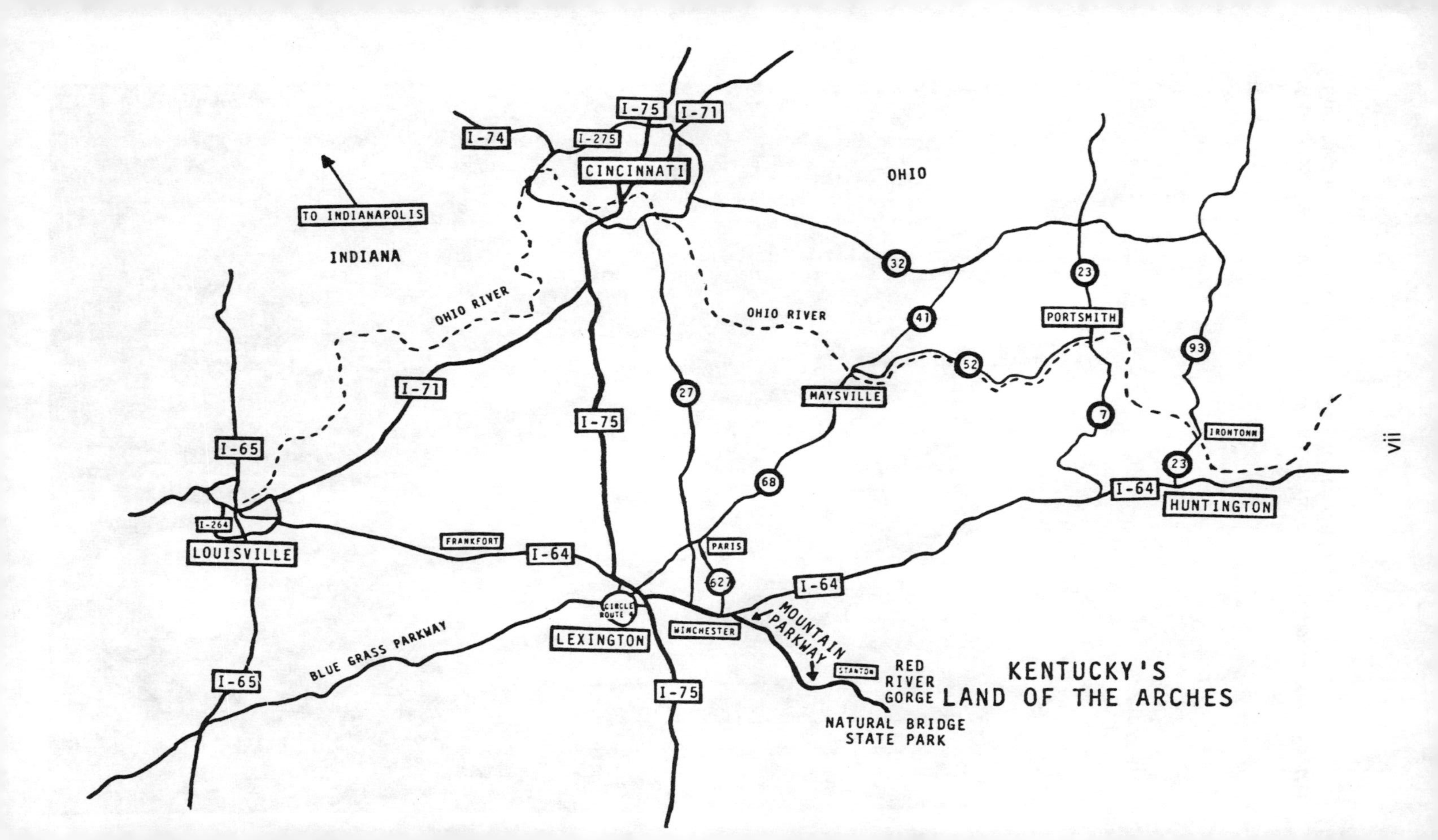
KENTUCKY'S
LAND OF THE ARCHES
RED
RIVER
GORGE
NATURAL BRIDGE
STATE PARK
STANTON
MOUNTAIN
PARKWAY
I-74
I-275
I-75
I-71
CINCINNATI
OHIO
TO INDIANAPOLIS
INDIANA
OHIO RIVER
OHIO RIVER
32
23
41
PORTSMITH
93
52
27
MAYSVILLE
I-71
I-75
7
IRONTOWN
I-65
23
68
I-64
HUNTINGTON
I-264
LOUISVILLE
FRANKFORT
I-64
PARIS
627
I-64
CIRCLE
ROUTE 4
LEXINGTON
WINCHESTER
BLUE GRASS PARKWAY
I-65
I-75

Ninety foot ice tower formed in 1977 below falls in the Torrent Rock Shelter (Courtesy of Larry Meadows & Red River Historical Society

I
HOW TO USE THIS BOOK

This volume is roughly divided into two separate parts; the first covers the introduction, the geologic formation of the arches and a brief chronicle of man's experiences in the Gorge. The second part describes the things to be seen and how to get to them. If you are reading these pages while planning a visit to the area or if you are already there, glance over the book in the evening before an exploratory trip, continue with the introduction and read through the geology and history sections. This will aid you in choosing the various trips you feel will be most worthwhile and give you a better understanding and appreciation of what you are going to see.

If you obtained the book just before you're ready to leave on a trail or drive, read the section called "Trail Tips-Safety and Suggested Hikes" beginning on page 30 , then turn to the specific place you wish to visit, saving the introduction, geology and history sections for evening reading. To aid those who are entirely new to the area, I have included a suggested itinerary for sightseeing and hiking in that same chapter to help you get the most scenic value for the time you have to spend. Several maps are included designed to make it easier for you to find your way around the area. The large area map located in the back of the book on pages 164 and 166 covers the roads and trails of the entire region. This map also shows the areas covered by the detailed maps in the text and the page numbers where both the maps and trail descriptions may be found. The page numbers for the trails as well as the individual maps are also given in the Table of Contents.

FIRST IMPRESSIONS: WHAT'S AROUND THE BEND

As you travel southeast on the Mountain Parkway, a dramatic scenery change occurs when you round a certain curve about seven miles east of Interstate 64. There, in the distance, you can see the rolling hills of the Bluegrass yield to what looks like a low mountain range. My own emotional reaction when I first rounded that curve several years ago was not unlike the ones I felt when approaching the Smokies near Sevierville, Tennessee, or the front range of the Rockies in Colorado. Since this sudden rise in east central Kentucky, known to geologists at the Pottsville Escarpment, tops out at an altitude of only 1,300 feet, it is questionable if these high ridges should qualify as mountains. The local people feel that they do and refer to the general area as the place where "the Bluegrass meets the mountains". If not high, the topography's sudden ruggedness can produce a similar emotional impact simply by its dramatic contrast.

Most people are attracted to the area by the famous Natural Bridge, not realizing that it is only one of several natural arches in the vicinity or that the combined acreage of the State Park and the National Forest holds a wealth of sightseeing adventures. I remember a lady I once met in the Natural Bridge Campground who told me, "When you see all those ridges in the distance you know that there must be hundreds of wonderful things to see."

And indeed, there are. In an area of about 30 square miles, the Red River Gorge and Natural Bridge State Park house a marvelous collection of palisades, rock promontories, solitary pinnacles and spires, numerous natural arches and a multitude of cascading mountain streams.

The Red River Gorge has even occasionally been said to resemble the Grand Canyon of the Colorado, although the Gorge is only about 1/10th as deep and in no way packs the emotional wallop one experiences when first looking into that awesome panoramic chasm in Arizona. There are, however, some features of the Gorge that suggest, in a far less spectacular way, its gargantuan cousin in the West.

The Gorge has its exclusiveness too. For example, nowhere else in the world are there as many natural arches as there are in the compressed vicinity of the Red River Gorge area. The known number of natural openings there has now passed 100. The only area in the United States that can boast anywhere near as many is Arches National Park in Utah. If many of the western arches are larger and more spectacular, the Gorge arches are more varied in their size and geological development. The Gorge arches are often found in the company of large cave-like rock shelters or recess caves which are not found in any abundance in the Utah park.

This is a blessed land for the lover of plants and wild flowers as well. Because of the altitude change in the Gorge and the variety of soils along the escarpment of the ridges, approximately 1,000 different wild flowering plants have been identified as blooming naturally in the area. Flowers bloom in the Gorge that are usually found only farther to the north in Michigan and Canada. Other varieties are found which more generally favor the warmer climates of southern Appalachia. The region has been called, without gross exaggeration, "The best natural botanical garden in the eastern United States."

With the completion of the Mountain Parkway in 1963, a modern chain of super highways, including I-75 and I-64 make this once remote area easily accessible by automobile. The constant increase in the number of visitors might lead you to expect an overflow of unsightly commercial establishments, giving the Gorge a honkey-tonk like atmosphere and destroying the solitude of this natural wilderness area. This, happily, has not happened, and most of the area remains in a largely unspoiled state.

On popular weekends from the spring through the fall, there are, indeed, hundreds of visitors, but most of them seem to cluster at Hemlock Lodge or the campgrounds. Usually the short trails to Natural Bridge and Sky Bridge are sometimes crowded, leaving the rest of the trails in seclusion for the more devoted hikers. Further, in the 50 odd miles of official trails, there are hikes for walkers of every ability.

PURPOSE OF THIS GUIDE BOOK

I remember that lady in the campgound telling me, "It just takes so long to find where everything is and how to get there. You waste half your time just finding out." This book will help you save those wasted hours for sightseeing.

Time and again, I have met people on trails who had no idea how difficult the trails were or any good idea of what they were going to see along the way. Too often I have found exhausted hikers who had bitten off more than they could chew. I have found them lost or confused because trail markers had been destroyed or turned around by vandals. There are sections of trail that are confusing because many unofficial paths have obscured the real path or natural growth and erosion have made it difficult to follow. When I first walked these trails I felt more than once like the old Indian who said, "Me not lost. Trail lost."

There are others who are simply unaware of how beautiful a land this is. I recall overhearing a very attractive young lady as she viewed that marvelous panorama extending out across the valley of Middle Fork from the top of Natural Bridge. Somewhat awestruck, she turned to the young man alongside her and said, "And to think all these years I thought Kentucky was just a place you passed through on your way to Florida!"

WHAT IS NOT IN THE BOOK

Although I have included all the official trails in the area and some off-trail locations, there are many beautiful off trail spots in the vicinity that I have not included for the simple reason that it would have made the book far too long and too cumbersome to carry on hikes. There are directions on how to find at least twenty arches and many other unusual natural formations worth a visit included in this book. That leaves about 80 of the less spectacular and more remote arches to be sought after by the more adventurous.

I have also avoided writing about the wild flowers for several reasons. Even the barest description of the hundreds of the most commonly seen blooms would have made this book encyclopedic in size. There are several excellent books already available written by knowledgeable naturalists who have done in-depth studies. The most complete is, *A Guide to the Wildflowers and Ferns of Kentucky* by Mary Warton and Roger Barbour, University of Kentucky Press, Lexington, Kentucky, 40506. The same authors have also written *Trees and Shrubs of Kentucky,* also published by the University of Kentucky Press.

Some may find it irritating that I have not mentioned specific places or trails for seeing wildflowers. Bitter experience has taught me that to do so would be the worst kind of folly. To mention a specific area for exceptional wildflower sightings would be to condemn it, for thoughtless pickers would turn the blooming profusion into a desert within a year. A general rule of thumb for finding wildflowers is usually the busier the trail the fewer the flowers. But even the popular trails offer a variety of wild blooms for the sharp-eyed visitor. I remember a walk I took along a very popular trail one September afternoon and identified fourteen separate species of blooming wildflowers in less than half a mile. Generally, late April and early May have the largest number of blooming plants, but the summer and early fall are almost as good. There are blooming plants in this area from early March through late November.

OTHER ACTIVITIES

Besides the great natural outdoor show, there are lectures given either in the Activities Center or Hemlock Lodge in Natural Bridge State Park on Friday and Saturday nights throughout the year. Guided trail hikes and motor caravans with the State Park Naturalist are occasionally scheduled leaving from the lodge on pleasant weekends. There is no charge for either the lectures or guided trips and you do not have to be a lodge guest to attend the evening lectures or to take the guided trips. Lectures are also often given in the Koomer Ridge Campground by a Forest Service naturalist during summer weekend evenings.

Organized square dancing is held every weekend on Hoe Down Island in the State Park during the season. The State Park also has a swimming pool and paddle boats. Both Mill Creek Lake and Swift Creek are stocked with trout. A variety of bass and pan fish as well as trout are found both in the lake and local streams. There is even a native variety of muskalonge in the Red River.

If you are looking for night clubs, go-go girls and a carnival-like atmosphere, the area is not for you. If a natural arch means nothing more to you than a place to throw an empty beer can or to carve your initials on its million-year-old surface, you will be bored here. If you feel wildflowers are there for the picking, the very essence of the Gorge's beauty will pass you by. But if you are looking for a variety of the natural world's unspoiled contrasts, the Natural Bridge-Red River Gorge area is a pleasant place to visit.

THE BEST TIME TO COME

More and more visitors are finding this area a four-season favorite. The spring with its abundance of wildflowers, and the fall with the color of the turning seasons are in many ways the best. Spring and fall weekends are terribly busy, but during the week one can actually feel lonesome on the trails. I once walked the trails for five straight weekdays in September with ideal weather conditions and met but two hikers in all that time.

Summer is the busiest week-day season, and it is busier still on weekends. It is not my favorite time of year for hiking in the area, for walking up and down the escarpments in the summer months can be very hot and there is little breeze for relief. Unless you like wall-to-wall people, tent cities, traffic jams on roads and trails, avoid the area as if it had an outbreak of the plague during Memorial Day, Fourth of July and Labor Day weekends. Too many people avoid the winter months who might otherwise enjoy them. If you are interested in things geologic, the absence of foliage opens up the ridges giving the viewer a much better panorama of the terrain. With the many pine and hemlock trees, the forest is never without a fair amount of greenery. If you can schedule a visit after the area has had several days of below freezing temperatures, you will find that the water dripping from hundreds of ledges and cliffs produces giant icicles by the thousands. Snow is uncommon, but when it settles on the undulating ridges and forests, it turns the area into a Currier and Ives wonderland.

WHERE TO STAY

Campgrounds:

There are three public campgrounds in the vicinity. Two of them, Whittleton Branch Campground and Middle Fork Campground are in Natural Bridge State Park and have entrances on Kentucky State Route 11 (#IX on large map). The exact entrances of these two campgrounds are shown on the Natural Bridge State Park map on page 52. There are electrical hookups, modern toilet facilities and hot showers at both camps. From May through October they fill up fast on weekends. Space is almost always available on weekdays. There are special areas for tents and small tent trailers, and many sites are available for larger trailers and motor homes. At least one of the two camps is open in all but the coldest of the winter months.

The other organized public campground is the beautifully situated Koomer Ridge Campground managed by the Forest Service on Route 15 between Slade and Pine Ridge (#III on large map). A few sites are available for large trailers and motor homes. One area is restricted to tents only. During the normal camping season water is available and there are pit toilets, but there are no electrical hookups. Although always open during the popular seasonal camping months, winter closing dates of this campground are affected by changing federal policies and budget considerations. It fills up fast on pleasant weather weekends during the spring and fall.

The forest service has also designated five areas as primitive campgrounds, which are mostly in open fields, each having a pit toilet but no water. Two are located on Tunnel Ridge Road, two on Chimney Top Road, and one on Rock Bridge Road.

Backcountry camping is permitted on the federal lands of the forest in the Gorge area as long as the campsites are at least 100 yards from a road or organized campground and out of sight of any official trail. Some popular areas of the Gorge, especially around Gray's Arch, have been overused by backpackers causing serious ecological damage. Such areas are occasionally posted as no camping locations to give the surroundings a rest and restore them to their natural state. Backpackers should not bury garbage (dogs and other animals dig it up). Pack out all litter and cut no green wood. No camping is permitted outside the organized campgrounds in Natural Bridge State Park.

Lodgings:

Hemlock Lodge and cabins are located in Natural Bridge State Park on Kentucky Route 11 (#IX on large map). The exact location of both the lodge and the cabins is shown on the Natural Bridge State Park map. Hemlock Lodge offers both food and lodging the year around. Because of its popularity, you should have reservations well in advance of a proposed visit even during the winter months. The cottages are open from the spring through the fall, and reservations for them are made through Hemlock Lodge.

Address:

Hemlock Lodge
Natural Bridge State Park
Slade, Kentucky 40376

Phone: Area Code (606) 663-2214

A modern motel is located on Route 11 between Slade and Natural Bridge State Park. It is:

Lil Abner Motel. Phone: Area Code (606) 663-5384

Lil Abner is closed during the winter months. Abner Motel has a restaurant.

Two small motels are located near the Gorge area on Route 15 between Slade and Pine Ridge. They are: Mountain Park Motel. Open all year. Phone: Area Code (606) 668-3551 Sky Bridge Motel. Open all year. Phone: Area Code (606) 668-3526

There is one motel in the nearby town of Stanton some 12 miles from the Gorge area. Abner's Motel is on Routes 11 and 15 in the center of Stanton about a block north of the Stanton exit of the Mountain Parkway. It is open year around. Phone: Area Code (606) 663-4379.

THE END OF THE BEGINNING

I hope your own personal discovery of the Red River Gorge Natural Bridge area will be aided and enhanced by the reading of this book. From the diminutive subtleness of tiny wildflowers to the grand spectacles of high ochre-colored cliffs and seventy-foot arches, I have found it an exciting outdoor world to explore. If some readers feel that my descriptions are overstated, I can only confess that my writing here reflects the emotional impact the area has made upon me by my many visits there through the years. No chamber of commerce hired me to write sparkling superlatives to attract visitors. I have been affected only by what I have seen and I have written what I believe is a fair description of the area. I sincerely hope that this book leads you to corners you otherwise might have missed, helps you do the type of sightseeing that suits your energies and abilities, and enables you to make the best use of your time in the Gorge area.

II
THE GEOLOGIC HISTORY OF THE GORGE AREA AND HOW THE ARCHES WERE FORMED

One day in 1923, when the first visitors' lodge was being constructed at Natural Bridge, a group of young workmen were sitting around the small hamlet of Slade, Kentucky, killing time on their day off. An automobile pulled up alongside and the driver asked if any of them knew the way to Natural Bridge.

"Gawd, I ought to," replied one of the young builders, "I helped build it."

There are a few people who come to this land of arches who are probably firmly convinced that Natural Bridge isn't natural at all. Most visitors know that these 100 odd arches are natural phenomena but haven't the foggiest notion of how all those openings got there in the first place. This section is devoted to the few who would like to find out.

TYPES OF SEDIMENTARY ROCK

All layers of rock in the valleys of the Gorge are what is called sedimentary rock. There are three basic types of sedimentary rocks: shale, limestone, and sandstone. All three are found abundantly in the Gorge area and they were all deposited in two geologic periods known as the Mississippian and the Pennsylvanian. If one understands how these three different sedimentary rock deposits were formed, one has the basic knowledge to appreciate the fundamental geological developments here.

Shallow seas, swamps and rivers covered the area on several occasions in the geologic past. Deposits from the water settled to the bottom. Each time these seas and swamps advanced and retreated, they left layers of mud and sand which were later compressed into rock by the tremendous weight of other layers deposited above them. The sedimentary rock type eventually formed was determined by the kind of material that was deposited.

Originally, the sedimentary rock known as shale was deposited as clay rich mud. After being compressed into rock, this clay mud became shale. Not all such shales are alike. Their variety is caused by organic differences in the clay deposits, as well as the amount of pressure they were subject to after they were laid down. These local shales are soft and are easily eroded away, therefore none of the natural arches are found in shale strata.

Limestone also began as mud. The original deposits consisted of a lime rich ooze known as calcareous mud often interspersed with many sea shells. It was compressed into rock by the same process that created the shales. Allthough limestone is far harder than shale, calcium carbonate, the rock's main mineral, dissolves easily with continuous exposure to running water. Such characteristics lead to the making of caves where limestone deposits are thick and there is continuous underground stream activity. These conditions caused Mammoth Cave and many other large caves in the western part of the state. Since the limestone beds are relatively thin in the Gorge area, the few caves discovered here are small and insignificant. Natural arches are sometimes formed in limestone, and such arches do exist in the vicinity of the Gorge.

As the name suggests, the basic ingredient of sandstone is sand. Deposited along ancient shorelines and stream beds, these sands were consolidated by the pressure of overlying beds and natural cementing agents. Like the other two sedimentary rocks, limestone and shale, there are several types of sandstone of varying hardness and grades. These variations are caused by the type of sand, the cementing agents and the pressure involved. One type is known as conglomerate sandstone. Conglomerates are formed when thousands of pebbles settle in among sand particles. The pressure and cementing agents glue all of them together in solid rock layers. This type of sandstone is also known as pebble rock.

MISSISSIPPIAN AND PENNSYLVANIAN PERIODS

The lowest layers of rock strata one can see exposed in the valleys were deposited during a long expanse of time known to geologists as the Mississippian period. When the Mississippian began some 300 million years ago, the climate was generally mild. Much of the rock strata was deposited on the bottom of shallow seas which rose and retreated, forming a series of layers that became the sedimentary rock of the Mississippian. Layers laid down in the late Mississippian forming the top levels of this geologic period are classified together in this area as the Waverly Formation. This formation forms the lower strata of the Gorge.

The uppermost layers of the Gorge were formed during the next geologic age, the Pennsylvanian. Beginning about 260 million years ago, the Pennsylvanian got its name from the great coal fields found in Pennsylvania, West Virginia and eastern Kentucky. Sediments of the Pennsylvanian were less marine than those of the Mississippian in the vicinity. They contain far more of the plant life which grew in many prehistoric swamps. This decaying matter became the basic ingredient of the coal deposits.

Only the very earliest deposits of the Pennsylvanian remain in the vicinity of the Red River Gorge, and they do not include significant layers of coal. The larger and more famous coal beds, however, were here at one time. When you stand on the span of Natural Bridge or on the top of any of the high ridges, you are on a rock stratum that was formed before the large coal layers and, at one time, was below them. Several million years ago these large seams of coal and other sedimentary deposits extended thousands of feet above the exposed ridge tops of today. Geologists believe altitudes here then exceeded 12,000 feet above present sea level. What happend to all that material, especially the valuable beds of coal? In Figure #1 you can see, in a somewhat simplified and generalized drawing, how the major strata were laid down across central Kentucky in flat horizontal beds. All of the upper Pennsylvanian, including the larger coal deposits have been eroded here by stream action over periods of millions of years. The erosion activity was speeded up by a change of position of the original beds throughout this area.

THE CINCINNATI ARCH

About 40 million years after the Pennsylvanian period, a twisting of the earth's surface caused a general uplifting of the geologic strata extending north and south through central Kentucky and into southern Ohio. Such an uplifting is known as an anticline. This anticline, called the Cincinnati Arch, left the beds warped in a dome-like structure as shown in Figure #2. With the beds of the Pennsylvanian and later deposits thrust upward in the highest part of the arch which was above the present area of the Bluegrass region today, they were subject to rapid stream erosion. Figure #3 diagrams the same area today with the top of the Cincinnati Arch eroded. The hardness of the sandstone and the conglomerate layers make them more resistant to erosion than the other layers in the original deposits. This has caused a sharp front of ridges known as the Pottsville Escarpement which runs roughly north and south and forms the caplayers of the ridge tops in the Gorge area.

THE CREATION OF THE GORGE

If you look across the valleys from Chimney Top Overlook, Raven's Rock, Sky

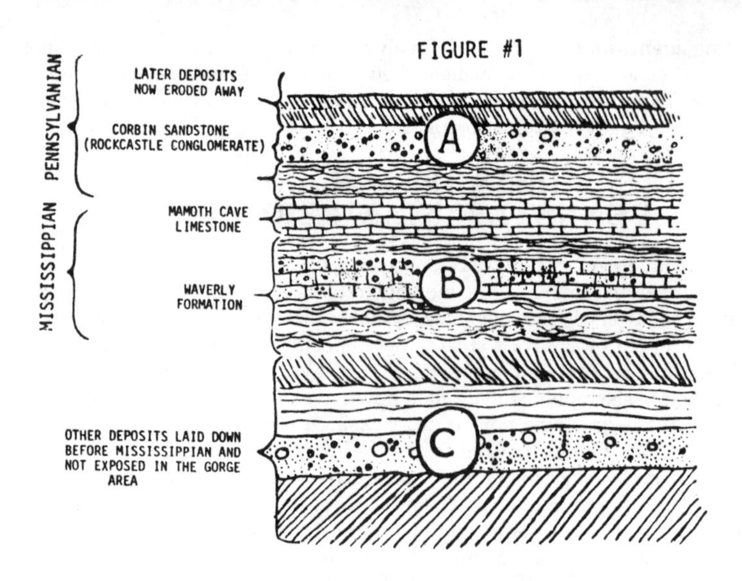

FIGURE #2

BEDS AT THE TIME OF THE FORMING OF THE CINCINNATI ARCH

PENNSYLVANIAN

MISSISSIPPIAN

AREA OF THE RED RIVER GORGE

CORBIN SANDSTONE

MAMOTH CAVE LIMESTONE

WAVERLY FORMATION

DEPOSITS LAID DOWN BEFOREMISSISSIPPIAN

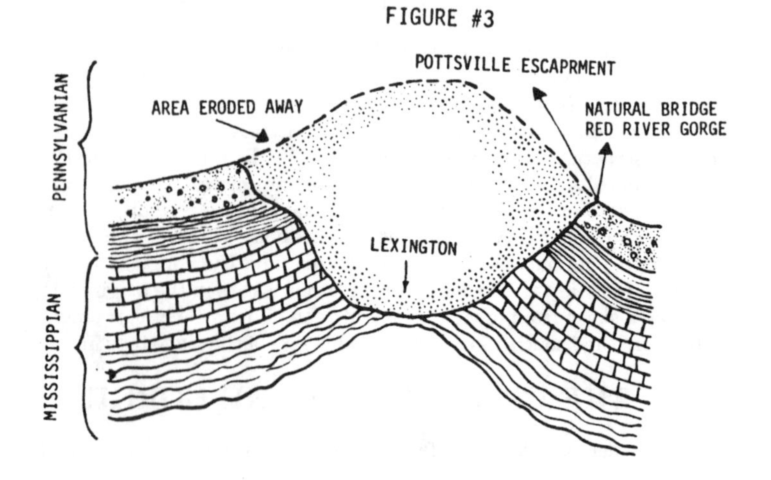

Bridge or Natural Bridge to the high cliff area on the far sides, you can see what the erosion process has done. Once there were no such valleys or gorges. Through a long period of geologic history, after the upthrusting of the Cincinnati Arch, the Red River and its tributaries began the slow work of cutting the gorge and valleys that are there today. The cliffs and ridges were formed because of the toughness of the sandstone layers. If these top layers had been less resistant to erosion, the valleys would now be surrounded by gentle hills rather than the ridge cliffs. Much of this sandstone was laid down, not on the bottoms of shallow seas, but by huge river deltas that once covered the area. Pebbles were deposited along with the sand on the bottom of the stream beds, making the sandstone a conglomerate or pebble stone. The cementing agent in this conglomerate is limonite, an iron oxide which gives these beds their rusty red appearance. Since limonite is an excellent cementing agent, it resulted in a particularly erosion-resistant pebble stone known locally as the Corbin sandstone (formerly called the Rockcastle conglomerate). This reddish colored conglomerate forms most of the capstone in the area. Most layers of sandstone were laid down under varying geologic conditions, explaining why some beds contain higher percentages of limonite than others. This means that some layers are stronger than others, and so the resistance to erosion varies from layer to layer.

WEATHERING

While there are at least four distinct ways that arches have been created in this area, all are caused by the geologic process called weathering. This is a process where rock is rotted away or destroyed by various natural agents, especially water. It seeps into the stone and dissolves the cementing iron oxide in the sandstone and calcium carbonate in limestone. With the removal of the cementing agents, the rock crumbles. Water seeping into cracks can fracture the rocks when it freezes and expands.

Other weathering agents are the roots of plants and trees that penetrate into crevices, splitting rocks, and wind which can blow the fractured particles away.

FORMATION OF ROCK SHELTERS, LIGHTHOUSES, RIDGE TOPS AND BUTTRESS ARCHES

There is no standard agreement among geologists about the name classification of different types of arch formations. Some of the following names and classifications used here are in general use and some are my own. My guide in the selection of names was to use those that I felt would most easily be understood by the average reader.

The most common type of arch found in the Gorge area is cut into narrow ridges among the sandstone layers of the Corbin sandstone (Rockcastle conglomerate). These are generally located near the top of the sandstone capped ridges, hence the name, ridge top arches. Although the basic rock formations in the Red River Gorge-Natural Bridge area were laid down between 250 and 280 million years ago, formation of the natural arches was a fairly recent geologic event. There is no certain way to accurately date the beginning of the formation of an arch. Geologists have suggested that the hollowing out process began less than 10,000 years ago. Before the arches could be formed, surrounding rock layers had to be carved into narrow ridges by stream erosion as shown in Figure #4 and #5.

Once the valleys and gorges were cut, leaving the hard cliff faces of Rockcastle conglomerate, conditions were right for the formation of rock shelters, light houses and ridge top arches. Along the rock cliffs, the lower weaker layers of rock began to weather faster than the strata above. Beneath the Corbin sandstone (Rockcastle conglomerate) is the Beattyville shale which forms the area's lowest Pennsylvanian rock. Beneath it is the Mammoth Cave limestone which is the top layer

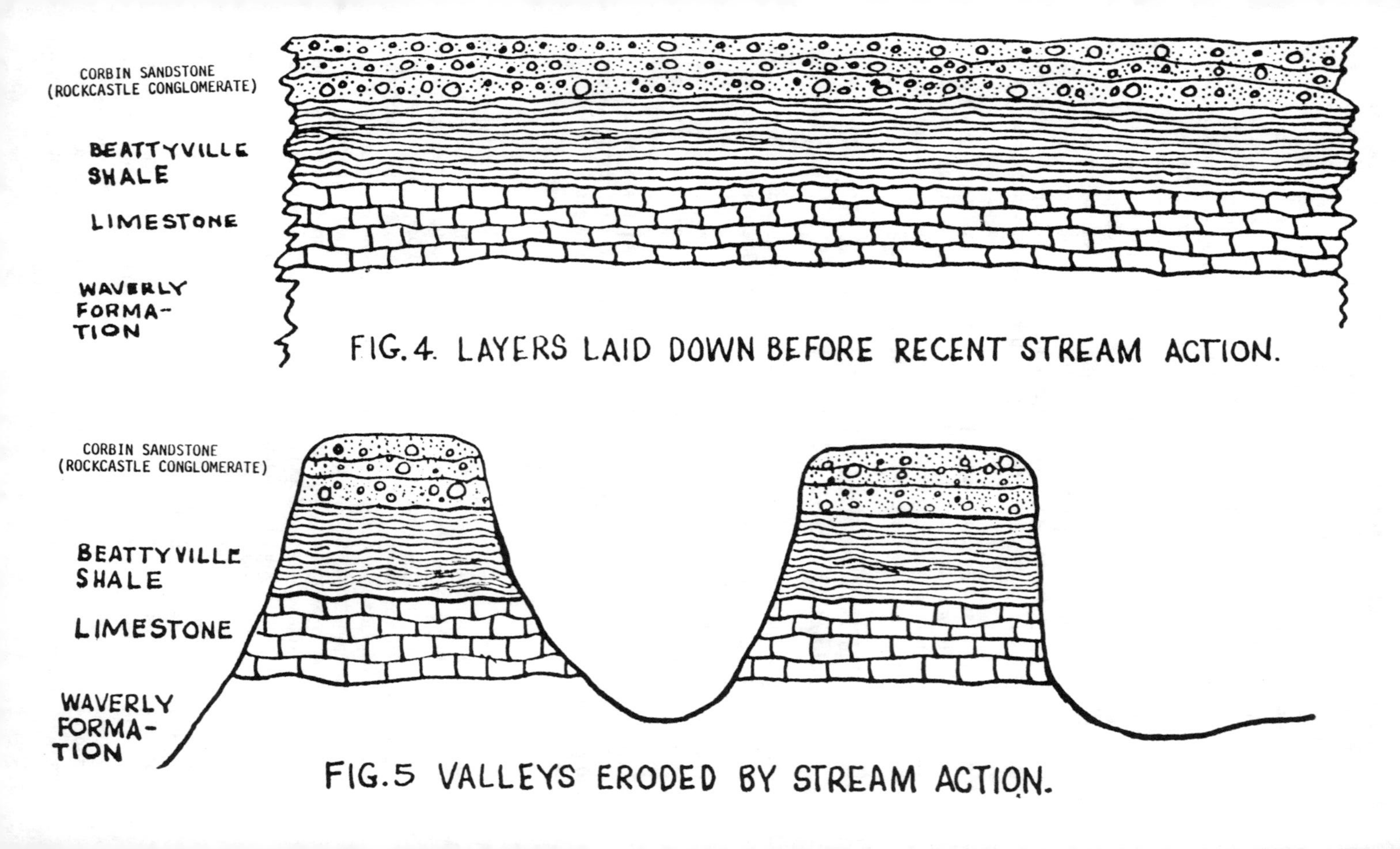

FIG. 4. LAYERS LAID DOWN BEFORE RECENT STREAM ACTION.

FIG. 5 VALLEYS ERODED BY STREAM ACTION.

FIGURE 6

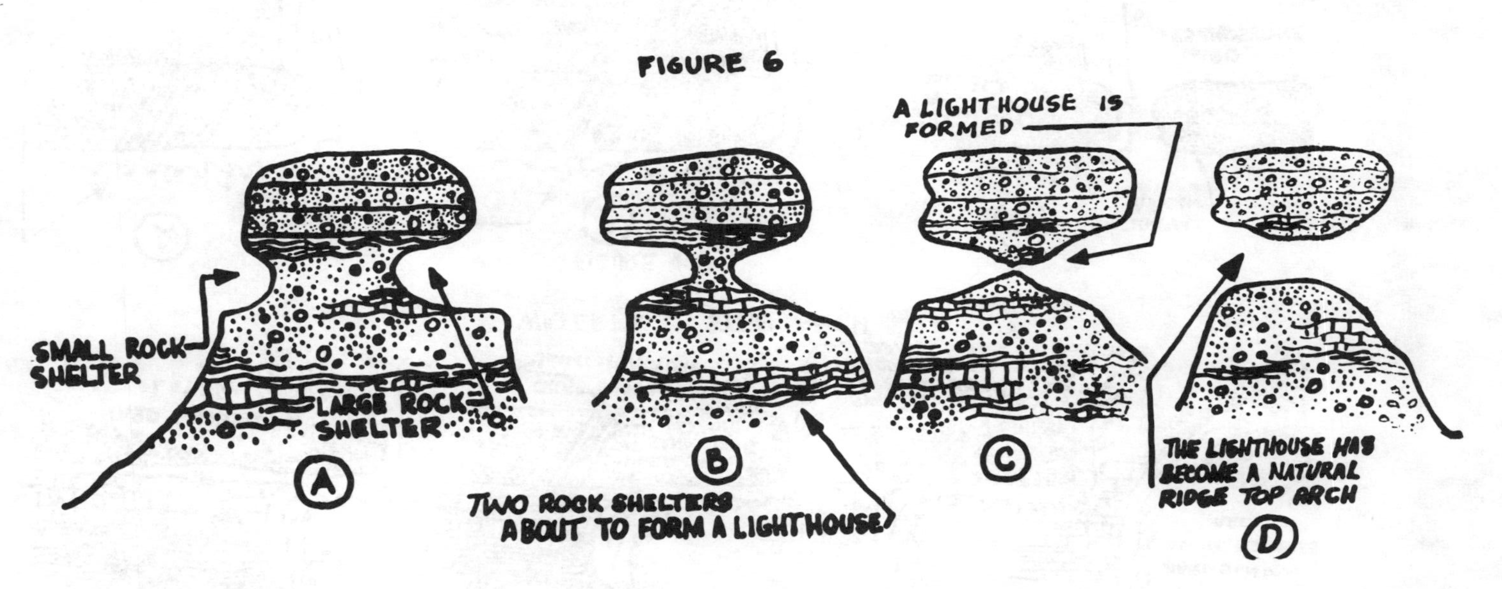
SMALL ROCK SHELTER
LARGE ROCK SHELTER
A
TWO ROCK SHELTERS ABOUT TO FORM A LIGHTHOUSE
B
A LIGHTHOUSE IS FORMED
C
THE LIGHTHOUSE HAS BECOME A NATURAL RIDGE TOP ARCH
D

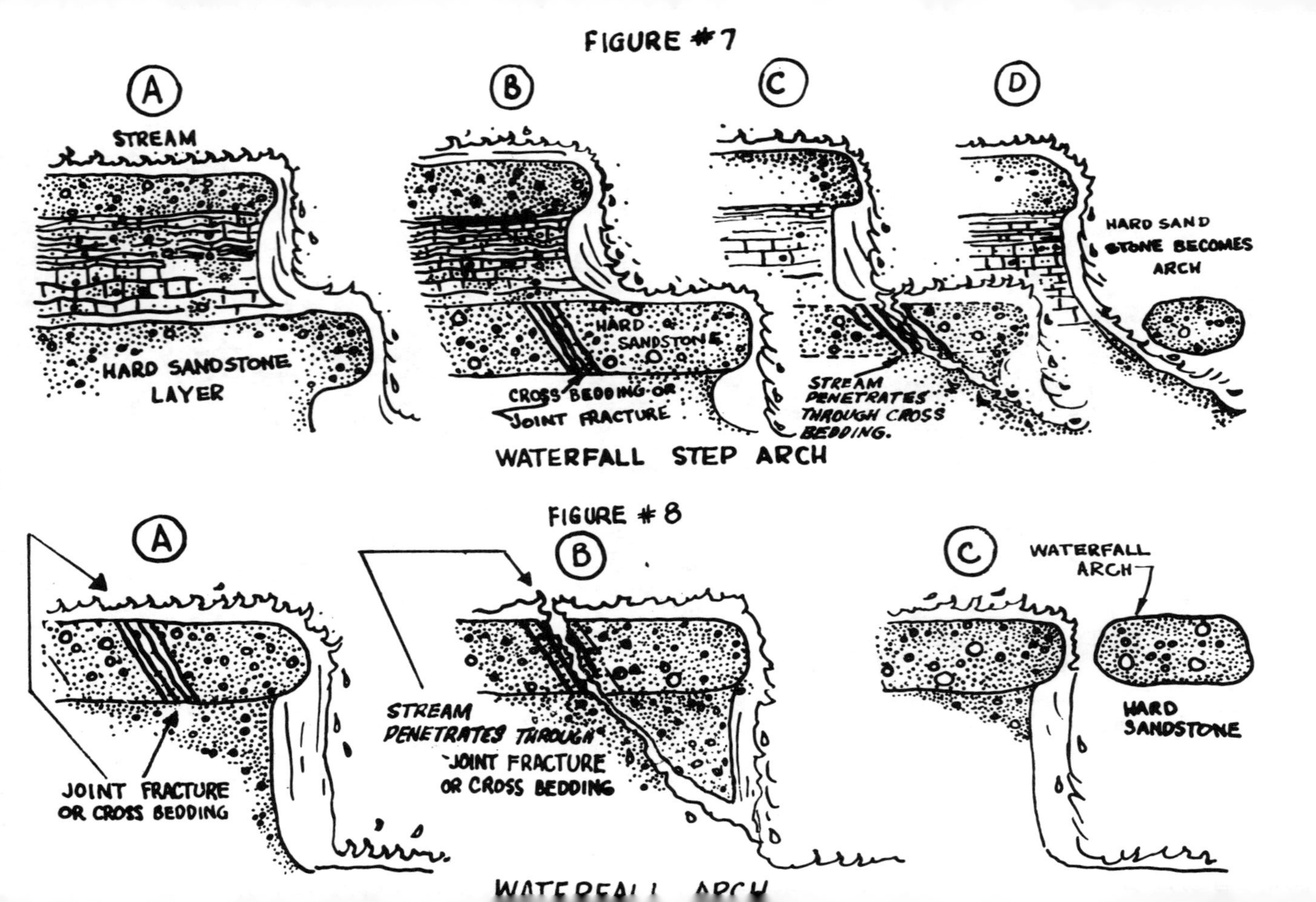

FIGURE #7
A
STREAM
HARD SANDSTONE LAYER
B
HARD SANDSTONE
CROSS BEDDING OR JOINT FRACTURE
C
STREAM PENETRATES THROUGH CROSS BEDDING.
D
HARD SAND STONE BECOMES ARCH
WATERFALL STEP ARCH
FIGURE #8
A
JOINT FRACTURE OR CROSS BEDDING
B
STREAM PENETRATES THROUGH JOINT FRACTURE OR CROSS BEDDING
C
WATERFALL ARCH
HARD SANDSTONE

of the Mississippian age. These two beds of shale and limestone are more easily eroded than the conglomerate sandstone. In addition, some of the less durable layers found in the Corbin sandstone, as well as some layers which appear to be tilted and are known as crossbeds, have eroded at a faster rate than those surrounding them. As sections of these layers weathered away along the sides of the ridges, they left an overhang of harder strata above, making a rock house, recess cave or rock shelter (Figure #6-A). These rock shelters do not extend deep into the rock as a cave would. There are literaly thousands of these rock shelters in the Red River Gorge-Natural Bridge area, their exposed entrances ranging in size from several feet to the length of a football field.

If a ridge is wide, as shown in Figure #6-A, rock shelters will remain rock houses for a long period of geologic time. If a ridge is narrow, as shown in Figure #6-B, it is likely that the deepest areas of two rock shelters on opposite sides of the ridge will eventually touch each other. A small hole would then be formed connecting the two rock shelters together as shown in Figure #6-C. Such a small hole is known as a lighthouse. When viewing one of these small openings as the setting sun shines through it, the intense pinpoint of light in the face of the otherwise dark cliff face suggests the bright illumination of an actual lighthouse. As this small hole increases in size, the lighthouse becomes a ridge top arch as shown in Figure #6-D. Although there is no set size on how large the opening must be before the lighthouse to natural arch transition takes place, some suggest that the name change should occur when an average sized adult is able to stand upright in the opening. As the arch increases in size, the outlines of the two rock shelters become less definite. Turtleback Arch, just off Swift Creek trail, is a good example of one of these openings that is in a transitory stage which is gradually destroying the general character of the two touching rock shelters.

As an arch increases in size, large chunks of rock will frequently break away from its underside. Such action results in very jagged edges along the bottom of the span and sharp rocks below. This is what is known as an arch in formation. Two good examples of this type are Castle Arch and Whistling Arch and both of them may be seen on the Gorge motor loop trip.

With time, the sharp edges are smoothed off by erosion, leaving a span of a more graceful appearance. Such arches are called finished arches. Both Princess Arch and Sky Bridge are good examples of this late stage of arch formation and both of them may also be seen on the Gorge motor loop trip.

While Natural Bridge is the best known ridge top arch in the area, there are certainly others one should see. For example, Sky Bridge is, in my opinion, the most beautiful and Gray's Arch the most awesome. All of the ridge top arches are in sandstone, well above the shale and limestone layers.

The buttress arch is formed in the same manner as the ridge top arch, but instead of being located in the middle of the ridge top, it is found at the declining end or finger of one. This rarer type of arch resembles the flying buttress of a French Gothic cathedral. Two classic examples of this type found in the Gorge are Gray's Arch and Indian Arch.

Sandstone arches are occasionally found well below the ridge tops, but these were formed by stream action and are found nearer the bottom of the valleys. Two types of these rarer arches are found in the Gorge Area.

WATERFALL STEP ARCH

The waterfall step arch, also sometimes called a valley head arch, begins when a waterfall with a precipitous drop hits a hard erosion resistant sandstone. As the top of the waterfall erodes, it washes away the weak sedimentary layers below it leaving a shelf as shown in Figures #7-A and B. Eventually, the retreating waterfall hits a weak segment in the harder sandstone strata such as a joint fracture

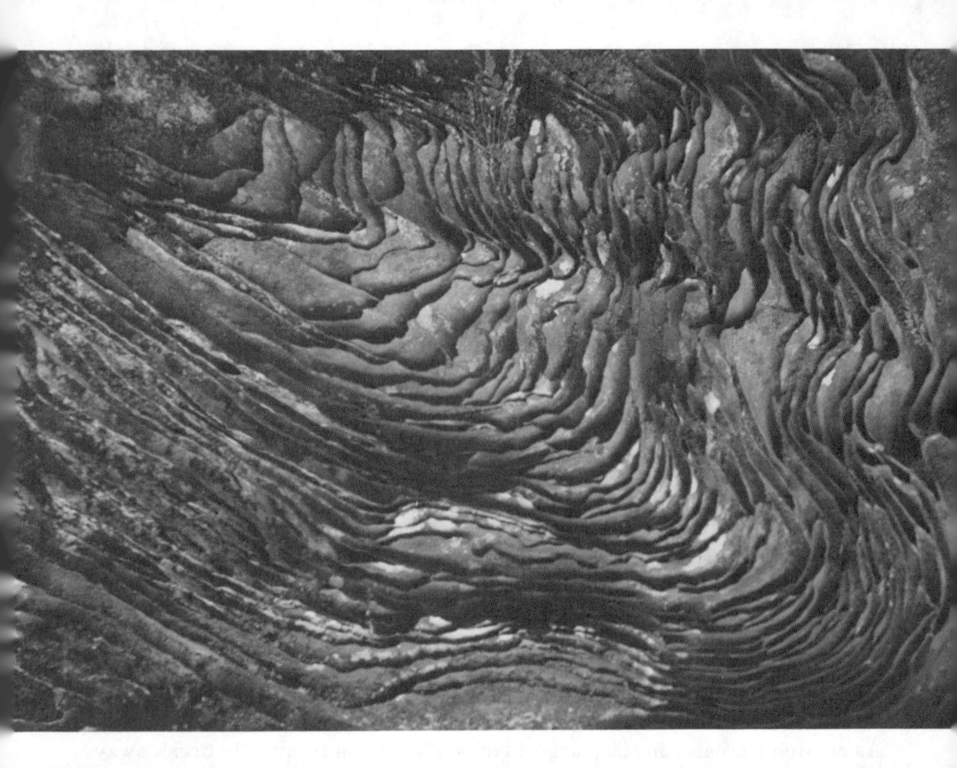

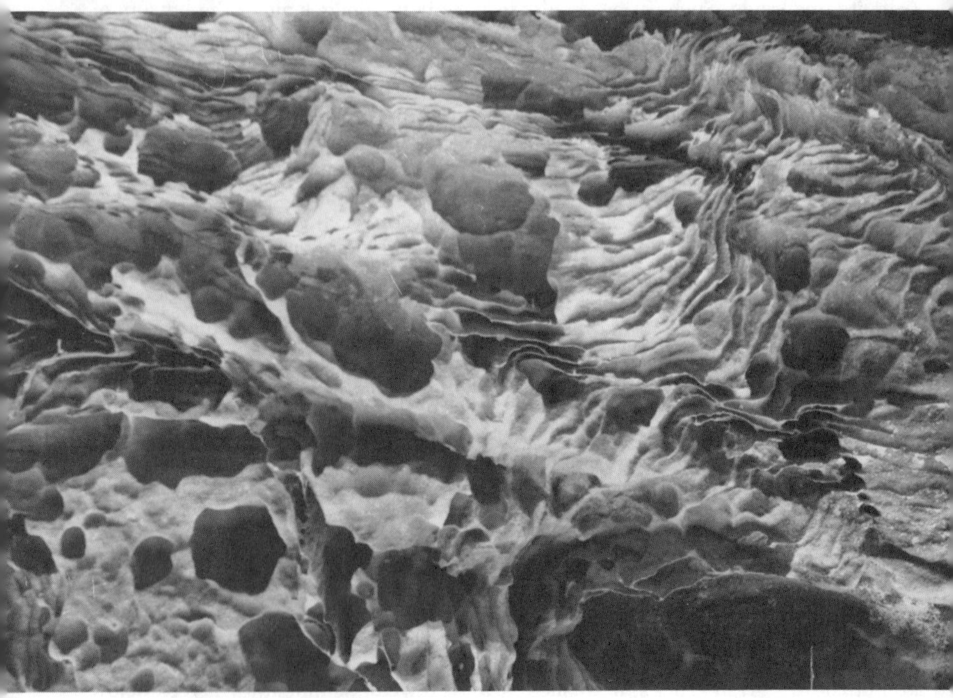

Interesting sandstone formations found near Rough Trail

or crossbedding as shown in Figure #7-C. Eventually, the waterfall undermines the shelf and isolates it creating an arch as seen in Figure #7-D.

There are two excellent examples of this type of arch in the Gorge area and both of them are on National Forest land. Whittleton Arch is the larger of the two with a front span of almost 100 feet. The smaller but equally interesting waterfall step arch is Silvermine Arch.

WATERFALL ARCH

The main difference between the waterfall step arch and the waterfall arch is that the forming arch is at the bottom of the waterfall in the former and at the top of the waterfall in the latter. Although the waterfall arch does not require a high waterfall, the arch was created in a manner similar to the waterfall step arch. The waterfall spills over the hard sandstone layer which forms the upper stream bed. This upper layer of sandstone also contained a weak section of a joint fracture or crossbedding as seen in Figure #8-A. As the stream begins a new watercourse under the old falls, the water erosion isolates the original face of the waterfall leaving a natural arch as shown in Figures #8-B and C. The only arch in the Gorge area created in this way is Rock Bridge. Many consider this to be the only true natural bridge because it is the only one that has a large stream passing under it.

LIMESTONE CAVE ARCH

When underground water seeps through a thick limestone layer, it will often dissolve enough of the stone over long periods of time to create caves. A limestone cave arch is created when the roof of both ends of a short cave collapses, leaving a short roof section of the cave as an arch. There are at least two such arches in the Gorge area. One is Moonshiner's Arch and the other is the diminutive Henson's Cave Arch in Natural Bridge State Park.

VERTICAL JOINT FRACTURES

The fractures are cracks in rock layers which descend more or less vertically. These joints were often "fractured" away from the original rock layers when these deposits were put under tremendous pressure by the upward thrust of the Cincinnati Arch. A good example of a vertical joint fracture is found at Chimney Top on the Motor Gorge loop trip. Another smaller but equally well known joint fracture in Natural Bridge State Park is Fat Man's Misery on the southwest side of Natural Bridge.

SLUMP BLOCKS

Slump blocks are the detached sections of a cliff wall that break away after a vertical joint fracture occurs. As time passes, gravity pulls them downhill, sometimes leaving a gap of hundreds of feet between them and the cliff face of which they were once a part.

BALANCED ROCKS

Although such formations are rarer in this area than natural arches, they are formed in the same way. This occurs when a solitary stand of rock is separated from a ridge by normal erosion or fracturing. The undersurfaces of this singular pinnacle erode faster than the top, leaving a much larger upper section which seems to be top heavy. The best example is Balanced Rock in the State Park.

III
A BRIEF HISTORY OF ANCIENT AND MODERN MAN IN THE VICINITY OF THE RED RIVER GORGE

When the modern visitor views one of the many large rock shelters that abound under the precipitous sandstone cliffs of the Gorge area, it is not hard for him to imagine what advantages these natural open caves would offer primitive people as living sites. Many of these "rock houses" are deep enough to be immune to wind and rain, yet the large, open, frontal areas allow plenty of natural light during the daylight hours and provide an easy exit for the smoke rising from open fires. Interiors in many of the larger caves would allow several families to live together for mutual aid and protection. We know today that that is what the aboriginal Indians did.

Excavations at these sites by archaeologists have unearthed a variety of Indian artifacts, bones of animals, and human skeletons. Strangely enough, grave sites are not common in the shelters and those few that have been found contain only the bodies of women and children. Why men were never buried in the shelters remains a mystery.

It is generally believed that these locations were occupied over long periods of time. These prehistoric Indians covered the ash beds of their fires with a mixture of sand and mud. Often another fire site was placed over the new surface and then covered again. Many shelter floors had a series of alternative ash and sand layers that were several feet thick. A few raised up the floor level of the shelter as much as ten feet. Such extensive thickness of these thin layers could have accumulated only over hundred of years of occupation. Other interesting proofs of the prehistoric Indians' existence here are the "hominy holes" and petroglyphs left behind in the sandstone surfaces of the rock shelters. The hominy holes were drilled in large sandstone rocks or floors of the shelters. Although they vary in size, the round cylindrical holes are usually about six inches in diameter and about a foot deep. It is erroneously thought that these aborigines used the holes to grind corn—hence the name "hominy". But the corn plant was unknown to these early people and was not introduced from Mexico until a much later time. The improperly named holes were used to grind not corn, but other seeds and nuts that were gathered from the wild plants in the locality.

Archaeologists have pieced together the following possible picture of these prehistoric people. The early inhabitants of these shelters were quite different from the modern Indians whom the white explorers encountered here in the eighteenth century. They were a far more primitive people whose ancient culture patterns were much less sophisticated than those of the red men whom Daniel Boone knew.

No one can be exactly sure when the first human inhabitants penetrated the area of the Bluegrass and Gorge area, but thanks to the modern carbon dating process, a more accurate and far older picture has been evolving. Ancient, primitive, nomadic groups known as the Paleo Indians were thought to be descendants of the Mongoloid peoples who were assumed to have crossed the Bering Straits many thousands of years ago. There were apparently two separate migratory periods that happened several thousand years apart, for there are two distinct blood types among American Indians today.

The Paleo Indians were primarily big game hunters who had no knowledge of agriculture, pottery making or weaving. They came to the grasslands and cane fields of Kentucky seeking good hunting grounds. At that time, they hunted the now extinct wooly mastodon as well as herds of buffalo, antelope and elk, which are no longer found in the area.

These Paleo Indians probably first penetrated the Bluegrass prior to 10,000

An Adena Indian "Hominy hole" located in a rock shelter near the Middle Fork of the Red River

Skeleton of pre-historic Indian woman excavated in a recess cave along Wolf Pen Branch Circa 1940 (Courtesy of Boyd Taylor)

B.C. It is thought that these earliest human inhabitants entered the Gorge area on hunting forays, using the numerous rock shelters, but, at this writing, irrefutable evidence of their doing so is sketchy.

The first Indians we can positively identify who lived in the rock shelters of the Gorge are known as the Archaic culture. They had more thoroughly adjusted to the environment of the forest, for they had the techniques of gathering many natural wild foods and hunting in ambush. They had apparently advanced enough to adjust their foraging according to the cycles of the seasons. Whether they were the direct descendants of the original Paleo Indian inhabitants or migrated from other areas is not known. Positive radio carbon dates place them in the rock shelters at least a thousand years before the birth of Christ, and some scholarly guesses suggest that they may have been there as early as 8000 B.C.

These dates have an interesting parallel to the geologic history of the developement of the arches. Geologists have guessed that the evolution of Natural Bridge from a sandstone ridge to a natural arch fits roughly into the same time sequence.

About 1000 B.C. the Archaic culture evolved into, or was replaced by, a new or more advance group known as the Woodland Culture. These people began growing crops instead of relying solely on food gathering. They were familiar with the use of bow and arrow and practiced both weaving and basket-making. These Woodland Culture Indians were the probable creators of the "hominy holes".

Sometime before the birth of Christ, the Woodland Culture was replaced by a more advanced group known as the Adena Culture. The Adenas relied more heavily upon plant cultivation. Along with weaving and basket-making, they acquired the skill of making pottery. Personal adornment was practiced, for they made ornaments from both mica and copper. By their time, Indian trade routes had been established, as neither mica nor copper ore are native to the area. The mica has been traced to its source in the present state of Michigan, and many pieces coming from the same Michigan location have been found in old Indian sites as far south as Florida. These early trade routes often followed old buffalo paths that were called traces. One of these traces traversed the Bluegrass just a few miles west of the Gorge area. The Adenas, who undoubtedly took part in this trading activity, are thought to be related to the famous Mound Builders of southern Ohio.

Somewhere around 800 A.D., the Adena Culture disappeared, and except for occasional hunting and war parties of modern tribes, the shelters were no longer occupied by Indians. We can only surmise what destinies befell the Adena culture. From their remaining artifacts, there is no evidence that they ever engaged in war-like activity. They apparently lived peaceably in small groups scattered widely among the hundreds of rock shelters. The rock shelter areas offered little good land for farming, while the Bluegrass, not far away, offered both land and an abundance of game. Their search for food may have caused the peaceful Adenas to leave the relative security of the shelters. In the open Bluegrass they may have come in contact with the more war-like tribes, who either absorbed or exterminated them.

THE MODERN INDIAN

The modern Indian lived mostly north and south of Kentucky. They viewed this area as a sort of no-man's land for habitation and a hunting ground for all. These tribes, such as the Shawnee, Miami and Iroquois to the north and the Cherokee to the south, developed into aggressive warring Indian nations. The old trade route that followed the buffalo trace became known as the "Warrior's Path", as it was frequently used for war parties invading the other's territory.

The first white explorers found that the tribes generally lived north of the Ohio River and south of the Cumberland River. The Indians called the Bluegrass the Great Meadowland, and they used it extensively for hunting. It was also ominously known as the "Middle Ground" since it acted as a buffer area between the powerful tribes that lived to the north and the south of the two border rivers. Both Daniel

Boone and John Filson, the first man to write extensively about Kentucky, knew that the Indians referred to it as "The Dark and Bloody Ground". Filson implied that the name came from the many war parties who clashed and spilt blood in the Great Meadowland. Some modern archaeologists have suggested that the name did not come from Indian warfare, but from the continuing hostilities between Indians and the white man, as the latter entered into this middle ground in ever increasing numbers.

ENTER THE WHITE MAN

Although earlier colonial explorers had penetrated the peripheral areas of Kentucky, one of the first white men of English extraction to enter Kentucky and write about it was Dr. Thomas Walker.

In 1750, exploring westward from his native Virginia in the interests of a royally chartered land company, Dr. Walker crossed and named the Cumberland Gap. From there, he headed in a northwesterly direction until he came upon the lower Red River. Then, following the Warrior's Path eastward, he arrived at the present site of Clay City. Even though he missed seeing the Bluegrass by less than a day's journey in taking this easterly turn, he was the first English colonial known to have come close to the Gorge area.

After Dr. Walker's trip, new explorers came in increasing numbers. One who had a direct effect on explorations of the area close to the Gorge was an itinerant wagoner, trader and explorer named John Finley. He made his first trip into Kentucky just two years after Dr. Walker's journey, and his second one in 1767.

On one of these adventures, the Shawnees took him deep into the Bluegrass to an Indian encampment called ES-KIP-PA-KITH-I-KA. Now known as "Old Indian Fields", this Indian outpost was just a few miles west of the Red River Gorge. Here Finley freely traded with the Indians and heard many stories of the Great Meadowland. He became increasingly aware of the opportunities for both hunters and farmers in this large open area.

Between his two forays into the Kentucky wilderness, he served with the British forces organized in 1755 under the command of General Braddock. Braddock's objective was to capture the French Fort Duquesne at the present site of Pittsburgh during the French and Indian War.

Another man on that ill-fated expedition was a young wagoner whose name was Daniel Boone. Cutting the road through the wilderness for the supply wagons was slow going, and as they sat around the nightly campfires, Boone undoubtedly heard Finley tell many tales of that lush wilderness called KAIN-TUCK. After the famous military disaster known as Braddock's Defeat, both men went their separate ways and did not meet again for fourteen years, two years after Finley's second sojourn into Kentucky.

At this meeting, Boone had a farm in North Carolina which was not doing well. In May of 1769, a small expedition led by the two men set out to explore and hunt in the Kentucky area. They crossed Cumberland Gap and by early June they established a base camp on Station Camp Creek just a few miles southwest of the Red River Gorge.

Moving a few miles northward, Finley rediscovered the site of ES-KIP-PA-KITH-I-KA, but the Indian village had been destroyed and was deserted. Today the site is a farm field, and its only distinction is a roadside marker along Kentucky Route 15, a few miles west of Clay City, which relates its brief known history.

Later the same year, Boone and his companions moved their camp northward to the banks of a small creek near the junction of the Kentucky and Red Rivers. The only book in their possession was a copy of Jonathan Swift's famous satire, "Gulliver's Travels". Often referred to as the first book in Kentucky, it furnished the name for this small creek. Although the spelling has been altered from Swift's original Lorbrulgrd, the stream is known today as Lulbegrud Creek. An historical marker on Route 15, west of Clay city and not far from Old Indian Fields, identifies the creek.

Did Boone penetrate into the Gorge area in his exploratory trips? Was D. Boon Hut, discovered in a large rock shelter in 1959, really built and occupied by the famous frontiersman? Although the evidence is only speculative, and we may never positively know, there is no doubt that he was very close to the Land of the Arches. The important factor is that explorations by Boone, Finley and Walker, who all came quite close to the Gorge, made possible the coming of permanent settlers.

THE LEGEND OF THE LOST SILVER MINES

Perhaps the most intriguing story about the mountainous area of Eastern Kentucky in the eighteenth century concerns the alleged adventures and discovery of a large silver mine by a man named John Swift. According to some written accounts, Swift was guided into the Kentucky mountains in 1760 by a Mr. Munday. Swift's journals relate that Munday had previously been held a captive by the Shawnees. During his captivity, the Indians took him to rock shelters where extensive silver mining and smelting operations were being carried out by the red men. Later, the Indians released him and he returned east, subsequently meeting Swift and telling him of his adventures. Some accounts identify Swift as a sailor; others say that he was a smuggler born in Philadelphia.

As soon as they could gather supplies, Munday, Swift, and a few companions returned to the Kentucky wilderness in 1760 or 1761. Munday easily relocated the mines which had been conveniently deserted by the Indians. Swift made six trips to the mines between 1761 and 1769, but all attempts to bring out silver bullion were frustrated in one way or another. After these disappointments, Swift went to England in hopes of raising enough funds to finance a larger expedition.

John Swift was still in England when the American Revolution broke out. Because of his outspoken feelings favoring the colonials, he was clapped into an English jail, where he languished for some years. During his incarceration, he lost his eyesight, and upon his release he was a broken man. Still undaunted, he returned to the newly formed United States and continued trying to whip up enthusiasm for new ventures to try to bring the valuable metal out of the wilderness.

With his eyesight gone, Swift and his followers could only turn to the journals he had written on previous trips to the mines. He had vividly described the topographical features where the lost mines and caches of silver could be found. But they were never rediscovered.

Shortly before his death in 1800, the disappointed old man admonished his associates, "Don't ever stop a lookin', boys. It's there and it'll make you and Kentucky rich."

How much of John Swift's story is true has been open to widely different interpretations. Several versions of this journal were in existence by the middle of the nineteenth century. It did bring many treasure-seekers into eastern Kentucky, but no one has ever found a trace of silver. Swift's descriptions of visible landmarks do match several well known geographic features in the Gorge area. His journals mention a natural bridge across a good sized stream that Swift and his company often used. The only natural arch over a sizeable stream in Kentucky is Rock Bridge. The creek that flows under Rock Bridge was named Swift Camp Creek, for it was believed that it was on the banks of this creek that Swift made his base camp. Other prominent geologic features that are found in the vicinity and mentioned by Swift are many rock shelters, a cliff resembling a half moon (seen from Chimney Top Overlook), a rock resembling a haystack (Haystack Rock) and a cliff with a hole in it (Sky Bridge).

A hoard of treasure hunters have searched every nook and cranny of the Gorge with no luck. Before you start packing your metal detectors and other mining paraphernalia and set out to seek the mother lode, consider these historical facts before you leave:

1. All geologic deposits in the Gorge area are sedimentary rocks, and silver ore is not produced in such rock formations.
2. The Shawnee tribes were known by many white men, but there is no evidence that the Shawnees had any appreciable amounts of silver nor knew

the complicated process of smelting silver from ore.

3. No documentary evidence exists that John Swift or anyone else ever brought as much as a thimble full of silver from any location in Kentucky.
4. There is no documentary evidence that a man named Swift ever wrote such journals or that the existing journals were even written in the eighteenth century.
5. There is no positive proof that this particular John Swift existed at all.

Unfortunately, many aboriginal Indian sites in the rock shelters have been ruined for serious archaeological investigation by treasure hunters. Many of the hominy holes were split open and destroyed because the treasure seekers mistakenly thought these cylindrical holes were molds for silver ingots. If there is little chance that the story of Swift's lost silver mine is no more than folk legend, it has enhanced the romance of the area. Whoever wrote the existing variations of John Swift's Journals was certainly aware of the many geologic formations found in this vicinity.

MINING SUCCESSES IN THE AREA

Successful, if not extensive, mining activities have been carried out in the vicinity of the Gorge during the nineteenth century. Many of the sandstone formations contain potassium nitrate (saltpeter), used in the making of gunpowder. During the period of the Napoleonic Wars, including our own involvement in the War of 1812, demand for saltpeter was high enough to initiate small mining operations in many of the rock shelters of the area. Niter mining was actively carried out in the vicinity of the Gorge between 1804 and 1814; this supplied several gunpowder mills operating in nearby Lexington. Following the cessation of hostilities, the high cost of extracting the potassium nitrate prohibited further operations.

There was a short period during the Civil War when some locations were again mined, but the activities were not extensive. Through the intervening years, the mines were forgotten, lost or destroyed. In recent times two such mines have been rediscovered. One of them is in Natural Bridge State Park. Unfortunately, vandals have either destroyed or carried off all evidence of the original mine.

The other mine was fortunately not rediscovered until 1959 in a rock shelter containing D. Boon Hut just off Tunnel Ridge Road and can be seen in its relatively well preserved state today.

PERMANENT SETTLERS IN THE AREA

With the heavily forested narrow ridges and the steep valleys of the Gorge, little acreage is available for farmland. Pioneer farmers preferred the rich open areas of the Bluegrass. Much of the Gorge area was not used for settlement, and most of its virgin forests were not cut until the late nineteenth and early twentieth centuries.

The Bush family was one of the earliest families to settle in the vicinity. They entered Kentucky quite early, coming with Daniel Boone along the Wilderness Road, and were among the original settlers at Boonesborough. Lou Ellen Bush, born in 1804, and a direct descendant of the Boonesborough Bushes, moved into the area near Natural Bridge State Park. At one time he owned much of the land that is now part of the State Park, as well as large sections of Whittleton Branch now in the National Forest. He married Martha Tondsen, who several members of the present family believe was half Indian. They also told me that her love for the woods influenced her husband to build their first homestead along Whittleton Branch.

Later, Lou Ellen moved his family south and began a little settlement which became the hamlet of Zachariah. Zachariah today is a small town just six miles south of Natural Brige on Kentucky Route 11. Many of Lou Ellen's descendants live in and around this little town today. In the center of this community is the Bush General Store, owned and operated by the great-grandson of Lou Ellen and Marth Bush.

THE FIRST INDUSTRY AND THE FIRST TOWN

Cottage Furnace, a nineteenth century iron smelter located off Route 213 near Stanton, Kentucky

Urban growth and activity in the area were greatly hampered by its inaccessibility. The existing wagon trails were meager and there were no railroads anywhere near the Gorge until late in the nineteenth century. The first town of any size near the Natural Bridge-Red River Gorge area began just down river from the Gorge. This came about when a geologic area beginning in central Ohio extending southward well into Kentucky was discovered to be rich in iron ore. Named the "Hanging Rock Iron Region", after a port of that name on the Ohio River where much processed iron was shipped, this ore rich area passes right through the Gorge.

Having discovered substantial deposits of iron ore in the beds of many branches of the Red River, two brothers, Steven and Joel Collins, decided to build an iron furnace along the banks of the Red River. In 1787, they built their first furnace, known as a bloomery, and the town that grew up around it was called Red River Furnace. Cannon balls were manufactured in this bloomery for the War of 1812, and some of them got to New Orleans in time for Andy Jackson to use them in the battle there against the British in 1815.

This iron works was operated profitably under various owners for better than 40 years, turning out nails, axes and strap iron for the Lexington market. Later, the iron manufacturing company moved south into Estill County. The original town then changed its name to Clay City in honor of Kentucky's Great Compromiser, Henry Clay.

Although the Red River Furnace has long since disappeared, two historic ruins of this type of nineteenth century iron making furnace are near the Gorge area and today are part of the Daniel Boone National Forest. Cottage Furnace on Kentucky Route 213 is just a few miles south of Stanton and the much larger Fitchburg Furnace is on Kentucky Route 975 just a few miles from Route 52. This latter historic ruin has a self guided historical trail through the furnace grounds. An interesting book relating the history of the Fitchburg Furnace has been authored by Don Fig who is the Forest Service Recreation Supervisor for the Red River Gorge area. For those who would like to see what one of these furnaces looked like during its operating heyday, the Ohio Historical Society has recently restored the old Buckeye Furnace near Wellston, Ohio to its original operating condition. More information may be obtained by calling toll free 1-800-BUCKEYE.

THE HARVEST OF THE FORESTS

During the last half of the nineteenth century, the wealth of the vast hardwood forests was realized, and large lumbering operations commenced. With the iron industry now gone, the new lumbering ventures offered Clay City another profitable economic venture. Many trees were as large as eight feet in diameter, consuming 400 years in their growth. The ensuing lumbering operations would denude the entire area of practically all of the virgin timber within fifty years, but it was a prosperous time for an area that has never known great economic wealth.

There are many legends told today of bloody feuds which erupted over disputed timber rights between various claimants in these rugged foothills of the Cumberland Mountains. One would like to think that the buying of such claims brought in great sums of money, but such payments were very low. Bloodshed over pittances points out the general economic difficulty of the inhabitants of the area.

The Red River and its large tributaries were used to float the logs out of the Gorge down to Clay City. There, large mills processed them into finished lumber. Often wooden dams were built across the tributaries to hold the newly-cut logs until they were needed at the mill and to maintain enough water to float the logs out to the Red River. A section of such a log dam can still be seen today along the banks of the north fork of the Red River.

ENTER THE RAILROADS

As early as 1850, speculators wanted to build a railroad from Lexington to Bluefield, West Virginia, to supply cheap coal for the industrial potentiality of that central Kentucky city. Such a proposed rail line would come close to the Red River Gorge. Although various companies were formed and reformed, no track was laid until 1886. With the increased lumbering operations at Clay City, the rail builders assumed that the commercial possibilities would be better for their new line if it passed through that town. Clay City had grown considerably since its early iron making days. A huge lumber mill was in operation there which would eventually produce over 200,000 board feet of lumber daily and become the second largest in the world. Accordingly, tracks were laid as far as Clay City by the Kentucky Union Railroad.

These were boom times for this town on the banks of the Red River, but, when the timber was used up, the great Swan and Day Lumber Mill closed its doors. No new industry appeared to replace the old one, as had happened previously after the demise of the iron works. Today, this once busy metropolis has dwindled to a sleepy segment of its former self and, in recent time, has lost its leadership to the neighboring town of Stanton, four miles to the east. Although there are almost no traces of the huge Swan and Day Lumber Mill to be seen today, one building still reflects the glory of its golden years. The old Clay City National Bank building, complete with its original safe, still stands in the center of town and now houses the Red River Historical Society Museum. Open on Sunday during the tourist season, it has a collection of both man-made and natural artifacts, many of which date from aboriginal Indian periods. Admission to the museum is free.

But while the boom was on, the railroad pushed eastward and track now reached Slade. If you exit the Mountain Parkway at Slade and head south on Route 11 in the direction of Natural Bridge State Park, look to the right, and you can still see the old wooden frame train depot not far from the road. The railroad kept building southeastward, following along the Middle Fork of the Red River. A railroad tunnel was built at McCormick, a few miles from Slade. This sandstone tunnel is less than a mile away from Natural Bridge, and the present Hemlock Lodge in the State Park sits almost directly over it.

Middle Fork was known as Graining Block Fork in the early nineteenth century, for the Indians used to grain their animal skins in the stream. Graining is a process where hair is scrapped from the hides in preparation for tanning. Although Natural Bridge is less than a mile from the stream, the Indians apparently paid

"The Dinkey." One of the climax-type locomotives used by the Mountain Central Railroad

Logging train of the Dana Lumber Company near Gray's Branch Circa 1900 (Courtesy of Elsie Kruger & the Red River Historical Society)

no attention to it. An old wagoner, long since dead, reported that his father had heard the red men call it "a hole in the wall" showing their indifference and literal frankness toward such unusual geologic features. But this also meant that the new rail line was just a little over a half mile from Natural Bridge, a coincidence that would play an important part in the later developement of Natural Bridge as a tourist attraction.

About five miles south of McCormick, at a place called Torrent, the rail builders turned away from Middle Fork and dug another tunnel in the direction of the rail line's final destination at Jackson, Kentucky. The original idea of building a line through to West Virginia had long since been given up. This tunnel, the longest on the line, stretched a distance of 11,100 feet. It was a hazardous tunnel to construct since it had to be dug through soft shale.

It has been generally believed that the tunnel at Torrent was built by convict labor. Tales have been told about troublesome prisoners becoming victims of shale slides. It has been suggested that such accidents were not accidents at all, but were arranged to make sure that these men would not menace society again. How much of this is true and how much is due to fertile imaginations is not definitely known. The tunnel has long since caved in, and only the entrance is visible today.

It was also at Torrent that the first attempts to utilize the area as a vacation and resort center commenced. In 1889, the construction of the first hotel in the area began there. But the big boom in the tourist business was yet to come, and apparently the railroad had not yet realized the commercial opportunities in promoting the area as a vacation center.

Although the line was completed to its final terminus at Jackson, it was plagued with financial difficulties and was reorganized in 1894 as the Lexington and Eastern Railroad. In 1910, the line was purchased by the Louisville and Nashville Railroad, which operated it until all rail activities on the line stopped in 1942.

Several narrow gauge railroads were built in the Red River Gorge-Natural Bridge area to facilitate bringing logs down to the mainline. Some of these were no more than tramways where timber was hauled in small flatcars pulled by horses or mules. Others, where the volume warranted it, were driven by steam locomotives. A good example of such a narrow gauge steam railroad was built by the Swan and Day Lumber Company of Clay City. That company held timber rights for over 7000 acres of good hardwood forests in the area of Chimney Top Creek. In order to get the timber down to the main rail line, it commenced building a narrow gauge railroad in 1898. Its junction with the main line was at McCormick, not far from Slade; this later became known as Campton Junction. Its track went up Whittleton Branch and crossed that stream 26 times in less than two miles. Topping out on the ridge along the present Mountain Parkway, the tracks descended to Chimney Top Creek with a total track length of approximately fourteen miles. By 1905, all trees suited for commercial purposes had been cut and transported from the Chimney Top area, and the railroad was no longer needed for logging. Since there were no real all-weather roads back into the communities of Pine Ridge and Campton, plans were made to turn the logging railroad into a freight and passenger line. Taking up the tracks along the Chimney Top Creek section and extending the track from the top of the Whittleton Branch to these two small isolated towns, a narrow gauge railroad named the Mountain Central formed a year-round link between them and the outside world. In 1907, the final track was laid, with a distance of twelve miles from Campton Junction to Campton. One way fare was 75 cents and took about an hour and twenty minutes. No great fortunes were made from the Mountain Central, known locally as the "Dinky", but it did manage to operate on a sliver of a profit for about twenty years. When Kentucky State Route 15, the first hard-surfaced, all-weather road to reach Campton, was completed in 1924, the fate of the "Dinky" was sealed. Railroad service was carried on until 1928 with ever-increasing operational losses. With no hope of restoring the railroad to profitable commercial use, it was dismanteled in 1930. A few traces of this old railroad can

The area's first resort hotel built at Torrent, Kentucky, a few miles north of Natural Bridge (Courtesy of the Red River Historical Society)

Pavilion once located in the large recess cave behind the L. Park Hotel. (Courtesy of Tim Tipton and the Red River Historical Society)

be seen when hiking the Whittleton Branch trail today where once the little Climax engines puffed up the ridge.

A more permanent landmark of the old logging railroads is found near the present town of Nada. At the beginning of this century, extensive acreage of hardwood forest still existed in the lower Red River Gorge. To have a rail access from the lower Gorge to the town of Nada and the mail line, a railroad tunnel was dug between 1911 and 1912. The Dana Lumber Company, which built the tunnel and the logging railroad, had a large sawmill close to the junction of their tracks and the main line, a couple of miles east of Slade at Lombard. By putting the last two letters of Dana in front of the first two, the name Nada was created for the town that sprang up around the mill. Nada Tunnel is just a mile and a half beyond the town and pierces through Tunnel Ridge. When all the timber holdings had been cut, the railroad tunnel was converted for one lane automobile traffic. Today, Route 77 runs through the ridge on the well-known Gorge loop trip.

FIRST ATTEMPTS TO ESTABLISH A TOURIST AND VACATION CENTER

By 1925, the logging operations were over, but before this economic resource gave out, the L. and E. Railroad had seen the possibilities of encouraging a tourist clientele by promoting the area as a locale of natural enchantment and a haven for hay fever sufferers. By 1900, the small town of Torrent had the only real resort hotel in the area. It was strategically located along the tracks of the L. and E. Railroad, which furnished the only convenient way to get to this scenic area. At the turn of the century the facilities were enlarged, and it was renamed the L. Park Hotel ("L." for Lake).

In order to entertain the guests, all waiters were required to play musical instruments, providing dance music for the guests until the wee hours. This resort was busy from the spring through the fall but was busiest during the hay fever season, since sufferers from Lexington and vicinity could escape by a rather easy, short and direct train ride. Hotel guests were charged eight dollars a day for room and board, which was rather expensive at the turn of the century.

Behind the location of the hotel, there is a very large box canyon which forms a natural amphitheatre. Tiers of wooden benches with a seating capacity of 1,000 were built under the overhang of the shelter. From here, the spectators look down on an outside dance pavillion and also could watch a waterfall descending 162 feet from the lip of the shelter. During conventions, famous orators were brought here. To aid the speaker, a cable was suspended from the ridge top, supporting a little cage-like speaker's platform. When the speaker began, the cage was raised to the level of the seats under the shelter. His voice was easily contained and amplified by the sandstone ceiling and walls of the shelter.

BLACK GOLD IN THEM THAR HILLS

In 1917, oil drillers hit pay dirt when they brought in a series of high-producing wells in the Big Sinking fields a few miles south of Torrent. Since Torrent was the closest railpoint to the fields, a boom town atmosphere began straining to the utmost the facilities of the only hotel in town. Tons of supplies were transferred here from rail cars to wagons. So much equipment was brought in by the railroads that teams of oxen sometimes waited as long as eight hours to get their loads. During rainy weather, the muck of the dirt road was so deep that oxen were reported to have sunk down deep enough in the mire to drown. As long as the oil boom lasted, the L. Park Hotel stayed busy the year around.

Some wells were later dug in the Gorge area, and a few pipes can be seen along the Whittleton Branch Trail. Abandoned wells are easily seen near White's Branch Arch close to Sand Gap Trail near the State Park.

When the oil boom subsided, the L. Park Hotel was still in business, although by that time the bulk of the summer trade had shifted five miles to the north at Natural Bridge. The hotel suffered its final blow when it caught fire in 1926 and burned to the ground. Today, Torrent is a ghost town on Kentucky Route 11. All the buildings from that era and the railroad that was its lifeline have disappeared, and its location is not even indicated by a road sign. Both the entrance of the Torrent Tunnel and the large rock shelter are still there, but they are on private property and cannot be seen from the highway.

But if Torrent and the L. Park Hotel are no more than memories today, visitors to Natural Bridge have steadily increased since the late nineteenth century. Special excursion trains passed through the sandstone tunnel at McCormick and stopped as soon as all cars were clear of the tunnel. Hoe Down Island in the State Park is the exact site where the visitors detrained, for this was the closest rail point for the walk to Natural Bridge.

Realizing the potential numbers of visitors who would make such excursions by train, the passenger department of the L. and E. Railroad published a booklet about 1900 entitled "Natural Bridge". In it were over 70 photographs which included not only the bridge, but scenes of the logging operations, the nearby towns, and the rail line itself. This fascinating historical brochure has recently been reprinted by the Red River Historical Society and is on sale at the museum in Clay City and at the Natural Bridge State Park gift shops.

At the turn of the century, since the nearest hotel facilities were five miles away at Torrent, the bulk of the visitors to Natural Bridge made excursions for a single day. The railroad had built several structures at the rail stop for the convenience of these one-day visitors. They included bowling alleys, a cafe, and dancing and lunching pavillions.

When the L. and N. Railroad purchased the line in 1910, they continued to improve the facilities to keep attracting excursion visitors who were coming in increasing numbers from such distant points as Louisviulle and Cincinnati. Extensive landscaping was carried out, and much of the area looked like a well-manicured outdoor botanical garden. Special trains from Cincinnati and Louisville left these cities early on Saturdays and Sundays for Natural Bridge and returned late in the evening. It was not until 1923 that the railroad built the first Hemlock Lodge, a large log building capable of lodging and feeding the many visitors who wanted more than a single day's excursion.

In 1926, the Louisville and Nashville Railroad deeded all of its lands in the Natural Bridge area to the State of Kentucky, and Natural Bridge State Park was the outcome. With the state operating the lodge, the railroad remained the most popular way to get there until the first all-weather automobile road was completed to the park in 1932. This began a slow decrease in the number of people traveling to the park by train. Sunday excursions by rail still remained popular and they were continued until 1939. In 1942, the railroad era came to an end when the War Production Board ordered the tracks to be taken up for use in the war effort. The iron horse that had played so dramatic a role in the development of the area was gone for good, and the automobile had taken its place.

DEVELOPMENT OF THE GORGE AREA

The Red River Gorge had no passenger railroad to advertise its beauties as did its southern neighbor, Natural Bridge; therefore, relatively few people knew of the natural wonders it had to offer when the once-denuded ridges had regrown into a new forest. Before this regrowth, the barren and difficult terrain was considered worthless. Since only the good bottom land of the Lower Gorge was suitable for profitable farming, the steep escarpments surrounding it were, more or less, deserted, allowing the slow process of reforestation to start anew. With the stock market crash of 1929 and the Depression of the early thirties, such marginal soil seemed useless except to a few whose family ties gave them a fierce loyalty to their land.

As early as 1914, the U.S. Forest Service began examining most of Kentucky for the possible creation of a national forest. With the financial holocaust of 1929, such plans had to be laid aside. They were taken up again in 1934 when the Cumberland Purchase Unit was established. Most of the land now owned by the federal government in the Gorge area was purchased in the late 1930's. This land became part of the Cumberland National Forest, established in 1937 by President Roosevelt. The first projects for an outdoor recreational development were begun about the same time when the C.C.C. boys began building new roads and trails

A Natural Bridge excursion train at the present site of Hoe Down Island Circa 1900 (Courtesy of William Franz and the Red River Historical Society)

in the area. Their old campsite is now Whittleton Branch Campground in the State Park. Short trails, such as the ones to Rock Bridge and Sky Bridge, were built before World War II, but no connecting trails of any length were laid out.

Not until 1960, when the federal government began the Accelerated Public Works Program to counter a rise in unemployment, were most of the existing trails laid out. Under this federal program, better than 35 miles of trail were constructed in the Gorge area.

In 1966, President Johnson changed the name of the Cumberland National Forest to the Daniel Boone National Forest. The Red River Gorge area of the forest consists of over 53,000 acres. Added to the approximately 2,000 acres of the neighboring Natural Bridge State Park, the reforested Gorge is a marvelous scenic recreation area. Recently, the federal government proclaimed about half of this acreage as a National Geologic area. With the beauty of its arches, rock houses, and cliffs, its wildflowers, streams and beauty of its forest, this land seems destined to remain a place where urban man can still find and enjoy these rare natural surroundings for as long as we have a government to protect them. This, I believe, is as it rightfully should be.

IV
TRAIL TIPS, SAFETY AND SUGGESTED HIKES

RATING OF TRAIL DIFFICULTY

To help you find what trails are within your capacity and those you can enjoy, I have devised six levels of trail difficulty: VERY EASY, EASY, MODERATE, MODERATE-TO-STRENUOUS, STRENUOUS, and VERY STRENUOUS. Any such system will tend to be slightly arbitrary, but the levels have been worked out by considering both elevation changes and distance.

Anyone able to walk one level city block without undue difficulty should be able to walk the trails marked VERY EASY with no difficulty. If you want to see if your definition of EASY is the same as mine, walk the Whittleton Branch Trail #216 from the Whittleton Branch Campground to Whittleton Arch and return. This round trip walk of about two miles has just enough gentle uphill grade to keep it from being a dead flat, city type stroll, and is long enough to have some significance as a test. If you complete this hike and feel that you have had a comfortable walk, your definition of EASY would be pretty much the same as mine. If you felt that this hike is about as much walking as you can comfortable stand in one day on your walking level, translate my classification of EASY to read MODERATE for you, and my word MODERATE to read STRENUOUS.

For those of you who could not complete the Whittleton Arch walk or were just able to do so feeling that the grim reaper was about to cut you down in route, turn to the Motor Loop Drive section of this book and enjoy the Gorge from the easily reached overlooks and take only the trails marked VERY EASY.

The necessary walking time to complete a trail is even more difficult to classify, since the range would stretch from tortoise speed walkers to human Ferraris. I have tended to lean toward the slower paced walkers, those who are in no hurry, have come to drink in the scenery and have no intention of pushing themselves. Any conditioned, serious hiker used to treks of many miles in a single day, can easily cover the trails in far less time than indicated, and will not find any trail in the area overly difficult.

WHY ALL THE SIGNS

In the trail descriptions I have included relevant signs at the trail heads and trail junctions. This is not to be redundant, which it often will be, but to aid the hiker when signs are missing or have been deliberately turned around to confuse hikers. The vandalism of trail signs by thoughtless hooligans has reached runaway proportions and this is an attempt on my part to help ease the problem.

TRAIL AND BACKCOUNTRY SAFETY

I was once asked by a newspaper reporter if I thought the Red River Gorge area is a dangerous place in which to hike. I answered that any place is dangerous for fools. If a person exercises reasonable common sense, none of the official trails or overlooks in the Red River Gorge-Natural Bridge area are dangerous. However, many sections have numerous high cliffs that can be potentially hazardous for the foolhardy. There are several places near overlooks, arches, trails and even campgrounds where a fall could result in serious injury or death. These areas can be extremely hazardous for those with little off-trail hiking experience or whose judgement is impaired by a mind altering substance.

Drugs, alcohol and camping near cliff tops is a lethal mixture which too often results in serious injury or death. If the natural rewards of camping and hiking in the Gorge escape you and your only real excitement in coming is to get spaced out, then, if we can't convince you to stay home, find a campsite on the valley bottoms rather than on the ridges.

Don Fig, who has been the forest service recreational supervisor for many years and who trains, co-ordinates and often leads volunteer rescue groups, is the proud recipient of a presidential citation for his many successful rescues. He explained to me the most serious mistakes often made by sightseers and campers. These include wandering around at night on ridge or arch tops to urinate, gather firewood or horsing around without a flashlight. One incredibly stupid stunt that has happened more than once has occured when an otherwise snug camper wakes up during the dark hours of a cold night finding his bladder under extreme pressure. In an effort to keep warm while answering nature's call, the half-awake camper, while still ensconced in his sleeping bag, bunny-hops over to the cliff edge to relieve the pressure and suddenly finds himself sliding off into the darkness below.

Another problem for people wandering off the official trails is getting lost. If you do lose your way or separate from your group, it is usually best not to try to find your way out at night. Stay put until morning. If you still have plenty of daylight and you are not on top of a ridge or high cliff area, cautiously follow a watercourse downstream for it will eventually lead you to a road. But never go over a rock face or down a ravine without visual contact of what is immediately below you for some streams have dangerous dropoffs even when they approach the valley floor.

If someone in your party gets lost, separated or falls over a precipice, carefully identify the location with visible landmarks and make sure you know how to get back to the same location. Too often panic-stricken people reporting to authorities their missing or injured friends become so disoriented that they cannot take rescuers back to the approximate vicinity. This makes rescue operations far more difficult, sometimes more hazardous, and always more time consuming.

A daylight activity that also can be lethal is getting too close to the edge of cliffs or arches to get a better view. On occasion, otherwise sensible and cautious people seem to be swept up by a mystic fascination while gazing over the sides of the better known arches. They keep inching out to get a better look below until they fall, often to their deaths. Remember, even though there are no hand rails on the arch tops, it's a long way down.

Common explanations by those who made the unexpected plunges and were fortunate enough to survive said from their stretchers or hospital bed, "The branch I was holding onto broke." "The little tree I was hanging onto came out by the roots." "I didn't know I was so close and lost my balance." There are about 60 accidents reported in the area each year. About 35 to 40 of these result in serious injury, with one or two deaths per year. The age of most victims fall between the middle teens up to the mid twenties, and they are usually male.

Too many visitors who do not understand the topography and size of the Gorge mistakenly believe that a well trained search and rescue team can find anyone in an hour or less. The following examples prove what a mistaken idea this can be. Despite intensive search operations involving many volunteers and thousands of man hours, it took over two weeks to find one such winter victim whose ice-encased body was eventually located frozen to the bottom of a waterfall. Another, who disappeared in May, remained missing until his skeleton was found the following January. Most lost persons, however, do not become such grim statistics and are usually found within a twenty-four hour period.

To avoid such mishaps, unless you are a skilled and knowledgeable cross country hiker, stay on the trail for often the edges of sheer cliffs are hidden in thick underbrush. Be cautious about peering over the edges of the larger arches and allow no horseplay on top of them. Following these rules eliminates the dangers of the cliff top areas, which can then be enjoyed in the complete and even casual comfort which common sense affords.

Team rescuing a seriously injured cliff fall victim (Courtesy of Don Fig)

If you have children who wish to go on trail hikes or viewing points, make sure a responsible adult accompanies them on all walks. Children who tend to be reckless, who will not stay on the trails but bound off in all directions should be sternly warned of the extreme danger of such undisciplined activity. Make them stay on the trails and stay in sight. Children who will not obey should not be taken on trails or to overlook points.

If you require the help of rescuers don't repeat the same mistake one mother made. She understandably become hysterical when her young child wandered off from a campground near a high cliff area after dark. Despite an intensive search of the immediate area by the child's parents and friends no clue to his whereabouts turned up.

The family wisely contacted local forest service authorities who quickly organized trained volunteer groups and began an intensive search which lasted through the night with no results. When daylight arrived, the search leader went back to the camp with the unpleasant news, but was prepared to tell the mother that the search would continue. To his amazement he found her peacefully asleep. She became very annoyed when he awoke her and curtly told the leader that her missing child had wandered back to camp about 20 minutes after the searchers had left. Because of her thoughtless indifference in neglecting to tell the authorities of her child's safe return, several volunteers spent a totally unnecessary search in hazardous cliff areas through the entire night.

SCALING THE WALLS

Another popular activity which occasionally leads to injurious falls and hazardous rescue operations is rock climbing. The serious mishaps in this increasingly popular sport usually occur when climbers have little or no training in proper climbing techniques and are using improper or inadequate equipment. Too many macho types challenge the walls with little know how using equipment that was not designed for climbing. Worse yet, they encourage others to follow them in their untrained efforts. These he-man types and those stupid enough to follow them often are seriously injured or killed. If you wish to become active in this exciting sport, get training from bona-fide experts who are trained to teach good climbing techniques and make sure at least one highly skilled and qualified person accompanies you on your initial climbs. I know of no serious injury in the Gorge suffered by experienced climbers with proper gear.

AUTO VANDALISM

A serious consideration that overnight hikers who drive to the Gorge trail heads must contemplate is the risk of having their vehicle looted and/or vandalized. I have been asked by many visitors why something hasn't been done to stop this pilfering and damage to vehicles parked in the Gorge and I can truthfully answer that a great deal has been done. The forest service has two full-time law enforcement officers on duty in the Gorge area during the popular seasons. The state police also patrol and occasionally conduct stake outs in the area as well. Due to these operations, several offenders have been caught in recent seasons. All were convicted in Federal Court and served prison sentences that were more than a slap on the wrist.

This has slowed down but not eliminated the problem. It seems that unfortunately, a few months after one group is caught and prosecuted another new group begins the pilfering anew. The problem is that the acreage in the Gorge is an overwhelming area for a few law enforcement officers to effectively handle. This is enhanced by the fact that the Red River Gorge-Natural Bridge area sits in the middle of a large economically depressed area of Appalachia. With the comparatively small number of visitors involved and stringent federal and state budget considerations, an increase in the number of law enforcement officers is unlikely.

While there is no guarantee that your auto will not be vandalized, here are a few suggestions that should decrease your chances of being victimized. Don't park along the paved public highways, for in these locations your parked car becomes an easy target for hit and run operations. Don't park at the Gray's Arch picnic area or the cement bridge (on Route 715 at the dividing point between the upper and lower Gorge) for both areas have been frequently hit. Park as far away from the paved highways as you can. Thieves don't like to go too far on the narrow dead-end gravel roads that the Forest Service maintains. If you have valuables such as cameras, jewelry, wallets and watches don't mistakenly think they will be safe by hiding them under your car seat or locking them in the trunk for these are the first places the thieves look. Take such items with you on your hike or leave them at home.

With a much smaller area to cover, the security force at Natural Bridge State Park is usually able to give adequate protection for vehicles left in their official parking lots. But since backpacking is not allowed within the confines of the state park, this is little help for those overnighting in back country areas of the Gorge.

If you happen to own a bicycle or moped, you might leave your car in a secure parking area, then return to the trail head on your two wheeler. Since bikes and mopeds are light you can hide them back in the forest and chain lock them to a handy tree.

ABOUT THE SNAKES

Besides several varieties of harmless snakes, there are two poisonous types, the copperhead and the timber rattlesnake, that are native to the area. Your chances of seeing one are very slim. Bruce Poundstone, who hiked these local trails for better than 40 years saw one rattlesnake in all that time. As Chief Fire Warden for the U.S. Forest Service, Clarence Henson covered every nook and corner of the area for over 27 years, and in all that time only one poisonous snake struck at him, harmlessly hitting his boot.

These snakes tend to shy away from areas frequently traveled by people. If you are walking any of the often hiked Natural Bridge Trails or such popular trails in the Gorge area as Rock Bridge or Sky Bridge, your chances of encountering a poisonous snake are only slightly better than finding a wooly mastodon perched atop Natural Bridge. Even on the back trails, sightings of any kind of snake are rare. If you should be one of the infrequent few who encounters a poisonous snake on the trail, remember that neither of the poisonous snakes is aggressive by nature and will not attack you unless he feels threatened. The poison, after all, is for hunting, not for attacking humans. In the very rare occasions I have seen rattlesnakes and copperheads, they quite docilely eyed me with much the same cautious curiosity I showed them. I once took my hiking stick and gently touched the ten button tail of a rattlesnake. Even then, he didn't coil or take any type of hostile action. To paraphrase the late F.D.R., the greatest thing to fear about these reptiles is fear itself. There are far more people who die every year from the bites and stings of insects than by snakebites. On the average, there are about 14 fatalities from snakebites in the United States every year, and only rarely does one of these fatalities occur in Kentucky. By checking every source in the Gorge area available to me, I found only four visitors had been bitten by poisonous snakes in the past several years. Since there are over one million visitors to the Red River Gorge-Natural Bridge area every year, the odds that you would be bitten are more than one in a million. Not one of these bites occurred along a trail and none of the victims died. You face a far greater hazard to your life from those vipers behind the steering wheel whom you encounter along the highway than those wigglers on the ground.

Nonetheless, certain precautions should be taken when hiking the back trails. Do not hike in bare feet or shorts. It is better to wear shoes that cover the ankle since about 90% of snake strikes occur at ankle height. Long pants are also advisable since a snake bites when he strikes a surface. If the snake strikes a pants leg, he is likely to penetrate no more than the air between the pants and the leg. Never put your hands under logs or rocks without first taking a look. Watch sunny spots on the trail on cool days and shady ones on hot days, since snakes are cold blooded creatures and must avoid extremes in temperature to survive. If you have an abnormal fear of snakes but still love to hike, wait until the first hard frost in the fall when snakes usually begin their winter hibernation.

SUGGESTIONS FOR TRAIL HIKES

Unless people have come for a specific purpose like a backpack, climbing or canoe trip, most first time weekend sightseeing visitors will use one day taking the short loop walks at Natural Bridge or at Koomer Ridge and the other day taking the Gorge motor loop trip. There are a variety of short loop walks up and back from Natural Bridge requiring no more than two hours and in some cases, considerably less. Other short and easy walks in the Gorge include the Sky Bridge loop walk, the Angel Window and Whistling Arch walks.

Other hikes of "short" duration but of high scenic value, lasting two to three hours, are the Rock Bridge loop walk, the Double Arch walk, the D. Boon Hut loop walk, the Auxier Ridge Trail, the Hidden Arch loop trail and the walks to Gray's Arch, Whittleton Arch and Silvermine Arch. These walks are not physically demanding and make good morning or afternoon hikes for families who don't want to take on too arduous an adventure. Look up the page number for the description of each of these hikes, as well as the day hikes below, in the Table of Contents.

DAY HIKES

Most of the following hikes are easily completed in a few hours for those who are in good hiking condition, but are primarily designed for a fuller hiking day.

ROCK BRIDGE-TURTLE BACK ARCH. Start this hike at the Rock Bridge parking lot. Follow the Rock Bridge Loop Trail #207 past Rock Bridge to the junction of Swift Creek Trail #219. Follow Trail #219 past the log dam, Hell's Kitchen and Bear Pen Branch Narrows. Take the short side trip to the old still, then continue on to Turtle Back Arch. After seeing the arch, retrace your steps back along Swift Camp Creek Trail to the intersection of the Rock Bridge Loop Trail. Turn right on the loop trail starting up the ridge. This section completes the loop ending at the parking lot. Total distance—about five miles.

KOOMER RIDGE DAY HIKE. A good day's loop hike for seasoned walkers can also be taken from the Koomer Ridge Recreation Area. Take Koomer Ridge Trail #220 down to Chimney Top Creek where it junctions with Rough Trail #221. Turn left on Rough Trail and follow it west until Pinch-Em-Tight Trail #223 exits on the left. Follow Pinch-Em-Tight Trail a short distance until Buck Trail exits on the left. Follow Buck Trail #226 back until it intersects with the Koomer Ridge Trail. Turn right and follow the Koomer Ridge Trail back to the parking lot. This is a good stiff walk of about seven miles. Although there are no arches to be seen on this long walk, it does offer some of the best views of mountain-type streams in the area, and it is often one of the least populated loops in the area.

GRAY'S ARCH DAY LOOP HIKE. There are two versions of this hike and both of them start at the Gray's Arch parking lot. For the shorter walk, take the Gray's Arch Trail for the short distance it covers to Rough Trail. Turn right on Rough Trail and follow it eastward to Gray's Arch. After seeing the arch, continue on the easterly direction of Rough Trail until Rush Ridge Trail exits on the right. Take Rush Ridge Trail to Pinch-Em-Tight Trail. Turn right on Pinch-Em-Tight Trail for the short distance to Tunnel Ridge Road and the parking lot. The distance of this short version is about four miles. For the longer version follow the same course as the shorter trip until you get to Rush Ridge Trail. Do not turn onto Rush Ridge Trail, but continue on Rough Trail until it joins with Pinch-Em-Tight Trail. Turn right on Pinch-Em-Tight Trail and follow it back to Tunnel Ridge Road and the parking lot. This longer loop hike is a little over five miles.

DOUBLE ARCH-COURTHOUSE ROCK—AUXIER RIDGE LOOP DAY HIKE. A more strenuous walk starts at the Double Arch parking lot at the end of Tunnel Ridge Road. Take the Double Arch Trail to the arch. Retrace your steps to the Auxier Branch Trail. Turn left and follow Auxier Branch Trail to Courthouse Rock Trail. Turn left and follow the Courthouse Rock Trail to the intersection of Auxier Ridge Trail by taking the wooden steps up to the top of the ridge. Turn right and follow the Auxier Ridge Trail back to the parking lot for that trail and onto Tunnel Ridge Road and walk back to your car. This is a moderately strenuous walk of over six miles and should be considered as a day hike only by hikers in good physical condition. A shorter version of this loop can be accomplished by cutting out the Double Arch Trail. Start out at the parking lot for the Courthouse Rock-Auxier Ridge Trails. Follow one out and return on the other.

BOUNDARY LINE HIKE. Another demanding day walk is the Natural Bridge to Whites Branch Arch boundary line hike. Details of this hike are given in the description of Sand Gap Trail in the Natural Bridge State Park chapter.

HOOD'S BRANCH LOOP. A less demanding and far more scenic loop hike can be walked by utilizing the new and attractive Hood's Branch Trail. Take any one of the popular trails up to Natural Bridge and return to the sky lift area on the Hood's Branch Trail. The length of this loop is between five and seven miles depending on which trail you take up to Natural Bridge.

INDIAN STAIRWAY LOOP. This off-trail hike takes off from and rejoins the Gladie Creek segment of the Sheltowee Trace National Recreation Trail. None of the loop is on official trails, and although it is not difficult to follow, it has some real scrambling particularly down Indian Stairway and is quite close to high cliff edges in several places. Hikers who are not particularly agile, in good physical condition or are afraid of heights should not consider taking this demanding but otherwise spectacular loop hike.

ADVICE FOR BACKPAKERS

Although primitive camping is not allowed in Natural Bridge State Park outside the official campground, it is allowed in the Red River Gorge area of the Daniel Boone National Forest. There are a variety of long hikes requiring overnight stays that will serve both the veteran and novice backpacker. It is a marvelous area for backpacking activities for a number of reasons. For the beginner, going up and down the escarpments puts just enough bite in the trail to make you feel any extra poundage you are carrying. It also offers the beginner many miles of trail which seldom cross roads but which have the safety factor of never being more than three miles from a road in case an emergency or exhaustion would require a hasty exit from the trails before the proposed hike was completed.

Besides the scenic rewards, the Gorge area offers the veteran backpacker several things. There is enough variety to offer the expert backpacker (and the novice, too) several different weekend trips, where he can isolate himself in the scenery far from the madding crowd. It is also a good place to test out and organize new equipment and to get into generally good shape for longer proposed hikes especially in our eastern or western mountains. Almost every trail has a useable natural water supply (purification tablets are recommended) so toting water is rarely a problem.

Although excellent for trail walks, the vicinity of the Gorge is not a good cross country area for two reasons. First, there are large patches of rhododendron that are extremely difficult to penetrate especially with a backpack. With a great deal of extended effort, one can force his way through, but the ecological damage to plant life is enough to drain away the rewards of a wilderness experience. Second, the area is lined with steep ridges and high cliffs whose edges are often hidden in thick underbrush. Even with topo maps, you will find cliff edges often alarmingly upon you before you can take precautionary measures. So except for experienced backpackers who are skilled in off trail techniques, cross country hiking in the ridge top areas is not recommended. However, novice backpackers with some experience and who wish to try some boondocking, might explore the hollow bottoms and valley floors of the Gorge area.

A SUMMING UP

Don't let horror stories deter you from doing sensible hiking and sightseeing at Natural Bridge or the Gorge. Remember thousands walk the trails, explore the back country and scale the cliffs every year with no mishap. When good common sense is applied, the official trails in the Natural Bridge-Red River Gorge area are hardly more threatening than a city sidewalk!

By following sensible precedures and not going over the limit of your own skills and capabilities, your chances of becoming a negative statistic requiring emergency help will be quite small. Both the Natural Bridge State Park and the Stanton Ranger District personnel do a first rate job in helping the many thousands of visitors a year to have an enjoyable and safe stay in the Gorge area. Since demands for the time of the naturalists and rangers is heavy, try to make requests for their services and help as reasonable as possible. They get more than their share of crackpot requests. An example of this kind of foolishness happened a few years ago when a camper from New Jersey staying at Koomer Ridge phoned the local ranger at four in the morning. He complained to the sleepy-eyed ranger, who lived more than twenty miles away, that he had just run out of firewood and demanded that the ranger immediately come to Koomer Ridge and cut him some more.

V
RED RIVER GORGE AUTOMOBILE SCENIC LOOP DRIVE

This Gorge drive is one of the most rewarding journeys that sightseers can take in the land of the arches. The trip features parts of the rim on the lower Red River Gorge with several scenic overlooks, views of several arches, and stretches of the Red River in the bottom of the gorge. The round trip is approximately 35 to 40 miles long and includes much to see both for the good hiker as well as those whose handicaps limit them to short walks or no walking at all. With a combination of a lot of motoring and a little walking, the loop trip can give you spectacular views of the Gorge and several good examples of ridge top arches. It is difficult to estimate the time to complete the journey, for this will be governed mainly by the interest of the viewers. The speediest could hardly do it less than two hours, while for the careful unhurried visitor it could take all day. Most people complete the loop during either a long morning or a long afternoon. By using the description below and the map found on page 164 and page 166, you can easily find your way along the loop drive.

At this writing the loop trip can be done in either direction, although there is talk of making at least part of it a one way road. It is described here in only one direction which, I believe, is the most scenic of the two. Most of the driving covers good but often narrow blacktop roads. One important side trip is on a one lane gravel road maintained by the U.S. Forest Service. I would also like to caution the driver that much of the loop road meanders, having numerous curves. Visibility is often restricted to a few yards, but with proper precautions, the drive is not a dangerous one.

FROM SLADE TO PINE RIDGE

Take Kentucky Route 15 east from the small hamlet of Slade in the direction of Campton and Pine Ridge. If the Mountain Parkway is on your right as you leave Slade, you are going in the proper direction. Just after leaving Slade, Route 15 crosses over the Mountain Parkway.

After that crossing, Route 15 climbs Slade Hill and goes through a series of tight curves. About 2½ miles from Slade, Route 15 hits the simultaneous beginning of Tunnel Ridge Road on the left and Whittleton Branch Trail on the right. Shortly after this junction, Route 15 again crosses over the Mountain Parkway. If you are familiar with the appearance of Indian Head (also known as Profile Rock, the Devil's pulpit and Lover's Leap) from earlier visits to Natural Bridge State Park, you can see them again shortly after this second crossing of the Mountain Parkway. If you haven't seen them at a closer range, it would be of little interest for you to stop and see them at this distance because they appear so small. If you do wish to take a look, pull off on the right hand side of the road about 100 feet after crossing the parkway bridge. Looking to the right, you have a view down the valley cut by Whittleton Branch. In the distance, a little over two miles away as the crow flies, both Lover's Leap and Indian Head Rock are seen in the hazy distance. Not far beyond this point and a little over four miles from Slade, the road passes the entrance to the Koomer Ridge Recreation Area campground on the left. Then Route 15 crosses over the toll road again and goes by the Mountain Park Motel. When you continue on Route 15, just after entering the small hamlet of Pine Ridge and passing the Sky Bridge Motel on the right Kentucky Route 715 intersects Route 15 from the left. Turn left here and follow Route 715. On this corner, set back from the road, is the Dessie Scott Children's Home whose story is another interesting part of the local mountain history. Before there were good

Half Moon (Chimp) Rock as seen from Chimney Top overlook

roads in this region, it was almost impossible for children to receive much formal education. Some dedicated teachers with missionary zeal penetrated these areas in an attempt to introduce rudimentary education and improve living conditions when and where they could. The Dessie Scott Childran's Home is a marvelous surviving example. In 1934, a lady named Esther Pushee came from the New England states to do missionary work in the mountains. When the mother of a large destitute family died, Miss Pushee began to care for the children. Soon other children came to her seeking aid, and before long this foster home was established. A disastrous fire claimed several lives in 1939, including that of the housemother, Dessie Scott. The home was named after her as a memorial.

Today, the home ministers to the needs of 30 to 40 children who range in age from two to twenty. When I asked Mrs. Winchip, the acting director, how long the children stayed, she replied, "They stay as long as they need us." The entrance to the home is a few yards east on Route 15, and visitors are welcome.

FROM PINE RIDGE TO CHIMNEY TOP ROAD

Just after you turn left and head north on Route 715, the road passes a tobacco barn on the left, then crosses over the Mountain Parkway. As you cross the bridge you can look left down the valley cut by Chimney Top Creek. The speck of a water tower seen on the horizon is at Frenchberg. Less than 100 yards beyond the bridge, Route 715 passes the beginning of the Rock Bridge service road on the right (#IV on map, pg.166). On the right side of the road a sign announces that you are entering the Red River Gorge National Geological Area in the Daniel Boone National Forest. At this intersection the Forest Service has a visitor center in a mobile home type structure. The times that it is staffed by forest service personnel varies with the seasons and the whims of the federal government and its funding allotments for paying seasonal employees.

The Rock Bridge loop hike beginning three miles down the gravel road on the right is one of the best in the area, but if you are trying to complete the Gorge loop trip in half a day or less, this worthwhile excursion may prove too time-consuming. See page 113 for details of this hike.

CHIMNEY TOP SCENIC DRIVE

A little less than two miles beyond the Rock Bridge Road, Route 715 goes by the beginning of Chimney Top Scenic Drive on the left (#V on map,pg. 166). In a little less than four miles, this side road leads to Chimney Top Overlook where you have one of the best scenic overlooks of the lower Gorge. Cars going in the opposite direction on this narrow gravel road can just barely pass one another if it is done at a snail's pace. If you take this highly recommended side trip, about a half mile from Route 715, the Parched Corn section of Rough Trail exits to the right and the Chimney Top section of Rough Trail exits from the left.

Just beyond this trail crossing, there is a well marked large parking lot to the left. Since Rough Trail passes through the parking lot it is a good point for taking day hikes on these two sections of trail. It is also the parking lot to use for primitive campsite #3.

A short distance beyond the parking lot there is a pullout on the right side of the road for an overlook view. The view is disappointing and most will find it not worthwhile. Not far beyond this pullout there is another one on the left that offers better scenic rewards. By walking just a few feet from your car, you can get a good view of the backside of Half Moon Cliff just to your right. From this viewing position it looks as if Half Moon Cliff is divided into three large rock sections. Although there is an arch in the ridge, it is not visible from here. If you look right, above those large sections at the end of the ridge, you can see both Raven's Rock and Courthouse Rock in the distance. These landmarks can be seen from this vantage point only on fairly clear days and otherwise can be recognized from here by people who have seen them previously at closer range. The perspective from this distant view makes these monstrous sandstone monuments rather abscure and tiny.

HALF MOON ARCH

If you are not pressed for time and would like to visit Half Moon Arch, you can walk to it easily on a little unmarked trail in about five minutes. It begins on the left side of Chimney Top road about 3.4 miles from Route 715. You will see a sign on the right side of Chimney Top Road that reads: **PRIMITIVE CAMPSITE #4.** Alongside it there is a refuse cage enclosed in chicken wire. The campsite, complete with privy, is in a field that opens up a few yards back from the road.

Across the road on the left you will see a bank of sandy, red-colored earth in the road-cut above the road. Go to the top of the bank and you will see the little trail. Although most of the trail is very easy, there is a challenging stretch just before you get to the arch which could prove too much for walkers who have difficulty going up or down rather steep embankments. If you decide that you want to see the arch, the walk should take you about ten minutes one way.

Follow the trail along the ridge top which, despite its unofficial status, is far more distinct than it was a few years ago because Half Moon rock is a favorite of rapellers and rock climbers. The trail will take a decided drop, then level off. When you come to where the ridge takes a second more decided drop then goes up the narrow rock spine of the ridge, you are close to the point where you leave the top of the ridge. Go almost to the bottom of the dip then start working your way down the left side of the ridge, keeping the ridge top on your right. The descent is steep, but you don't have to go many feet before you arrive at the arch. It is six feet high and eight feet long. Just beyond the arch there are about a half dozen

Princess Arch

much smaller openings that go entirely through the ridge. It is rather rare to see so many ridge piercing holes so close together and they might vaguely remind you of a giant piece of Swiss cheese.

PRINCESS ARCH

Just as you approach the turnaround loop at the end of Chimney Top Road, where there are Forest Service toilet facilities for each sex, a sign on the right indicates the trail to Princess Arch. A very easy trail, which is less than half a mile round trip leads you to the top of this very lovely arch. With its 32 foot length and 8 foot height, it is not one of the biggest or most spectacular arches, but its gently curved surfaces give the viewer an attractive example of what is known in geologic terms as a finished arch. The walk to the top of the arch can be made by almost anyone, and it warrants a visit from all but the most hurried visitor. Getting to the bottom of Princess Arch is difficult for those whose walking is generally restricted to level surfaces.

The trail takes you right over the top of the arch. If you want to see it from underneath there are two ways to get there. First, once you know you are on top of the arch, turn around and walk back up the trail for about 70 feet. Look to the right and you should find a small path that quickly takes you down to the underside of the arch. It is a steep but not dangerous grade. The other way is to continue across the arch and walk about 70 feet beyond it on the ridge top. There is a tree growing quite close to the ridge on the left side. By using the tree as a support and some natural stepping stones in the sandstone ridge, you can lower yourself down to the bottom section of the arch.

CHIMNEY TOP OVERLOOK

Even if you decide to skip Princess Arch, you shouldn't miss the short walk to Chimney Top Overlook-especially if it is a nice day. Go around the loop turn-around at the end of the road. Just as you complete the circle, you can see the beginning of Chimney Top walk on the right. A wide and easy paved trail with a round trip distance of ⅔ miles makes the walk a gentle one for almost anyone who does not have a serious physical handicap. This trail takes you right to the cliff top of the Gorge. Chimney Top, about 200 feet high and 600 feet above the Red River, is a slump block created by a joint fracture that has broken away from the cliff face and is about 3½ feet from it. It all sounds very spooky if you suffer from acrophobia but it really isn't, for the Forest Service maintains steady guard rails that lend the neccessary sense of security. It will take the average walker about ten to fifteen minutes to reach the viewpoint atop Chimney Rock. There you have an unobstructed view of several miles of the lower Red River Gorge and the panoramic view is spectacular, especially when the fall colors are at their peak.

On reaching the overlook, look sharply left and you will see a high cliff with a crescent top-hence its name, Half Moon Rock. I also like to think of it as Chimp Rock, as the upper middle section protrudes outward and is shaped very much like the head of a giant chimpanzee. If you have trouble seeing this natural sculpturing, note that there is a small tree growing from his nose.

Half Moon Rock tapers off to the right into the valley cut by Chimney Top Rock.

At this writing you can see a house and a small barn below you in the valley formed by Chimney Top Creek which was part of a small farm owned by the same family for many generations. But the property has recently been sold to the federal government for inclusion in the Daniel Boone National Forest. How long the buildings will remain is something the forest service will have to decide.

The high cliffs directly behind the farm constitute the end of Pinch-Em-Tight Ridge. Note that there is a low section or saddle between the top sections at the end of the ridge. That is Pinch-Em-Tight Gap. This gap gave the ridge its name for the children who lived on the farm a few generations ago used to visit children who lived on another farm on the opposite side of the ridge. Since going through the gap was, in places, a narrow squeeze the children named it Pinch-Em-Tight. The right end of this ridge that overlooks the Gorge is also known as Revenuer's Rock. In the moonshining days before roads were plentiful in the area, federal agents used to scramble up this high point looking for tell-tale traces of smoke rising from the fires of illegal stills hidden in the trees.

At the bottom of the valley between you and the farm is Chimney Top Creek, which flows into the Red River to the right. Looking straight down the Red River, to your right, the large rock promontory with a rounded stone top is known as Cloud Splitter Rock.

PARCHED CORN OVERLOOK AND ANGEL WINDOWS

After returning to Route 715,turn left on the black top road. In a little over a mile, Wildcat Trail commences on the right side of the road. Another 7/10 miles takes you to Parched Corn Overlook with parking area on the left side of the road. The overlook itself gives one a view of a heavily forested valley cut by Parched Corn Creek. It is not a spectacular view, but it is here that another pleasant walk begins to Angel Windows.

When you face Parched Corn Overlook from the road, Angel Windows Trail begins at the left end of the parking lot. Angel Windows are two small arches that are just a few feet apart at the end of the same ridge. The first one is approximately 4½ feet high and about 5 feet long. The second arch is approximately 5½ feet high and about 7 feet long.

When this area became part of the government forest, a very devout local resident showed these twin arches to a Forest Service employee and told him that a halo is sometimes visible through the opening-hence the name, "Angel Windows". This effect is probably caused by sunlight filtering through the very large hemlocks that grow in the hollow behind the arches. Despite several visits to the windows, I have never seen the halo effect. Even without glowing nimbuses these arches are still worth seeing, for their charm is in their diminutiveness. The trail is easy to follow, and the round trip walk is only a little over half a mile. This easy trail should not prove at all difficult for any healthy walker.

Leaving Parched Corn Overlook and continuing north on Route 715, in about 3/10 mile you will pass a parking lot on the left. At the far end of this parking lot the northern end of Swift Camp Creek Trail meets the eastern end of Rough Trail. This lot is well situated for doing day hikes along short sections of these trails. (For Trail descriptions see pages 123 and 137.)

WHISTLING ARCH

About 1 mile from the Parched Corn Overlook, Route 715 makes a sharp hairpin turn to the right and begins a rapid descent into the Gorge. Sky Bridge Road comes in from the left and joins Route 715 at this point. To the left of Route 715, just before the curve and the intersection, Whistling Arch Trail commences. A small and not very spectacular opening, Whistling Arch could be missed if your schedule is cramped. It does, however, offer some things in its favor. First, it has the easiest and shortest walk, being less than 2/10 mile round trip. Secondly, its 11 foot span, which is only 4 feet high, is a good example of what is known as an arch in formation. Contrast its rough jagged edges with the smooth lines of Princess arch or Sky Bridge and you can see the difference between what the geologists call an arch in formation and a finished arch. In high winds air rushing through the low opening whines, giving the arch its name. This whine is something that happens very rarely.

ON THE WAY TO SKY BRIDGE

At the Sky Bridge intersection do not turn right down Route 715, but take the Sky Bridge Road left. This trip to Sky Bridge should not be missed even by the most hurried visitor, for this arch is one of the great scenic wonders of the Gorge. Along the road to Sky Bridge you will pass some scenic overlooks. The first of these, called Devil's Canyon Overlook, is on the left side of the road with limited parking space on the right. It looks down into a section of the Red River Gorge where high cliffs are easily seen. Those cliffs that are farthest from you are on the opposite side of the Gorge.

SWIFT CREEK OVERLOOK

Just 2/10 mile further down the road the Swift Creek Overlook is on the right side of the highway. Overlooking the valley of Swift Camp Creek, this is an exceptionally interesting viewpoint, even though Swift Creek itself is out of sight, buried in the trees below. If you look straight ahead through the V in the valley, you will see distant cliffs that are on the other side of the Red River. Between the V and the Cliffs, Swift Creek empties into the Red River. You will see another cliff promontory on your left with a visible guard rail on its top. On the other side of that viewpoint, you get an excellent look at Sky Bridge, the next stopping place described on this trip. Looking to the right, across the valley cut by Swift Creek, you can see what looks like a large rock shelter, and indeed that's what it was in the not too distant geologic past. But it now has broken through to the other side and is Castle Arch. Although a view through the arch is impossible from this overlook, there is one location further along the trip where a look through Castle Arch is possible.

Sky Bridge as viewed from the Sky Bridge overlook

SKY BRIDGE OVERLOOK

When you reach a fork in the road you will see one of the Sky Bridge parking lots ahead on the right. Before going into the lot,take the right fork of the road for the best view of this beautiful arch. A sign there says:

BRIDGE OVERLOOK CAMERA POINT

Drive the short distance through a picnic area until you come to the loop at the end of the road. There is very little parking space at the loop. If you arrive on a busy day, it would be better to use the new parking lot found on the left just before the turnoff to Sky Bridge Overlook. From the loop there is a blacktop footpath that, in less than 100 yards of easy walking, brings you to the overlook. At the guard rail, look left, and the view of the arch is before you. Measuring 74 feet in length and 23 feet above the ground, it is one of the largest and, perhaps, the most beautiful arch in the Gorge. Like Princess Arch, it belongs in the finished arch class since its surfaces are graceful and smooth. Many of the lost siver mine hunters believe this is the "hole in the cliff" mentioned in John Swift's journals.

After you have drunk in the splendor of Sky Bridge, turn and look over the opposite side. You again are looking into the valley cut by Swift Camp Creek. The closest rock outcropping almost directly across the valley is the ridge that contains Castle Arch, though from here you can see only its top. Look to your right, and among the trees you can see the railings of Swift Creek Overlook where you were probably standing a few minutes earlier. You can't see Swift Creek from here either, but it curves around the base of the ridge that contains Castle Arch. Looking down into the valley of Swift Creek, you can easily see a section of Highway 715 below you. If you are completing the Gorge loop, you will cover that section of road on your way to the bottom of the Gorge.

SKY BRIDGE WALK

After returning to your car, drive the short distance back to the fork and turn right into the parking lot. At the far end of the lot, the walk to Sky Bridge commences. There are rest rooms here and a drinking fountain. Next to the drinking fountain the black top trail commences. At the end of the auto turnaround there is a sign which says:

SKY BRIDGE TRAIL NO. 214
SKY BRIDGE 1/4
SKY BRIDGE LOOP 1

Another sign nearby explains that there are over 750 species of plants found in the Gorge area representing ecosystems that are found from Atlanta, Georgia in the south to Montreal, Canada in the north.

There are three different alternatives here for the sightseer. The first is to take the very easy walk to the top of the bridge where both the Red River and Swift Camp Creek are visible. The second is to continue on to the end of the ridge which is just a couple of hundred yards of easy walking after you cross Sky Bridge. From there you can see a bridge that crosses the Red River and look into the upper Gorge. The third alternative is to take a loop trail that continues on from the end of the ridge, doubles back from the end of the ridge and takes you under the arch. Except for a set of 77 wooden steps at the end of the loop, the walk is an easy ¾ mile stroll. The steps themselves are not frightening for they have sturdy handrails and four platforms where you can catch your breath. But 77 steps is about the same as walking up to the sixth floor of an average building. If a couple of stories leaves you huffing and puffing you had better stop and weigh the consequences. The rest of the loop trip is baby simple.

The first part of this walk is paved and quite wide. Don't let children stray off the trail for this is a dangerous high cliff area. After a short distance you arrive at an overlook with guard rails on your left. Here, through the trees in all seasons of the year, one bend of the Red River and a stretch of Route 715 are visible. You will pass over that section of road later on the loop trip.

A few yards past the overlook you arrive on top of Sky Bridge. The upper surface of the arch has, unfortunately, become easily identifiable by the illegally carved names and initials of vandals and fools on it. Even though it is a federal offense, the desecration of these natural landmarks goes on at a frightening rate.

When you reach the center of the span, the view to your right looks down into the valley of Swift Creek, visible for the first time on this trip. You can also see a stretch of Route 715 that you cover later on the loop drive. Looking down from the other side of the arch you view a rather unexciting part of the north fork of the Red River.

After crossing Sky Bridge, the paved trail continues along the ridge top with a metal guard rail to aid you.There is an overlook at the end of the ridge which is enclosed in a wooden guard rail. At this spot you can see the cement bridge on Route 715 crossing the Red River about 400 feet below you. This bridge is the division point between the upper and lower sections of the Red River Gorge. If you look straight ahead up the river, you can see the precipitous cliffs on each side of the narrow upper Gorge. It is a magic wonderland of scenery now designated by state law as a "Wild River". To me, the Upper Gorge is as ruggedly beautiful as any area I have seen in the Eastern United States, but there are no roads or overlooks for the Upper Gorge. About the only way to see the entire Upper Gorge is by floating through with a canoe or kayak, a trip that should be considered by experienced whitewater paddlers only.(For description see page 145) Hikers can walk the first two miles along the river bank by taking the Douglas Trail (see Pg.161).

If you want to go under Sky Bridge and complete the loop walk, turn right at the guard rail and start down the trail that begins to descend the side of the ridge. Another easy 200 yard walk and 40 wooden steps lower you down to the underside of Sky Bridge. From here you can see that the underside of this arch is divided into two distinct sections. A pinnacle hanging down from the central span of the arch thins out to a column touching the ground. This forms two separate openings under the span; the smallest measures 9 feet long and 6 feet high, the larger being 73 feet long and 23 feet high.

To continue the loop walk, after passing the arch, you will soon descend ten wooden steps and pass by some small rock shelters. It is conceivable that sometime in the geologic future a few of these rock shelters might become new arches. But don't wait around watching, for a prospective new arch won't be completed till long after we are beyond speculating about such earthly matters.

Just beyond the rock shelters near the 77 wooden steps that take you back up to the ridge top there are interesting geologic formations etched in the side of the cliff wall consisting of many swirling stone lines that were created by stream action in the river deltas and shallow seas many millions of years ago. Once you have negotiated the 77 wooden steps a short blacktop walk completes the loop by returning you to within sight of the drinking fountain. When you return to the parking lot you may want to use the toilet facilities here since they are the last you will encounter on the loop drive.

TO CASTLE ARCH VIEW

Take the Sky Bridge Road back to the junction of Route 715. Check your mileage indicator at the intersection, then turn left on Route 715 in the direction of Frenchburg. When you have gone exactly ½ mile from the intersection, look carefully through the top of the trees on the right side of the road and almost parallel to it for a view of Castle Arch. It is more easily seen when the leaves have fallen, but is still visible here during the spring and summer months. This is the arch that looked like a rock shelter from Swift Creek Overlook, This arch in formation measures 13 feet high and 45 feet long.

MOONSHINER'S ARCH

In less than half a mile from the road view of Sky Bridge, you arrive at the bottom of the Gorge and cross the cement bridge over the north fork of the Red River. After you have crossed the bridge you will see a parking lot of sorts on the right side of the road. This is the area to park if you want to take the short walk to Moonshiner's Arch or the unofficial Douglas Trail (see page 161).

Moonshiner's Arch has not been included because of its beauty, for it isn't really a very attractive span. I include it because of its unique geologic and historical interest. It is a limestone arch and formed in an entirely different way than the sandstone arches you have seen. It is also the only limestone arch that is close to the road and easy to get to.

Its name also is a result of an odd geologic formation. There is a round hole about 5 feet in diameter which goes from the underside of the span clear through to the top. It made a marvelous natural chimney, so before good roads were built in the lower Gorge, moonshiners placed their smoking stills under it. Although the arch has a rather large front opening, the smaller opening in the back which completes the span is only 16 feet long with a height of 9 feet.

If your decision is to see Moonshiner's Arch walk toward the river from the parking area and you will see a well used trail heading down toward the river bank. This is the beginning of the Douglas Trail. Moving upstream, the trail then parallels the river. In a very short distance the trail threads its way through an area of boulders where an underground stream surfaces from under two large rocks before it tumbles into the Red River some 30 feet away. A short distance beyond this

Moonshiner's Arch

stream, the trail takes you to within sight of Moonshiner's Arch which is off the trail to the left. It's about a five minute walk from the parking lot.

Returning to the road, you will find that just beyond the bridge and the parking lot you can see a narrow road to the left (with a gate that is often closed) that goes down to the river. The bridge is the dividing line between the upper and lower gorge and this is the take-out point for the whitewater paddlers shooting the upper gorge and the put-in for those canoeists who wish to do the easier but far less scenic lower gorge. If you would like to canoe this Class One section of the river and do not have a canoe you will see a sign on the right hand side of the road which says: Red River Canoe Rental, and is in operation at this writing during pleasant weekends in season when the river has adequate water levels.

After returning to your vehicle, continue westward along Route 715. For the next few miles the road follows along the Red River. This area along the Lower Gorge is a pleasant and very curvy woodland drive.

About a mile beyond the cement bridge, you can see some very large boulders in the Red River. These huge rocks are the same ones Al Cornett painted in the large oil painting which hangs in Hemlock Lodge at Natural Bridge State Park.

Continuing on Route 715 you will soon get glimpses of Tower Rock to the right and above you. This solitary pinnacle, standing better than 200 feet above the level of the road, was made from more weather resisting sandstone and has survived, while the ridge that once contained it has now eroded away. A trail has recently been added that circles the tower. Look for a trailhead sign at the right side of the road.

This trail was constructed to aid rock climbers in getting to the bottom of Tower Rock.The trail has a moderate to moderately steep climb with a round trip distance of a little over a mile. It will take 30 to 45 minutes walking time to complete the hike. I am told the views from atop Tower Rock are impressive but I've never seen the view. Neither will you unless you are a serious rock climber for the trail only circles the base of the rock and does not take you to the top. Rock climbers consider this an easy climb but, for people not trained and equipped for this activity, the ascent up its walls is nearly impossible. The trail itself, although easy to follow, is disappointing for it remains largely closed in and offers no panoramic views. When you reach the base of the rock the trail takes you through one interesting geologic feature. It passes through a vertical joint fracture of a very large slump block.

BELL FALLS

Slightly over a half mile from Tower Rock there is a sign on the right side of the road announcing Bell Falls. It is a quite short but somewhat difficult walk back to the falls because the contour of the ground is quite steep and often slippery. With water trickling over a sandstone ledge and falling about 25 feet, this is a pretty but hardly spectacular falls. Unless you have a strong waterfall addiction and your emotions are set afire by every falling rivulet, you can bypass Bell tell Falls and feel certain that you have not deprived yourself of one of nature's great natural wonders.

TO CHIMNEY TOP VIEW

About ¾ of a mile beyond the falls the road crosses the bridge over Gladie Creek. The bottom of the Gorge is wider here and one can see that this bottom road curves sharply left. In a few more yards it curves sharply right. If the foliage is not too heavy, look left at this curve across the road and field until you see a deteriorating ridge on the other side of the Gorge. In the edge of that ridge there is a profile of a human face visible in the winter months. This profile rock looks very much like a dour faced George Washington.

Approximately 1½ miles further on, look for a sign for Chimney Top View on the left side of the road. From this viewpoint, you can easily see the 3½ foot crack that separates this precipitous joint fractured slump block from the cliff. You can also see the guard rails where you stood earlier in the day if you made the short walk to Chimney Top. The highest level of Chimney Top is more then 500 feet above the level of the road.

TO SILVER BRIDGE AND RAVEN'S ROCK

Continuing approximately a mile beyond Chimney Top View, you can look left across the flood plain of the Red River to the ridges rising on the other side. You can see the erosion caused by Chimney Top Creek, Rush Branch and others, leaving this series of ridges where many of the forest service trails are located.

Route 715 dead ends into Kentucky Route 77. Turn left on South 77 in the direction of Nada. In less than a mile a gargantuan solitary rock promontory known as Raven's Rock becomes easily visible. For years it was believed that ravens used its pock-marked cliffs for nesting places. Birds do nest in them but they are vultures, not ravens. If you arrive here late in the afternoon, you may be able to see a small opening (lighthouse) that is called Raven's Window high up on Raven's Rock.

Highway 77 then turns left and goes over the Silver Bridge. If it is late in the afternoon, go about .1 mile beyond the bridge and stop. Look right, in the general direction of Raven's Rock and you may be able to see another small lighthouse known as Goldfinch Window or Goldfinch Eye.

Over a decade ago a former automobile dealer from Mount Sterling, Ky. envisioned turning Raven's Rock into a major tourist attraction. He spent considerable sums of money on the project, which included building a steep paved road to its top, so people could drive up to what is probably the most spectacular overlook in the entire Gorge area. Further plans included the eventual building of a restaurant atop the rock with the view to whet the appetite of the diners. A fee was charged for driving private autos to the top. Serious problems soon arose. In September of 1976 a two day hang gliding tournament was held atop Raven's Rock

Chimney Top Rock

with the participants sailing off the 600 foot cliff into the valley below. On the first day of the meet a young pilot from Cincinnati was killed. It was thought at that time to be just an unfortunate freak accident and the meet was allowed to continue. A second fatality occured on the next day. Again, the victim was also from Cincinnati. Since both men were experienced hang glider pilots and had soared from Raven's Rock on several previous occasions, it was never fully determined whether the dual deaths were due to peculiar wind shifts around the rock, or to pilot error. Hang gliding has been forbidden from the rock since these accidents.

The number of autos making this steep and somewhat hazardous trip up and down did not produce enough revenue to keep the inclined road in repair so the whole enterprize was abandoned. Raven's Rock has since been purchased by the federal government and is now part of the Daniel Boone National Forest. Serious erosion cuts in the road have made it impassible for even F.W.D vehicles but hiking up the abandoned road can be a pleasant experience. Even though the view is outstanding, there are several things to consider before making the ascent. The round trip of almost four miles will take at least a a couple of hours with an altitude gain of 500 feet in about ½ mile. At this writing there is no parking area on public ground and there is no drinking water at the top. But for those in good condition and who have time for the climb the view offered from the top of Raven's Rock certainly makes the hike worthwhile (see pg. 157).

UP TO NADA TUNNEL

Beyond the Raven's Rock turnoff, Route 77 begins a gradual climb out of the Gorge. About 1¾ miles from Silver Bridge, the Martin's Branch section of Rough Trail begins on the left. It is just beyond a little red cabin on the left side of the road.

Beyond here, the climbing on Route 77 becomes steeper. As your vehicle negotiates the rise, notice the very high cliff to the left. That is Tunnel Ridge, and you

View about half way through Nada Tunnel

Digging Nada Tunnel in 1911 (Courtesy of Elizabeth McCoy and the Red River Historical Society)

Rapelling from Half Moon Rock

will soon be passing through it. After a series of curves you arrive at Nada Tunnel.

Built as a logging railroad tunnel in 1911, its rather scanty dimensions of a 12 foot height and 13 foot width allow only one-way traffic. Those with large campers or trailers in tow may find the squeeze a bit uncomfortable, but I've seen Full-sized school busses go through with no difficulty. There are no lights in the tunnel so when you peer through its 700 foot length, the opening on the other end looks suspiciously tiny. Some drivers believe that the other end of the tunnel isn't big enough to accommadate a car. It is, but headlights are necessary. A word of caution for those on bicycles. If your bike does not have a headlight, walk your bike through, for it is only too easy to collide with a wall in the darkened interior. If you are in a car remember to turn your lights off when you have cleared the tunnel.

NADA AND BEYOND

A mile and a half beyond the tunnel you begin passing through the town that gave the tunnel its name. Sixty years ago Nada was a thriving community with a population of over a thousand people, the center of a profitable lumbering operation. Once the forests were cut, the town's major economic activity was at an end and no new enterprise emerged to take its place. Those people who chose to continue living in Nada have found steady employment difficult to come by. The result has meant abject poverty for many of the town's inhabitants, an all too common sight for many small communities in Appalachia.

After passing through the town you go under the Mountain Parkway and hit Route 15. If you wish to return to, the Slade Interchange, turn left on Route 15 and in about two miles you will again be in Slade, completing the loop trip.

VI
NATURAL BRIDGE STATE PARK, ITS TRAILS AND OTHER FEATURES AND WHITTLETON BRANCH TRAIL OF THE DANIEL BOONE NATIONAL FOREST

Natural Bridge is the best known of the many arches in the Red River Gorge area. It is, in some ways, the largest and by far the most frequently visited arch in this region. For this reason some people shy away from visiting this span, but the views from the ridge top on and near Natural Bridge are distinctive and beautiful enough to make it worthwhile for the most insular of souls. If you are coming to the park by way of the Mountain Parkway, exit at Slade and head south on Highway 11 in the direction of Beattyville. In about two miles you will enter Natural Bridge State Park (number IX on large map). Use the smaller fold out map of the state park on page 52 to help you locate the various points of interest in the park.

After entering the park, you must decide whether to walk up the half-mile trail to the Bridge or to ride up the

SKYLIFT

If you opt for the ride, turn right on the first road you come to after entering the park. A sign there indicates that it will take you to Hemlock Lodge and the Sky Lift. After crossing a bridge, you make another right hand turn and travel on this road until you see the parking lot for the Sky Lift on the left. For those who are badly out of shape, obese, physically handicapped, just plain lazy or really interested in taking the ride, the Sky Lift is a safe and effortless way to get to the top of the ridge within easy walking distance to the arch. The ten-minute ride is about a half mile long and rises 600 feet in altitude. At this writing, the Sky Lift operates daily from the Sunday closest to April 15 to the last Sunday in October. If you use the Sky Lift, turn to page 61 for descriptions of what to see after you arrive at the top of the ridge. Many prefer to ride up, then take the easy walk down one of the trails. This is a nice plan, but it has one drawback. It is about 1.1 miles from the end of the trails back to the Sky Lift parking lot. It is an easy downhill walk but might create a problem for some. If you decide to walk up to the Bridge, your next step will be

FINDING THE NATURAL BRIDGE TRAILS

Two automobile parking lots are close to the beginning of the trails. See which one suits your purpose. The first of them is the **HEMLOCK LODGE PARKING LOT.** (Letter X on the Natural Bridge Park map). If you are staying overnight at Hemlock Lodge or plan to use their dining facilities, the lodge parking lot may best suit your purpose. Turn right off Route 11 at the Hemlock Lodge sign, cross the bridge and turn left up the hill to the lodge parking lot. If you are pulling a trailer, driving a large motor home or truck or have no particular reason to go to the lodge, do not use this lot. It is very narrow, on a dead end road and has limited space in which to turn around. Excessive amounts of motor vehicle traffic, especially on spring and fall weekends, often leads to large traffic snarls. This can be avoided by using the gift shop, nature trail and swimming pool parking lot (see below). To find the trail heads from the Hemlock Lodge parking lot, walk on the road past the lodge until the road dead ends at the far end of the lodge. Don't drive to the end unless there is a compelling reason to do so, since the natural contour of the land restricts the paved area at the end of the road to a very narrow turn-

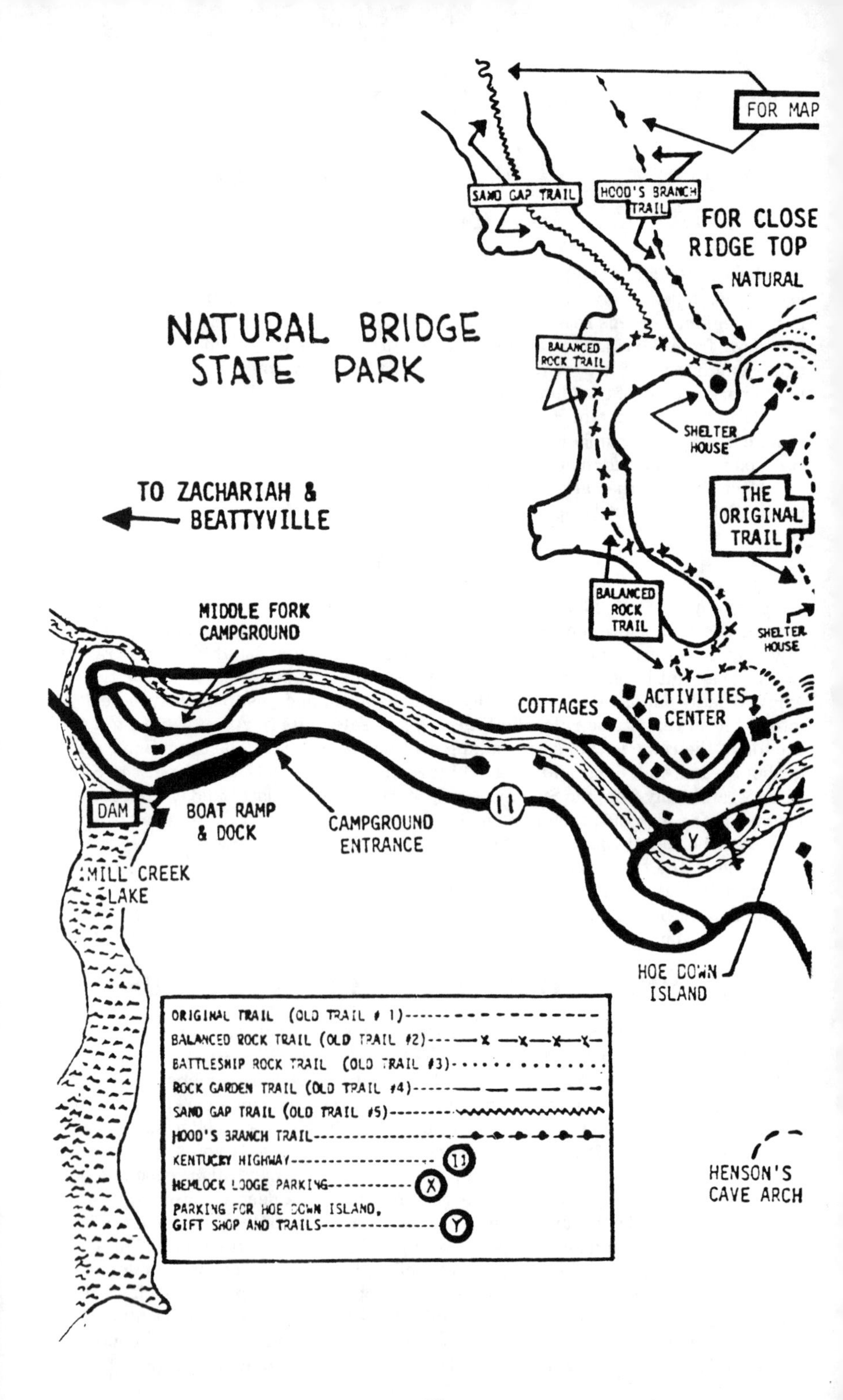
NATURAL BRIDGE
STATE PARK
FOR MAP
SAND GAP TRAIL
HOOD'S BRANCH TRAIL
FOR CLOSE
RIDGE TOP
NATURAL
BALANCED ROCK TRAIL
SHELTER HOUSE
TO ZACHARIAH & BEATTYVILLE
THE ORIGINAL TRAIL
BALANCED ROCK TRAIL
SHELTER HOUSE
MIDDLE FORK CAMPGROUND
COTTAGES
ACTIVITIES CENTER
DAM
BOAT RAMP & DOCK
CAMPGROUND ENTRANCE
11
Y
MILL CREEK LAKE
HOE DOWN ISLAND
ORIGINAL TRAIL (OLD TRAIL # 1)
BALANCED ROCK TRAIL (OLD TRAIL #2)
BATTLESHIP ROCK TRAIL (OLD TRAIL #3)
ROCK GARDEN TRAIL (OLD TRAIL #4)
SAND GAP TRAIL (OLD TRAIL #5)
HOOD'S BRANCH TRAIL
KENTUCKY HIGHWAY
HEMLOCK LODGE PARKING
PARKING FOR HOE DOWN ISLAND, GIFT SHOP AND TRAILS
HENSON'S CAVE ARCH

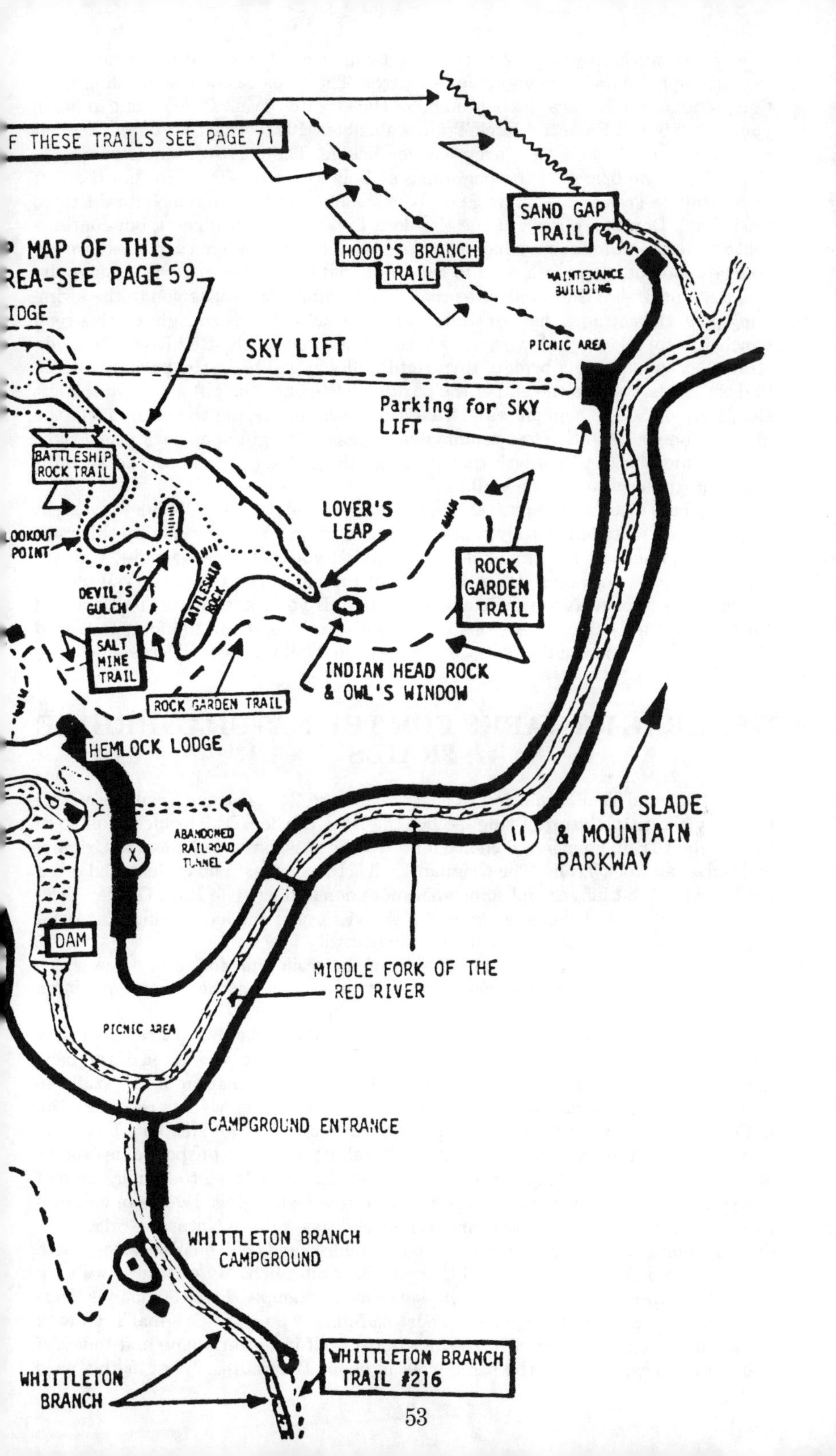

F THESE TRAILS SEE PAGE 71
P MAP OF THIS
REA-SEE PAGE 59
IDGE
SKY LIFT
HOOD'S BRANCH
TRAIL
SAND GAP
TRAIL
MAINTENANCE
BUILDING
PICNIC AREA
Parking for SKY
LIFT
BATTLESHIP
ROCK TRAIL
LOOKOUT
POINT
DEVIL'S
GULCH
BATTLESHIP
ROCK
LOVER'S
LEAP
ROCK
GARDEN
TRAIL
SALT
MINE
TRAIL
INDIAN HEAD ROCK
& OWL'S WINDOW
ROCK GARDEN TRAIL
HEMLOCK LODGE
ABANDONED
RAILROAD
TUNNEL
TO SLADE
& MOUNTAIN
PARKWAY
11
X
DAM
MIDDLE FORK OF THE
RED RIVER
PICNIC AREA
CAMPGROUND ENTRANCE
WHITTLETON BRANCH
CAMPGROUND
WHITTLETON
BRANCH
WHITTLETON BRANCH
TRAIL #216

around. From the turning circle there is a wide asphalt foot path that takes you to a drinking fountain within just a few yards. The steps beside the drinking fountain going up the hill are the beginning of the Original Trail. If you want to begin your trail hike on Balanced Rock Trail, walk about 100 feet farther on the asphalt path and you will come to a large wooden bridge. The narrow stone stairway to the right of the bridge is the beginning of Balanced Rock Trail.To find the Gift Shop, Nature Trail and swimming pool parking lot. (Letter Y on the Natural Bridge Park map). Don't turn right at the Hemlock Lodge-Sky Lift turnoff, but continue south on Route 11 for about a half mile. After the road climbs a hill and goes through a large road cut, there is a road to the right that starts downhill rather steeply. The state park sign there indicates that this downhill road takes you to the swimming pool, the cottages, nature trails and picnic area. You turn right on this road which quickly takes you down and over the middle fork of the Red River. Immediately after crossing the bridge, turn right and you will be in the parking lot. To find the trails, walk to the end of the parking lot toward the gift shop. On the left side, you will see an asphalt walk. Take this path up, passing the entrance of the gift shop on your right. When you have have passed the gift shop do not turn right on the wide blacktop footpath that parallels the gift shop, but proceed straight ahead on the crushed stone walk.

In a short distance the path starts uphill. Soon the path will divide. Turn right here and you will immediately cross a wooden bridge. You continue up this path until it dead ends at a large asphalt footpath. If you look to your right, you will see a drinking fountain on the other side of the path. The Original Trail begins at the stone steps next to the drinking fountain. If you want to start on Balanced Rock Trail, turn left on the asphalt walk and continue about 100 feet. Balanced Rock Trail begins at another set of stone steps just before the walk crosses a large wooden bridge.

GENERAL REMARKS FOR THE NATURAL BRIDGE TRAILS

The Original Trail, Balanced Rock Trail and the Rock Garden Trail are official trails for hiking to Natural Bridge. Since the Rock Garden Trail branches off from the Original Trail, your initial choice for a trail head is narrowed down to Original and Balanced Rock Trails. The Original Trail is the shortest and easiest. Balanced Rock Trail is a bit longer and somewhat more demanding. The Rock Garden Trail is the longest trail of those beginning in the vicinity of the lodge which take you to the Bridge. It is not, however, a difficult trail.

Check the general description of each of the trails that follow and see which one suits you best. Many visitors take one trail up and another down, making a nice loop hike.

There are three trails that start at the Bridge itself. Sand Gap Trail (formerly Trail #5), the longest in the state park, follows around the perimeter of the park and ends at the Sky Lift. Battleship Rock Trail is a combination of old Trails #6 and #3, which takes you to several interesting overlooks as well as the site of an old niter mine, Devil's Gulch and a small arch known as The Needle's Eye. The newest trail in the park, and possibly the loveliest and most unspoiled, is Hood's Branch Trail. For anyone in good physical condition and used to hiking, none of the trails leading to Natural Bridge is physically challenging. I've seen children as young as two and senior citizens in their eighties walk to Natural Bridge with little discomfort. However, most very young children and octogenarians, along with many others in between, will find these trails a bit much. My own first walk up to the Bridge several years ago might serve as an example. I was 30 pounds overweight and badly out of shape. The short half-mile trip up the Original Trail took me an agonizing half hour. I have since got myself in better shape and today, if I am in a hurry, I can do the same walk in about 12 minutes. Even at this pace

I can be passed by healthy teen-agers with such speed that I feel like a giant sloth with an underproductive thyroid gland.

When you look at the short distance of the Original Trail you might say, "Simple. Anyone can walk a half mile." Well-almost anyone. Frequently, I have seen people in an advanced stage of exhaustion on that short trail, swearing that the half mile distance sign at the beginning of the trail was a bigger snow job than the "Unsinkable Titanic". But the sign is exactly right. It isn't the distance that tires people, but the climb in elevation. Except possibly for Devil's Gulch on the Battleship Rock Trail, none of the trails to Natural Bridge are excessively steep, but the gain in elevation is almost 500 feet. To realize what this means, think of how many stairs you would have to climb to get to the top of a 40 story building. Of course, the trail gradient is less demanding than a stairway, but you still gain about the same altitude.

For those whose health is impaired by emphysema, obesity, heart trouble, arthritis or any other crippling handicap, the trails to Natural Bridge can present formidable obstacles, and the option of taking the Sky Lift should be seriously considered. However, if you are in good general health and want to punish yourself for not taking up jogging or an exercise program, for always waiting for the elevator for one flight up, or for avoiding taking positive action to lessen the dimensions of that 25 pound spare tire around your middle, try the Original Trail. It won't kill you, but it will make you groan just enough to show that the sedentary life is not adding to your longevity. If you wish to do extra penance because of excessive laziness and gluttony and feel the need to purge yourself even more, try going up Balanced Rock Trail. The 450 odd steps of that trail will cleanse the souls of the unconditioned of any sign of guilt for at least a week.

To aid those walkers who want to make a loop hike for the journey to Natural Bridge, I have described the trails in both directions. The uphill description of all trails begins below, while the description of the same trails in the opposite direction begins on page 67 . There is a detailed map of the ridge top area around the Bridge on page 59 . This map and the section entitled, **WHAT TO DO AND SEE AT THE TOP OF NATURAL BRIDGE** (page 61), will help you find the most interesting things to see on your walk to the arch. Before you set off on a hike, you might want to read the short chapter entitled, **TRAIL TIPS, SAFETY AND SUGGESTED HIKES,** beginning on page 30 if you have not already done so.

THE ORIGINAL TRAIL (formerly Trail #1) TO NATURAL BRIDGE

Distance: ½ mile one way
Hike: MODERATE
Walking Time: 15 to 30 minutes one way

GENERAL REMARKS. The recent renaming of old Trail #1 seems appropriate since it was the first trail to this famous arch and has been in constant use since the opening of the park in 1895. It is the most heavily used trail in the state and has now been declared a National Recreation Trail by the U.S. Department of Interior. Although the routing is the same today as it was when I first walked it several years ago it had changed more than any other trail in this book. In comparing the terrain in photographs taken of Natural Bridge taken about at the beginning of this century and the present, over four feet of soil has disappeared from under the Bridge in the ensuing four score years. Because of this constant erosion caused by the thousands of hikers that walk it every year, over 40 tons of gravel have been added to the base to keep the trail from becoming a canyon. Despite this heavy use, the trail can still give you the exotic feeling of entering a deep unspoiled woods. This is especially true if you walk the trail during the early morning hours before the hordes come on their often littering ways. You will no linger find lady slippers blooming alongside the trail as you could 40 years ago, but with the gargantuan efforts of the state park personnel, the trail surroundings look remarkably natural and fresh. It remains the quickest, easiest and most traveled foot path to Natural Bridge.

TRAIL DESCRIPTION. At the trail head just to the left of the stone steps next to the drinking fountain a sign there says:

THE ORIGINAL TRAIL
SHORTEST ROUTE TO NATURAL BRIDGE

Here, the trail starts up nine stone steps and very shortly there are 50 more. At the top of the steps, a smaller trail comes in from the left, but the Original Trail continues straight ahead. About 40 feet beyond the steps, the Rock Garden Trail exits to the right. A sign there says:

ROCK GARDEN TRAIL
HEMLOCK LODGE 1.6 MI.

Not far beyond this point, the trail passes a little shelter house on the right. Off the left side of the trail, almost directly across from the shelter house, is a typical limestone sinkhole that is more common in the Mammoth Cave area. If you climb down in the sinkhole (which is perfectly safe to do) you can see a narrow opening in the limestone wall. This opens into a limestone cave that connects with a rock shelter on Balanced Rock Trail. In the days when the park was owned by the L & N Railroad, electric lights illuminated the interior for those wishing to walk through the cave.

Through the years the opposite end of the cave became silted up making passage though it almost impossible. Most of that silt has now been removed, and, providing you're not too claustrophobic and you have a flashlight, a walk through this narrow limestone cave is now fairly easy.

Not long after passing the sinkhole, the trail begins climbing again and soon makes a switchback to the left. Now you have a nice pock-marked sandstone wall on your right. I remember walking by this wall one February afternoon when it sparkled and glittered like an ice palace, covered with dozens of huge icicles—some over 20 feet high.

When the path reaches the other end of the wall, the trail switches back again and goes by a second shelter on the left. Since the grade here is a little stiff many out of shape walkers rest here, possibly thinking the trail goes on forever into some sort of endless void. Actually, the shelter house is over ⅔ of the way to the Bridge. From here you have only a little over 200 yards-all uphill- to bring you to the underside of the arch.

After leaving the shelter house and climbing up some substantial wooden steps, a few yards more finds the trail cutting to the left. You continue up until the trail cuts sharply to the right and Voilaı-a few feet more and you are under the span of Natural Bridge.

To locate various trail beginnings, stand facing the arch with the direction of the lodge at your back. To the right on this side of the arch you will see the sign for the Battleship Rock Trail. Also on the right side of the arch but after passing under it, you will see the sign for the Rock Garden Trail. If you look left on this opposite side of the Natural Bridge you will see the narrow passage for Fat Man's Misery which takes you to the top of the arch and just to its right you will see the sign for the Hood's Branch Trail. Now turn to the section entitled **WHAT TO DO AND SEE ON TOP OF NATURAL BRIDGE** beginning on page 61.

BALANCED ROCK TRAIL (formerly Trail #2) TO NATURAL BRIDGE

Distance: ¾ mile one way

Balanced Rock alongside a popular Natural Bridge trail

Hike: MODERATE
Walking Time: 30 to 45 minutes one way

GENERAL REMARKS. If you don't like climbing steps, you won't like Balanced Rock Trail for you go up over 450 of them to reach the top of the Bridge. If you don't mind walking down steps, a nice short loop hike can be made by going up on the Original Trail then returning on Balanced Rock Trail. There is an interesting rock shelter in limestone along this trail which has the beginning of a short cave at its rear which goes through to the Original Trail. It used to be the only rock shelter of any consequence found on a trail in the state park, but there is now a very large and attractive one alongside the new Hood's Branch Trail. Since most of the really unusual rock shelters are in sandstone strata, this limestone shelter is not at all common in an area with many shelters. The unusual geologic formation that gives this trail its name is found close to the trail. Balanced Rock is a very large hunk of sandstone with much of its foundation eroded away, leaving it seemingly balanced precariously on its little stem. This trail also has two or three nice peek-a-boo views of Lookout Point and the valley leading up to Natural Bridge.

TRAIL DESCRIPTION. Balanced Rock Trail begins just 100 feet east of the Original Trail on the same asphalt walk. A sign to the left of the trail reads:

BALANCED ROCK TRAIL
NATURAL BRIDGE 0.75 MI

The trail immediately goes up 100 stone steps. At the top of the steps, the trail turns left in front of a small rock shelter sometimes known as "the cave". Although it is nowhere near as big as some in the Gorge.This is the limestone shelter mentioned previously.

At the back of this shelter, you can see a small opening which often has water flowing from it. This little hole was once many times larger permitting easy access to a small cave that comes out at the sinkhole on the Original Trail. During the railroad days, electric lights were strung through it to aid visitors in the dark interior.

In recent times the entrance to the cave at the back of the rock shelter was silted up so badly that it was nearly impossible to get through, but now the silt has been removed and passage is fairly easy. It is best to have a flashlight along if you want to follow this short cave through to the other trail.

It is not much of a walk beyond the shelter before Balanced Rock appears just off the left side of the trail. At the turn of the century, when the park was owned by the Lexington and Eastern Railroad, this local landmark was known as the Sphinx. Somehow the name got changed but photographs taken in the late nineteenth century show that it has changed very little in the last 85 years.

It is just beyond Balanced Rock that the real climbing begins with three long sections of wooden stairway containing over 90 steps. Afterwards, the trail begins to swing around the head of Rocky Point. There are several groups of stone stairways in this section, the longest having about 50 steps. The trail then works its way around on a ledge of the cliff face of Rocky Point. There is a metal guardrail along the trail here since there is a considerable drop-off. It is not frightening, but it is best to supervise closely rambunctious young children in this area.

Most of the climbing is now over and you will soon come to a second ledge with a metal guard rail on the right much like the first one. If you look through the trees, not only can you see Lookout Point directly across the valley from you, but by looking left, you can see the top of Natural Bridge.

The trail soon works its way to the top of the ridge, and after an easy ridge top walk, you will see the junction sign for Sand Gap Trail. A sign there says:

SAND GAP TRAIL
WHITE'S BRANCH ARCH 3.0 MI
HEMLOCK LODGE 6.0 MI
CAMPING-FIREBUILDING PROHIBITED

Shortly after passing by this junction, you go up and over an exposed sandstone knob unfortunately scarred by nefarious initial carvers. There is large shelter house on the right. Keep this shelter to the right and by walking a few more yards, you will be on top of Natural Bridge. Immediately on the left you will see a set of stone steps which lead you to Fat Man's Misery and then under the arch. Turn to page 61 for the section entitled **WHAT TO DO AND SEE ON TOP OF NATURAL BRIDGE.**

ROCK GARDEN TRAIL (formerly Trail #4) TO NATURAL BRIDGE

Distance: 1.6 miles one way
Hike: MODERATE Walking Time: 45 minutes to 1 hour 15 minutes

GENERAL REMARKS. Since this is the longest trail beginning in the vicinity of Hemlock Lodge that takes you to Natural Bridge, it is understandably the least travelled of those trails. The trail is not difficult for a healthy walker, and it has enough interesting things to see along the way to make it a pleasurable walk. It is also the best of the short trails in the state park for wildflowers. It follows along the bottom of some beautiful cliffs and is the only trail that passes under the Sky Lift below the ridge top. It is also often used for a loop hike, using one or the other trails going up and returning by the Rock Garden Trail. The trail gradient is never steep, and the only demanding section is three series of stone steps that are quite close together and have about 100 steps in all.

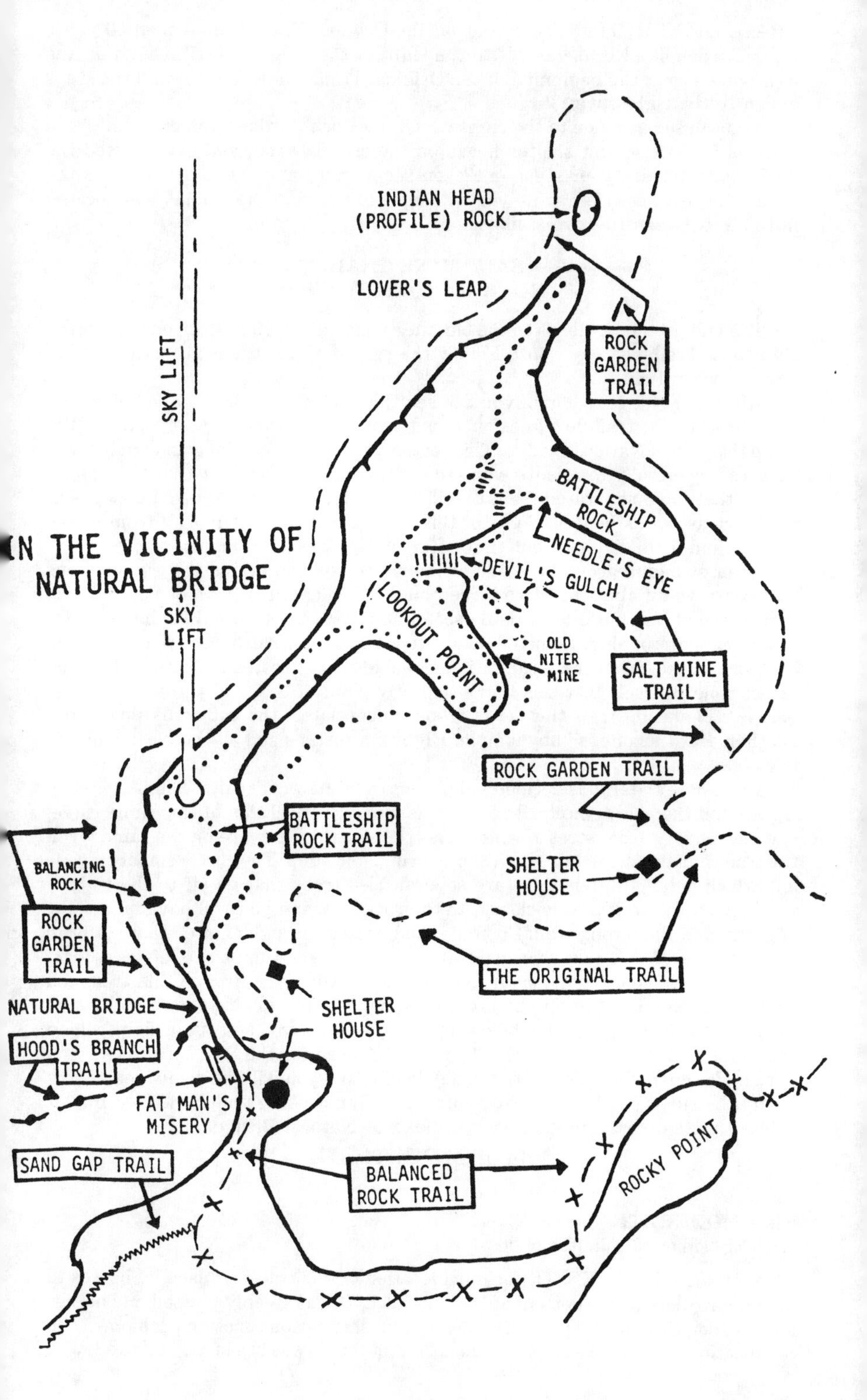
IN THE VICINITY OF NATURAL BRIDGE
INDIAN HEAD (PROFILE) ROCK
LOVER'S LEAP
ROCK GARDEN TRAIL
SKY LIFT
BATTLESHIP ROCK
NEEDLE'S EYE
DEVIL'S GULCH
LOOKOUT POINT
OLD NITER MINE
SALT MINE TRAIL
SKY LIFT
ROCK GARDEN TRAIL
BATTLESHIP ROCK TRAIL
SHELTER HOUSE
BALANCING ROCK
ROCK GARDEN TRAIL
THE ORIGINAL TRAIL
NATURAL BRIDGE
SHELTER HOUSE
HOOD'S BRANCH TRAIL
FAT MAN'S MISERY
SAND GAP TRAIL
BALANCED ROCK TRAIL
ROCKY POINT

TRAIL DESCRIPTION. Start out on the Original Trail. In less than 50 yards Rock Garden Trail branches off to the right of the Original Trail. Climb up the 50 stone steps at the beginning of the Original Trail. A few feet beyond the steps a sign to the right says:

You can see a ravine to the right which the Rock Garden Trail crosses. If you walk as far as the first shelter house on the original trail, you have passed the trail head. Retrace your steps until you see a trail to your left that crosses the ravine. Once across the ravine you will come to a fork in the trail. A sign located in the V between the two trails says:

←——— SALT MINE TRAIL
ROCK GARDEN TRAIL ———→

The trail to the left leads to the old niter mine and Devil's Gulch on the Battleship Rock Trail (see page 60). Follow the right fork for the continuation of the Rock Garden Trail.

After a slight, easy climb, you can see the roof of Hemlock Lodge below you on the right. The trail now goes on a long swing around the northern part of the ridge that forms Natural Bridge. This section of trail is easy hiking and fairly level. The trail eventually makes its way around many huge boulders known as slump blocks that have separated from the cliff face and slid down the slope. Some of them are as big as houses. Parts of this area are often a bit mucky from active springs and little rivulets, but they offer no significant problems.

After swinging around the end of the ridge, you will arrive at 34 stone steps that carry you up between two large boulders. In another 100 feet you will run into a second and more formidable set of about 60 steps carved in the face of a sandstone outcropping. Some of these steps are somewhat higher than what we are accustomed to, so the unconditioned walker may groan a little here. But you can console yourself that this is the half-way point of the trail and the prettiest part is still ahead. After this set of steps is negotiated, the trail runs smack into another. But this one is baby simple. Eight more steps and all the hard climbing is over.

From here the trail is decidedly different from the woodsy first half. After coming around the ridge, the trail now works along the backside of this same ridge, and except for a brief stretch where the trail and ridge top are on the same level, the trail remains at the bottom of some formidable cliffs. The cliffs remain on your left which is helpful, for there are several false trails that go off to the right.

Stay on the trail that is closest to the rock wall and you will have no danger of getting on the wrong trail. Soon the trail passes through an area that suffered a small forest fire a few years ago. A few blackened stumps are left as a grim reminder of this potential danger. Not long after you pass through this area, you walk under the Sky Lift. If the lift is running, it is fun to pause here and watch the people ascend slowly from below, soon to pass over you and out of sight behind the ridge wall. Because the trees had to be cleared for the Sky Lift access, you have a nice open view here of the valley below, and you will get some idea of how far up the ridge you have already climbed. After walking under the Sky Lift, it is less than a quarter mile of easy walking to Natural Bridge.

SALT MINE TRAIL

Distance: .4 mile
Hike: MODERATE
Walking Time: 10 minutes or less

GENERAL REMARKS. The original location of this trail was used by horses to take their riders to the bottom of Devil's Gulch. It was steeply pitched and horses hooves soon tore up the protective foliage causing serious erosion problems. The combination of the trail's steepness and the fact that it was in a straight line allowed

Through Fat Man's Misery next to Natural Bridge

heavy rains and the continuing action of the horse's hooves to turn the path into an ugly gully wash. But recently the trail was rerouted and is now an attractive short way to get up to the vicinity of the old niter mine, Devil's Gulch and Needle's Eye stairway. It also furnishes an interesting alternate way to Natural Bridge. By utilizing it and following Battleship Rock Trail up from the junction, then completing the loop by taking one of the available trails down on your return, this becomes one of the most scenic loops in a relatively short distance that a sightseer can take. It is somewhat steep, but its briefness makes it well within the capacity of a healthy walker.

TRAIL DESCRIPTION. To find the trail head follow the Rock Garden Trail. It is only a short distance from the point where Rock Garden Trail turns off from the Original Trail to the beginning of the Salt Mine Trail. A sign between a V in the trail says:

← SALT MINE TRAIL
ROCK GARDEN TRAIL →

By taking the left fork, the trail soon takes you across a wooden bridge to assist you over a steep slope on a rock outcropping. It then arrives and goes up 12 wooden steps and switches back to the right, soon arriving at the junction with the Battleship Rock Trail. By turning right you will be headed toward Devil's Gulch and the Needle's Eye stairway. A left turn will quickly take you to the steps that lead to the niter mine site. (see Battleship Rock Trail on page 62).

WHAT TO DO AND SEE AT THE TOP OF NATURAL BRIDGE

To help you locate the various points of sightseeing interest, I have included a map of the ridge top in the vicinity of the Bridge. Since both the Original Trail and the Rock Garden Trail end under the span of the Bridge, I will start with the lower section. Of course, you can alter the order of sightseeing to suit yourself. Those who have come from the Sky Lift can get to the bottom of the span by walking across the Bridge. Once across the Bridge, you will see a set of stone steps going down on the right side of the Bridge. Those stone steps take you down through Fat Man's Misery to the bottom of the arch. If you approach the arch from Balanced Rock Trail you will find these steps on the left shortly after you pass the shelter house on the right.

UNDER NATURAL BRIDGE

The diagram below shows the position of the four trail heads and their signs that begin under Natural Bridge.

LODGE

↑

BATTLESHIP ROCK TRAIL

THE ORIGINAL TRAIL SHORTEST ROUTE TO HEMLOCK LODGE

(FAT MAN'S MISERY)

ROCK GARDEN TRAIL HEMLOCK LODGE 1.6 MI

HOODS BRANCH TRAIL

Some believe that Natural Bridge is the largest natural arch in the state. In this they are wrong, for there are two arches in the southern part of the state whose measurements exceed Natural Bridge both in height and length. Those who say that Natural Bridge is the largest in the area are closer to the truth, but some modification is required. When you stand under the arch and look up, that magnificent span is 65 feet above you, by far the tallest in the area. It is 78 feet long from one end of the span to the other, which makes it almost the longest as well. Gray's Arch out distances it by a mere two feet and the front side of Whittleton Arch measures about 100 feet. Probably little has changed on the underside of the arch in the last few hundred years, but the ground level below it has altered significantly. If you look at photographs taken of the Bridge over 70 years ago, you will see that two to three more feet of the large sandstone rocks under the bridge are exposed above the ground level today.The millions of visitors who have walked under the Bridge have simply caused the ground surrounding the rocks to erode away. Alas, someday the area under the Bridge may have to be blacktopped in order to slow down the erosion.

Because of the heavy growth of trees, the view of the valleys on each side is pretty much blocked below the Bridge. This is not so when you get to the top. There is only one easy and safe way to reach the top quickly nearby the arch and that is to use Fat Man's Misery. This is a rock cleavage from the cliff face whose natural separation geologists call a vertical joint fracture (see Geology section). You make your way between the walls of this joint fracture for a distance of 83 feet. Fifty-five of the feet are between very high walls which confine you to a very restricted walking space. Although the passage is narrow, fat people or anyone else for that matter, needn't worry about getting stuck, but it only allows for one-way traffic. After you pass through Fat Man's Misery, a few sandstone steps take you to the top of Natural Bridge. Many will prefer to follow a longer loop trail leading the hiker to many interesting viewpoints which is described below.

BATTLESHIP ROCK TRAIL (formerly Trail #3 and #6)
From Under Natural Bridge to the Top

GENERAL REMARKS. This walk is a good one for seeing many of the sights and overlooks in the vicinity of Natural Bridge. Although going up through Fat Man's Misery is a much easier way to get to the top of Natural Bridge, the Battleship Rock Trail offers a loop hike which will lead you to many of the best overlooks in the vicinity. It will also take you to many interesting places as well as the best location for a panoramic view of Natural Bridge. To get up to the ridge top one must either go up Devil's Gulch or the Needle's Eye stairway which are steep enough that people with a physical handicap should avoid them. The grade up the Gulch is a rough but interesting climb. Because of its 250 foot length and its steepness, I believe it is easier to climb than to descend. Erosion has made this stairway rather treacherous and despite a Herculean effort on the part of state park personnel to keep the stairs in fairly walkable condition it still remains a rather difficult ascent. The Needle's Eye stairs are far easier to negotiate but still demand a fair amount of physical effort. Other attractions on Battleship Rock Trail include the site of an old niter mine where saltpeter was leached from the sandstone to make gunpowder for the War of 1812. The mine is not much more than a big sand hole today, but it is located under a spectacular cliff which in itself is impressive enough to make the walk worthwhile. If you walk this trail during the months when the leaves are off the trees, you will be able to get a nice view of the Needle's Eye, which is a small arch in the cliff face. Once up the ridge top it is just a short walk to Lover's Leap, which places you on top of a sheer cliff and gives an unobstructive view of the valley of Middle Fork almost 600 feet below. The return loop takes you by Lookout Point and takes you under the Sky Lift.

TRAIL DESCRIPTION. A sign at the trail head facing you says:

BATTLESHIP ROCK TRAIL.

This trail has no serious up or down sections until Devil's Gulch a little under a half mile away. Moving along the bottom of the cliff face, the trail eventually swings right to get around the bottom of Lookout Point. Just as the trail makes a left swing to get around the base of Lookout Point, look back through an opening in the trees and you get a very fine view of Natural Bridge. Once you are around Lookout Point, you won't have to walk very far before you can see the Needle's Eye dead ahead if the leaves are not on the trees. As you approach that cliff, you come to look to the left for a sign that says:

SALT MINE.

Next to the sign there is a series of steps that take you up to the level of the mine's location. At one time there was a sign here that read:

**AN OLD OVEN, PARTS OF IRON KETTLES
AND WOODEN TROUGHS
USED TO SEPARATE SALTPETER FROM ROCK**

All of these items were once there, but along with the sign, every trace of them has been destroyed or carried off by vandal souvenir hunters. All that is left is the sand which remains as mute testimony to the fate of unprotected historical sites. Just to the left there is a large sandy hole which is all that's left of the mine. Behind the hole there once was a sign which said:

**SALT MINE
HERE A COMPANY OF SOLDIERS MINED SALTPETER FOR
GUNPOWDER DURING THE WAR OF 1812**

Above the hole where the sign once stood, there is a spectacular overhanging cliff. If you wish to see an old niter mine with much of the original equipment still intact, take the D. Boon Hut hike in the Gorge, for there is an old mine in the same large rock shelter as the hut, and this mine remains in a largely unspoiled condition.

To continue, retrace your steps back to the main trail and turn left. You will

The Needle's Eye

shortly come to a sign to the right of the trail which says:

SALT MINE TRAIL ⟶
TO HEMLOCK LODGE

This trail, which goes downhill to the right, is a quick way back to the lodge area. Shortly beyond this point you will soon arrive at another junction where one trail goes straight ahead and a set of 16 wooden steps go off to the left. This set of steps plus 22 more take you to the bottom of Devil's Gulch. Even after a great deal of improvement by park personnel, the constant battle of erosion makes a walk up these steps a bit of a challenge and they can be hazardous especially if they are wet.

Over 250 feet long, the uneven and often treacherous steps of the gulch raise you 150 feet in altitude. If you have a strong desire to traverse the gulf it is easier to go up than to go down and there are now guardrails to aid you in the more hectic locations. If you wish to avoid climbing up the gulch but still desire to go to the top of Natural Bridge ridge, you can take the alternate Needle's Eye stairway.

Instead of taking the steps to the left, continue straight ahead until you come to another set of stone steps. You will go up over 80 of these steps which brings you to a narrow level area. Look to the right and you will see a narrow path which will take you to the Needle's Eye. If you get spooked when you get close to a drop-off, it might be better to skip the Needle's Eye for the ledge out to this small arch is quite narrow. Sure footed people who are careful should have no trouble.

The Needle's Eye is a classic example of two rock shelters on each side of a narrow ridge whose back walls have finally touched leaving a small opening called a lighthouse. The Needle's Eye is now in a state of erosion that classifies it somewhere between a lighthouse and an arch.

Returning to where you left the first set of stone steps, you can look to the left of the stone steps and see a second set of 26 stone steps which take you to the top of the ridge. If you turn right you have a short walk to Lover's Leap or by going left you will pass the top of Devil's Gulch, Lookout Point and under the Sky Lift. (See **SCENIC WALK TO LOVER'S LEAP.**) The points of interest described there, in reverse order, complete the Battleship Rock Trail loop.

TOP OF NATURAL BRIDGE

First, a word of warning. You are now on a ridge top where in many places there are sheer cliffs exceeding 100 feet in height. Keep your eye on your children. It isn't dangerous except for the ignorant and foolhardy. Better than half a million people walk near these precipices every year with no problem, but a few accidents do occur. The cause is almost always sheer recklessness and stupidity. Although no one has been killed falling from this area in recent years, from the antics and behavior I have too frequently witnessed in this area, I'm surprised that it doesn't happen almost daily.

Walking out on the span of the Bridge you can see the valleys open up on both sides of you. The biggest one is on the lodge side which was cut by the Middle Fork of the Red River and its tributaries. In my opinion, this panorama over Middle Fork is the best view from the top of an arch in the entire area. I've heard people exclaim, "Wow& Terrific& Unbelievable&" when first looking across this valley. And there are several equally spectacular views within a few hundred feet of this spot. The large rock promontory you see on the left is Lookout Point, where the view might be considered even better. The valley on the opposite side of Natural Bridge, cut by Upper Hood Branch, is more restrictive and not as spectacular.

I know that people often wonder when standing on the middle of Natural Bridge if anyone has ever been struck by lightening there. It happened once several years ago, and the man struck was killed. When I confirmed the accuracy of this story with Clarence Henson, he told me about a rather bizarre coincidence concerning the tragedy. The victim's home was in the vicinity of Lexington. On the same day, and possibly the same storm, his next door neighbor was killed by lightening on a golf course.

SCENIC WALK TO LOVER'S LEAP

After you cross the Bridge, you will see there a sign which reads:

BATTLESHIP ROCK TRAIL
LOOKOUT POINT
BATTLESHIP ROCK
LOVERS LEAP

You take the trail to the right of the sign to all of these places. But before you do, you may wish to see Balancing Rock. If you do, go up over a rock outcropping just to the left of the sign mentioned above. Directly behind the rock, you will see a well worn path. As you start up this path, almost immediately you will see another smaller path to the left. Take this left walk, and in a very short distance you will arrive at Balancing Rock. Use caution in approaching the rock, because part of it extends over the cliff face.

To begin the walk to Lookout Point and Lover's Leap, take the trail to the right of the large sign, previously mentioned, at the west end of the Bridge. The walk from here to Lover's Leap is less than ⅔ mile of very easy walking. This walk includes three more excellent scenic overlooks as well as a look down Devil's Gulch. The walk is fairly level and easy. By using the short cut indicated on the map on the way back from Lover's Leap you can cut the distance back to the Bridge for a round trip walk of just over a mile.

In less than 200 feet you will pass two overlooks to the right of the trail with substantial guardrails. The view from them is not exceptional. Just beyond the second of these two overlooks the trail then swings across the other side of the ridge to the Sky Lift. As you walk to the left of the Sky Lift, you will see a sign

Balancing Rock near Natural Bridge

parallel to the left side of the trail which says:

←NATURAL BRIDGE
500 FEET

and under it another sign saying:

LOOKOUT POINT →
LOVER'S LEAP →

To the left you will see another substantial guardrail and overlook slightly below the level of the Lift. Walk down to it. Not only does it give you the best view of people going up and down the Sky Lift, it also offers an exceptional mountainous panorama of a series of ridges and knobs where the Pottsville Escarpment begins eroding down on the fringe of the Bluegrass area. You can see a curve on Route 11 and look right into the parking area of the Li'l Abner Motel more than 600 feet below you. Looking off in the distance from this overlook, you can often see the blue haze that is so familiar in the Smoky Mountains and gave them their name.

From this overlook, walk under the Sky Lift. The trail now swings out to the end of Lookout Point where another excellent view awaits you. When you stand on the point with Natural Bridge on your right, the exposed rock outcropping across the valley and directly in front of you is Rocky Point. The Balanced Rock Trail skirts around this point and follows along the ridge behind it. As you look left into the valley of Middle Fork, part of the shallow pond in front of the lodge is visible. A view of the lodge is usually blocked by trees, but you will know its approximate location, as part of the parking lot is also visible. Across the valley, you can see the area that goes back into the Whittleton Branch Campground.

When you proceed on around Lookout Point, you will see the trail follows along the cliff edge to the right. Very shortly, the trail runs into a wooden guardrail and turns abruptly left. This guardrail is to keep people from falling into Devil's Gulch. Immediately after the trail turns left, it forks. The right fork is the continuation of the Balanced Rock Trail down through Devil's Gulch. The left fork in only .2 mile takes you to Lover's Leap. If you want a good view of the gulch from the top, take the right trail fork, and in just a few feet it will take you to the top of the Devil's Gulch stairway. From here you can get a good look at the gulch without having to walk down it.

The left fork curves around the top of the gulch and in a very short walk dead ends at Lover's Leap. This overlook offers possibly the most awesome straight-down view in the area. You can easily see the road that leads to the Sky Lift about 600 feet below you. The sandstone knob that is just a few yards in front of you at Lover's Leap and about as high is called the Devil's Pulpit. It is also known as Indian Head or Profile Rock, since a view from below presents the outline of a human face. Neither the face nor the lighthouse opening in this rock pinnacle known as the Owl's Window are visible from Lover's Leap, but they both can be seen down along Route 11 in the late afternoon near the entrance to Whittleton Branch Campground. If you look directly across the valley cut by Middle Fork to just below the horizon line, you will see a tiny white line. That is the Mountain Parkway and a road bridge that carries Route 15 over the road. As the crow flies, that spot is just a little over two miles away, but it seems more like ten. If you want to take the Red River Gorge automobile loop trip, I have included that spot in the description so you will be able to look back the other way and see how these high precipices shrink when viewed from that distance. The large finger of the ridge you are standing on that you can see jutting out into the valley on your right is Battleship Rock. During the railroad days there was a flagpole at the end of the rock, and each day an employee worked his way out there to raise and lower the flag.

TRAILS FROM NATURAL BRIDGE BACK TO THE PARKING AREAS

THE ORIGINAL TRAIL (formerly Trail #1) from Natural Bridge to the parking area

Distance: ½ mile
Hike: EASY
Walking Time: 10 to 15 minutes

TRAIL DESCRIPTION. For those who used the Sky Lift or other trails up to Natural Bridge and want the easiest and quickest way back, the Original Trail is the answer. It doesn't offer as many scenic rewards as the others, but is still pleasant enough. The trail head starts under the span of Natural Bridge. To find it, walk to the lodge side of the Bridge (opposite side from Fat Man's Misery). While facing in the direction of the lodge, walk to the right side under the arch where you will see a sign which says:

THE ORIGINAL TRAIL
SHORTEST ROUTE TO
HEMLOCK LODGE

After walking a short distance past the sign you will see that the wide trail curves sharply left and starts down an easy grade. In less than 100 yards the trail has another sharp curve to the right.

You will shortly go down past a shelter house on your right. The trail then curves around to the left, with a large pock-marked rock wall on your left. In just a few yards, the trail cuts right again, goes gently down and passes a second shelter house on the left.

Right across from the shelter house on the right side of the trail there is a big sink hole which is a common geologic feature in limestone cave country. If you look into the sink hole, you can see a narrow hole in the limestone wall. This is the beginning of a small limestone cave which comes out in the rock shelter on the Balanced Rock Trail. Many years ago, when the L & N Railroad owned the park, there were electric lights to aid visitors through the cave. The lights have not been maintained. During the ensuing years, the little underground stream running through the cave has silted up the other end so badly that human passage was almost impossible. Recently state park personnel have dug out the silted passage and, if you are not too claustrophobic and have a flashlight, you can walk through this very narrow limestone cave which takes you to the rock shelter alongside Balanced Rock Trail.

If cave walks are not to your liking, just a few yards beyond the shelter house on the Original Trail you will pass the trail head for the Rock Garden Trail on your left. A few more feet takes you to the top of a set of 50 stone steps. At the top of the steps there is a little trail that goes off to the right. In a very short distance it junctions with Balanced Rock Trail next to the rock shelter where those using the cave will exit. If you haven't seen the shelter, you might want to return that way. If not, go down the steps. You will soon run into nine more steps which bring you to the end of the trail alongside a drinking fountain.

BALANCED ROCK TRAIL (formerly Trail #2) From Natural Bridge to the Parking Area

Distance: ¾ mile
Hike: EASY
Walking Time: 20 to 40 minutes

TRAIL DESCRIPTION. The Balanced Rock Trail is the most popular return route for those coming up the Original Trail who wish to make a loop hike of their walk. Its biggest difficulty is the 450 odd steps stretched out over the length of the trail. At least from this direction, you have the easier chore of walking down them. Balanced Rock Trail begins at the same end of the ridge where the steps down to Fat Man's Misery are located. When you are standing on the Bridge, with those steps on your right, walk away from the Bridge, keeping the large shelter house on your left. You walk down over a well worn sandstone outcropping, unfortunately marred by many human initials. The trail then ascends slightly up some sandstone steps which have been eroded almost into uselessness. The beginning of the Sand Gap Trail starts here, exiting off to the right. From this point, the Balanced Rock Trail takes the left fork and follows the ridge north. You will run into several small groups of steps carved into the sandstone as the trail works itself down the side of the ridge. As the trail approaches the end of the ridge known as Rocky Point, it hangs on a ledge which has a steep drop-off to the left in two distinct areas. Both places have good metal guardrails to prevent you from straying over, but keep an eye on any daredevil children. Each of these ledges offers panoramic views, and from the first one the top of Natural Bridge can be seen through the trees. Beyond the ledges, as it curves around the front of Rocky Point, the trail starts losing altitude in earnest and you will run into a series of stone steps, one of which has about 50 steps. Then you will come upon three sections of a long wooden stairway that contain over 90 steps. This is the last large series of steps you will run into until the very end of the trail.

Not far beyond the wooden stairways, Balanced Rock comes into view on the right side of the trail. Known as the Sphinx during the latter part of the nineteenth century, photographs taken then show that it has changed very little in 85 years.

About 1/10 mile beyond Balanced Rock, the trail skirts a moderate sized rock shelter on the left. You can see water trickling through a hole at the back of the shelter. Although this rock house is much smaller than the largest ones in the Gorge area, it is unusual because it is in limestone rather than the more common sandstone.

This is the beginning of a short cave that ends at a sinkhole near the beginning of the Original Trail. If you have a flashlight and don't mind being enclosed in a confining area, you can walk through to the Original Trail and finish your walk from there. To complete the Balanced Rock Trail, turn right just beyond the rock shelter and go down the long stone stairway. The trail ends at the bottom of its 100 steps.

ROCK GARDEN TRAIL (formerly Trail #4)
From Natural Bridge to the Original Trail

Distance: 1.6 miles
Hike: MODERATE
Walking Time: 35 to 45 minutes

TRAIL DESCRIPTION. Rock Garden Trail commences at the base of Natural Bridge on the same side of the ridge as Fat Man's Misery but at the other end of the span. There are two rather large rocks on each side of the trail and a trail sign there that says:

ROCK GARDEN TRAIL
HEMLOCK LODGE 1.6 MI

As you start your return walk, the cliff face of the ridge should be above you on your right. On this gentle return walk there are many false trails that go down the escarpment on your left. You can easily avoid them by keeping on the trail to the right, following along the base of the ridge cliff. If you keep your eye on that stone cliff as you proceed down the trail, it won't be very long before you come to a tiny miniature arch in that cliff face. Unlike its gigantic big brother, this midget-sized opening doesn't penetrate the ridge but pierces through an extended finger of the cliff wall and measures only about two feet high and a yard long.

In less than a quarter mile you will come to the cleared area where the Sky Lift passes over your head. This is a fun place to watch the suspended people rising slowly from the valley floor and disappearing behind the bluff above you. Soon after passing under the Sky Lift, you will walk through an area of many blackened tree stumps, the remains of a small forest fire that raged briefly here a few years ago. The trail then goes under a little rock shelter whose roof is so low that adults will have to duck their heads slightly when they pass through. Then the trail works around the bottom of a high cliff that rises majestically on the right. Sometimes there are droplets of water coming over its side, and my children have had great fun trying to catch them in their mouths.

Not far beyond these cliffs the ridge drops down to almost the level of the trail for a brief period until three sets of steps again lowers the trail well below the ridge top. This is the one section of the Rock Garden Trail where the drop in altitude occurs rather suddenly. You proceed down a set of eight stone steps carved in the fork face. This is just a warm up, for you quickly come to a second set that goes down a sandstone knob with approximately 63 steps cut in its surface. Much of the stairway is rather steep and some steps are about a foot high, so approach them cautiously. When you reach the bottom of this set, you are about half way back to the Original Trail. A hundred feet further on you run into another set of 33 stone steps lodged between two large stone sections. These steps are not high, easy to descend and are the last steps on the trail.

The trail has moved into the forest at this lower altitude as it curves around the end of the ridge. Now traffic can occasionally be heard from the roads that are out of sight below you. The trail weaves around between hugh boulders known as slump blocks that broke away from the ridge in the geologic past. In this area there are a few places where springs and runoff water have made the trail a bit mucky.

Not long after you have passed the area of the large boulders, you will be able to see the roof of Hemlock Lodge below you on the left side of the trail. Don't try to short cut to the lodge here, for there is a dangerous drop-off between you and that building. Also in this section, there is a fork in the trail, where the left fork heads invitingly down in the direction of the lodge. Don't take the left fork for it soon ends in a cul-de-sac by a little pump house. By staying on the correct right fork, you will see that the trail soon junctions with another very wide trail. This was used as a horse trail some years ago, but it was discontinued for that purpose because of serious erosion problems. It is again being used by hikers and has been named the Salt Mine Trail. It ends at the Battleship Rock Trail between the Devil's Gulch and the Needle's Eye. Beyond this junction the Rock Garden Trail takes you down to the bottom of a small ravine and part way up the other side where it junctions with the Original Trail. Turn left here and in less than 100 yards you will be back at the drinking fountain at the trail head.

SAND GAP TRAIL (formerly Trail #5) From Balanced Rock Trail to White's Branch Arch, and the Maintenance Building,

Distance: From Balanced Rock Trail to White's Branch Arch: 2.2 miles one way
Hike: STRENUOUS
Walking Time: 45 minutes to 1½ hours one way Distance for complete loop walk, including the side trip to White's Branch Arch: 6.8 miles
Hike: VERY STRENUOUS
Walking Time: 5 to 8 hours

GENERAL REMARKS. Sand Gap Trail and Hood's Branch Trail are the only ones not included in the general state park map. They are, however, included on the map found on page 71 . Named after Sand Gap Arch, this trail never gets really close to that large ridge top opening nor is it ever visible from this path. At one point, however, both arch and trail are on the same ridge and are close enough that the easiest and shortest cross country approach to the arch is from this trail which can be covered in about ⅔ mile of off trail walking.

This trail has also been known as the Boundary Line Trail because it skirts the borders of Natural Bridge State Park for a good part of its distance. It is the longest trail in the park and despite its length, is perhaps, mile for mile, scenically the least rewarding. It follows the top of a long ridge in the shape of a huge natural "U" with no prominent overlooks. Enclosed in a secondary forest growth, most of the trail is amazingly level. Though the views are not spectacular, the walk offers a quiet isolated solitude with no need to expend a great deal of energy in climbing and descending various ridges. Except for its descent down to the maintenance barn, which is rugged walking indeed, Sand Gap Trail offers three level miles of easy walking, the longest by far of any trail in the Gorge area that has no series of ascents or descents.

Its length and lack of spectacular views are responsible for its infrequent use. I've walked the trail on four different occasions and have never encountered another human being. Despite the fact that it is seldom walked and has had little maintenance for a number of years, it is easy to follow and the few trees that have fallen across the trail in the ensuing years are no problem to skirt around. If you like a long, isolated walk, this may be a trail that you would really enjoy.

Sand Gap Trail also leads to the turnoff that goes to White's Branch Arch, the only natural arch in the area that has a road across its top. If you envision watching automobiles using this natural phenomenon from some handy overlook, speculating on the magnificent combination of the natural and the practical, I'm afraid you will be disappointed on two counts. First, the road is extremely rough, suitable only for jeep-type vehicles. It is seldom used and I have never seen a vehicle on it. Second, despite its 48 foot span and an opening 12 feet high, White's Branch

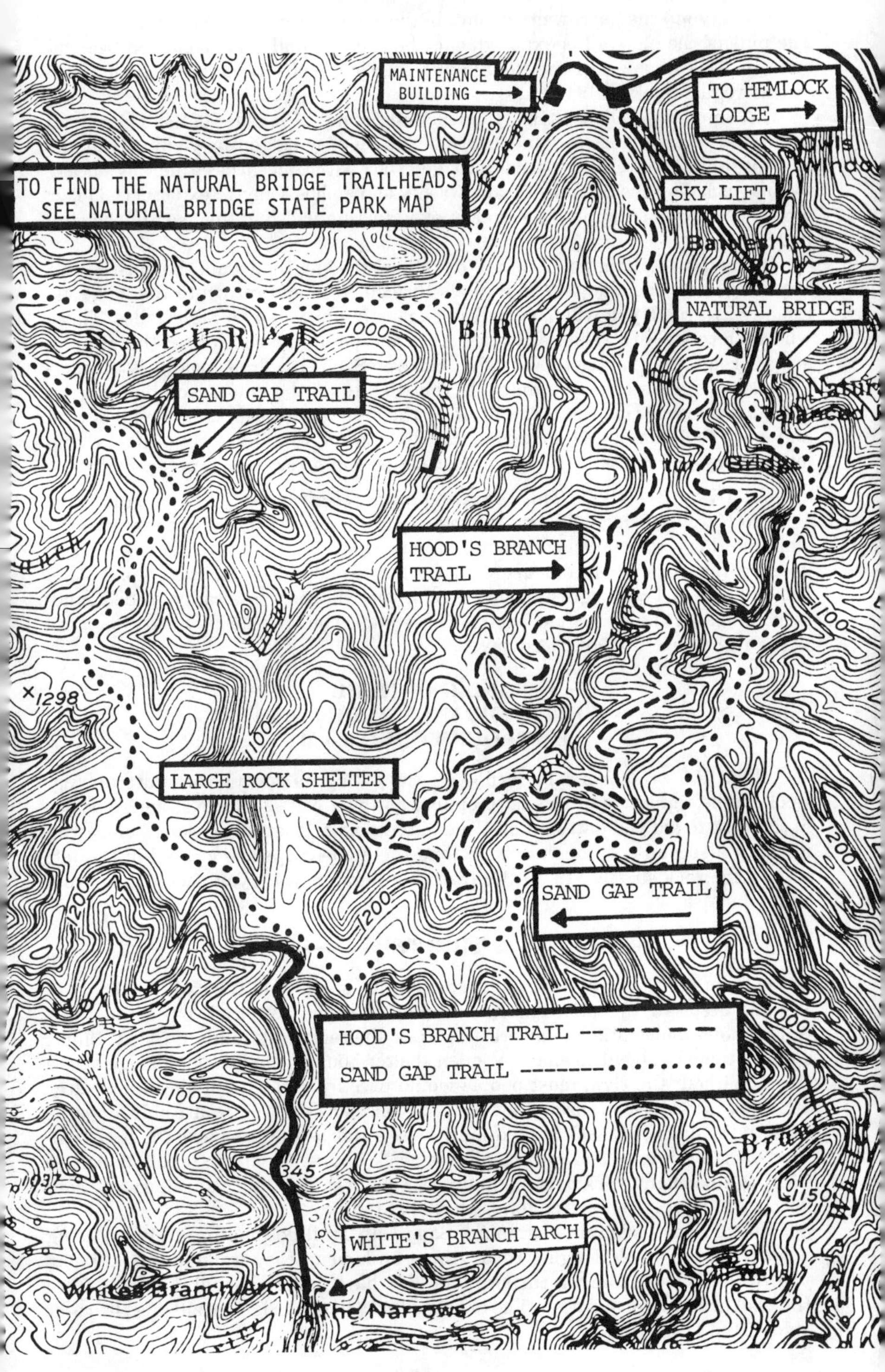
MAINTENANCE BUILDING
TO HEMLOCK LODGE
TO FIND THE NATURAL BRIDGE TRAILHEADS SEE NATURAL BRIDGE STATE PARK MAP
SKY LIFT
NATURAL BRIDGE
SAND GAP TRAIL
HOOD'S BRANCH TRAIL
LARGE ROCK SHELTER
SAND GAP TRAIL
HOOD'S BRANCH TRAIL
SAND GAP TRAIL
WHITE'S BRANCH ARCH
Whites Branch Arch
The Narrows
1298
1000
1100
1200
1150
345

Arch is dangerously difficult to see. There is no trouble walking across it, but seeing the opening is a very tricky matter.

Just beyond the narrows that contain the arch, there is an abandoned oil well. The pipe of the old well is exposed, and the area around it is blackened from oil spillage. This was part of the Big Sinking Oil Field which brought on an oil boom in this region back in 1917.

On completing the loop trail, you will find the next 1½ miles of Sand Gap Trail beyond White's Branch junction continues to be easy ridge top walking. But the descent to the maintenance barn is a rugged walk with trail surfaces offering uneasy footing, including the bottom of many washes and gullies. Only an experienced hiker who is used to making his way over uneven terrain will find this part of the trail not difficult.

If you use the Original Trail up to Natural Bridge, then walk the entire Sand Gap Trail, plus the side trip to White's Branch Arch and return to the lodge via the Sky Lift road, you will have had an exhausting hike of over eight miles. Those who wish to walk to White's Branch Arch and enjoy the solitude of this trail on an easier jaunt can return the way they came on Sand Gap Trail, making it a moderate hike of a little over five miles. If you wish to do the whole loop but shorten it a bit, you could ride the Sky Lift up to the arch, eliminating a half mile of trail and a 500 foot climb, and have your car waiting for you at the Sky Lift parking lot to carry you back to the lodge or campground after your hike.

TRAIL DESCRIPTION. This trail head branches off Balanced Rock Trail quite close to Natural Bridge. To find it, walk from the top of Natural Bridge with the stairway down to Fat Man's Misery on your right. Walk away from the Bridge, keeping the large shelter house on your left. Follow down a little dip. As the Balanced Rock Trail begins to climb again, you will see a few badly eroded sandstone steps on the trail. Just beyond these steps the trail forks. Sand Gap Trail is the right fork. A sign there says:

SAND GAP TRAIL
WHITE'S BRANCH ARCH 3.0 MI
HEMLOCK LODGE 6.0 MI

About 100 yards from the trail head, the path goes down a rock outcropping. Look to the right side of this outcropping and you will see some stone steps cut in the rock to aid you getting down the outcropping. It isn't very long before you run into a second outcropping. This time the stone steps are located in the left side of the rock surface. In a little over five minutes walk you should come to a sign which says:

SHELTER ⟶

which points in the direction of some small rock shelters to the right of the trail. When I first saw this sign I wondered why someone bothered to put up a sign to point out some rather uninteresting rock shelters, only to learn that it didn't refer to them at all but to an old wooden shelter house that sits on the ridge above them. Without the sign, most people would pass by without noticing the shelter at all as I have done on three previous occasions. The shelter is quite old and dates back to the days of C.C.C. and possibly back as far as the days when L & N Railroad owned this area and ran the old Hemlock Lodge. Complete with a flagstone floor, the excellent workmanship indicates that in times past this trail was walked with considerably more frequency that it is today.

About a mile from its beginning, Sand Gap Trail becomes quite wide, using what was once an old logging road. About an hour of easy walking should bring you to the White's Branch turnoff. You will have covered about 1.5 miles from the trail head to this junction. The old road forks here. A sign paralleling the right side of the trail reads:

ENTERING
NATURAL BRIDGE STATE PARK
NO HORSES OR MOTORIZED VEHICLES ALLOWED

The right fork is the continuation of Sand Gap Trail, while the left fork soon takes you out of the woods and joins a more prominent but still primitive road. If you turn left, the distance is ⅔ mile to the top of White's Branch Arch and ¾ mile to the abandoned oil well on the other side of the arch, which you should reach in about 15 to 20 minutes.

If you opt for the White's Branch trip, follow the left fork, and in about 150 feet it breaks out of the forest and passes under a power line with a telephone pole just to the right of the road. After you pass under the power line, you hit a more prominent but still primitive F.W.D. road. Turn left on this road. You will shortly come to a high cliff area where the road goes down into a saddle and then up again. The ridge here is not much wider than the road and has steep drop-offs on each side. This section is known as The Narrows, and White's Branch Arch is directly underneath the far end of it. If you follow the road across the saddle and up the other side, you will see a large oil-blackened area on the right side of the road with the pipe of the old oil well sticking up in the middle of the black area.

There is no easy place to see the arch, and for most people a walk across it will have to suffice. But there is one area where it can be seen without too much danger. Turn around and walk back across the narrows. As you cross the saddle, you can see large cliff promonotories extending from both sides of the road on the other end of the Narrows. There is a small road that goes out from the left which soon ends in a circle near the edge of this ridge finger. Carefully walk toward the cliff edge and you should be able to get a somewhat restricted view of the arch. Remember when fighting through the underbrush that the cliff edge is often hard to see among the foliage and the drop-off is sheer. A fall here would probably be fatal.

After returning to Sand Gap Trail, you have two different ways to complete your walk. If you are tired, it would be best for you to return the same way you came, for the last part of Sand Gap Trail can test your endurance. If you decide to proceed on the loop, you will see that it continues to follow along a forested ridge top. In about a mile, the trail makes a decided turn to the right and continues along the ridge. Then the trail makes a wide swing right going around the ridge. Not far beyond this, there is a little manway that comes in from the left. Stick to the trail on the right. The manway is the trailless direction to Sand Gap Arch. Shortly beyond this point, the trail begins its descent by starting down the right side of the ridge. As you start down this section, you will notice a small sandstone cliff developing on the left. There is one small but very interesting rock shelter in this wall whose interior dimensions are spherical in shape. These interior walls also have some interesting geologic folds on their surfaces.

The trail now follows the bottom of gullies which become streams in wet weather. There is a long, difficult and very rocky stretch which crosses a tributary of Lower Hood Branch a couple of times. After crossing a clearing, the trail forks at the waters of Lower Hood Branch. Take the fork on the right that crosses the branch. You cross Lower Hood Branch again turning right on a primitive road and almost immediately hit a second road. Shortly thereafter, the road takes you past the maintenance building. From here you follow the paved road past the Sky Lift parking lot and up the hill to the lodge.

HOOD'S BRANCH TRAIL

Distance: from Natural Bridge to the Sky Lift parking lot—3.7 miles
Hike: MODERATE
Walking Time: 1 hour 45 minutes to 2 hours 15 minutes.

GENERAL REMARKS. The natural setting of this newest and second longest trail in the state park is perhaps the loveliest and most unspoiled of all the park trails and one of the most quietly attractive in the whole Gorge area. Because of its length, it is walked only by a small percentage of the hordes that regularly invade Natural Bridge by the shortest trails or the Sky Lift, so it escapes the over-used appearance of the Original Trail and is nicely isolated from that busy world of the lodge. Conceived and laid out by Wilson Francis, the park's very knowledgeable naturalist, his love for the area's unspoiled beauty influenced his choice of routes. Part of it reuses a trail built by the C.C.C. over 40 years ago which had fallen into disuse for at least two decades. Although shorter than the Sand Gap Trail, its scenic rewards are far richer. Both trails loosely form U's, but their great difference is that the Sand Gap Trail is almost entirely a ridge top trail while Hood's Branch Trail follows paths part way down the escarpment and the bottom of the valley of Upper Hood Branch. Because of its isolation and lower elevation it doesn't have that picked-over feeling. Enough years have elapsed since this valley was logged to give it the appearance of being unspoiled and pristine.

Among the outstanding geologic features in the Red River Gorge are the large sandstone recess caves or rock shelters found there. Many of them can be viewed alongside or near trails in the national forest, but until recently, nary a single one was located near any trail in the state park.

The only shelter of any appreciable size found near a Natural Bridge trail was the rather small limestone shelter alongside Balanced Rock Trail. The new Hood's Branch Trail has changed all of that, for there is one large two-tiered beauty that the trail passes under as well as a very unusual one which looks like a large entrance to the more traditional type cave.

Hood's Branch Trail also puts little strain on the conditioned hiker for it is mostly a downhill trail with easy grades. For those in reasonably good physical condition who like to ride the Sky Lift, either because they enjoy the ride or who don't want to sweat out the 500 foot climb up to Natural Bridge but would still like to take a leisurely but beautiful long walk back, Hood's Branch Trail is ideal, for the trail ends at the Sky Lift's parking lot. But—Sunday strollers, beware! There are some uphill sections on the trail and 3.7 miles to someone who is not used to hiking can be a formidable distance.

TRAIL DESCRIPTION. The trail head is found below Natural Bridge next to Fat Man's Misery. A sign to the left of the trail says:

HOODS BRANCH TRAIL

In less than five minutes of walking you will pass a small rock shelter on your left where you can see that the front of the shelter has fallen away in recent years. You then have a couple of switchbacks before coming to a long sturdy wooden footbridge. After crossing the footbridge, the trail curves to the right giving you a good view of the cliff face you have been following. Then, after you swing back to the left around a high point of land, you will soon negotiate a couple of switchbacks and some moderately steep downhill grades.

There is another crossing of a second long wooden bridge followed by crossings of a few side branches, sometimes using stepping stones, small logs or small bridges. After following a rounding curve to the right where two small hollows join to form a larger one and the trail begins to climb easily, you can see the hollow floor dropping off quite a distance below you on the right.

Not long after you cross a third long wooden bridge, the trail passes over a mucky section using some long logs that are laid lengthwise, about 40 feet of it. When you cross a slightly larger wash where the trail turns sharply left briefly following the watercourse upstream, you have your first uphill climb that is moderately steep. It takes you into a side hollow to a large recess cave. Twenty natural stone steps lead you down to the upper ledge of this shelter. At its opposite end you can see the wooden bridge that leads you away from its extended rock roof.

This footbridge rests on the foundation of the original bridge built by the C.C.C. over 40 years ago. You can still see the ruins of the original bridge below the present one.

Watch young children in the recess cave for a fall off the shelter's ledge could result in serious injury. If you are tiring, the knowledge that over half the distance of this loop is now behind you might stimulate your adrenalin for a second wind.

After leaving the shelter you will cross a fourth long wooden bridge. It is not long before the trail swings left into a side hollow with another interesting recess cave about half the size of the previous one. It is more unusual than other large shelters in that its arch-shaped opening looks more like what most people would envision as the entrance to a more traditional tunnel type opening of a very large cave. It also recesses far enough back that its interior is far darker than most shelters. For no particular reason, it reminds me of a Neanderthal's cave apartment. Wilson Francis calls it his garage shelter because it could easily serve as a sheltered location for at least four large automobiles.

After leaving the vicinity of this shelter you will soon go briefly up two side hollows with bridges, then return to the main hollow of Upper Hood Branch. The trail is now following alongside that stream in its flat bottomed but not particularly wide hollow. For those with observant eyes, there is a pile of stones to the left that once was a foundation for an old log cabin. At one time there was a narrow dirt wagon road to this cabin and the trail follows along its path. One large black stone and some little ones help you cross Upper Hood Branch and it is not long before you recross the branch on another set of stepping stones.

After this crossing, the outline of the log road is more definite. The road divides with the left fork going uphill while the right one follows along the stream. A sign indicates that you follow the left one but you can go either way, for it is a turnaround once used by vehicles and the two segments soon join up. It is slightly under a mile from here to the trail's end at the Sky Lift.

You will soon pass what looks like a new wooden shelter house on the left. It was actually built over 40 years ago by the C.C.C. and restored in 1979. Just beyond it on the left, part way up the hill, you may see a little natural grotto which is visible during the winter season when the foliage is not heavy. If you walk up to it you can see that it is in limestone and has a little lighthouse type of natural rounded hole in its stone sides. It is also in this vicinity that during the warmer months you may hear the voices of people that are out of sight. They are riding the Sky Lift which soon comes into view during the less leafy seasons. When the road starts steeply down, look for a sign on the right which says:

TRAIL ⟶

Here the trail turns right, leaving the road and proceeds quite steeply down to the Sky Lift parking lot.

OTHER PLACES OF INTEREST IN NATURAL BRIDGE STATE PARK

HENSON'S CAVE ARCH TRAIL

Distance: 1/3 mile (one way)
Hike: MODERATE
Walking Time: 10 to 15 minutes (one way)

GENERAL REMARKS: When Clarence Henson was the superintendent of the state park, his youngest son, Dean, found this arch on the hillside near his home. Mr. Henson has been actively associated with the area for over 30 years with both the federal and state governments and was responsible for laying out many of the present trails in the Gorge area. Thus it pleased many of his friends, including myself, when this little arch became known by his family name. If you are looking for one of the larger and more graceful natural spans, you can skip this one, but for the geology buff it is a little jewel. Its formation in limestone is quite different from the ridge top sandstone arches that are far more common. Once it was a limestone cave about 20 to 30 feet long. At one end of the cave, a small stream eroded away the top of a sink hole until the roof collapsed. At the other end a sink hole formed causing the collapse of the roof there. The remaining roof of the cave formed the existing arch which is about ten feet long and nine feet high. The Henson's dog had fallen into one of the sink holes and Dean, while looking for the family pet, found the dog, quite unharmed at the bottom of the sink hole.

TRAIL DESCRIPTION. To locate the arch, first proceed to the Whittleton Branch Campground. Upon entering the campground, follow the campground road across the ford of Whittleton Branch until that road curves around the back of the restroom and shower building. Near campsite #24 you can see a small ravine where a sign facing you says:

HENSONS ARCH TRAIL

The trail immediately crosses the small stream at the bottom of the ravine and begins climbing in the upstream direction. Arrows painted on yellow signs soon indicate that the trail swings to the right as a moderately steep climb develops up the side of the ridge. Less than half way up the ridge the trail again turns right and begins to follow what once was probably an old trace road. At this point the worst of your climb is over for the road is fairly level as it curves slowly left around the end of the ridge. When you come to a second ravine where water erosion has cut a break in a small rock outcropping, the trail swings left, goes up through that break and in less than 50 yards the trail climbs up to the first sink hole. Alongside it there is a sign which says:

HENSONS CAVE ARCH

A sturdy ladder there aids you in getting to the bottom to give you a better view of this limestone arch. But before you descend, look around, for one time a copperhead fell in and couldn't get out any better than the dog could. If you walk under the arch, you will see the typical cylindrical shape of a sink hole on the other end. Be wary if you approach the sink hole from above, for it is slippery around the edges and falling in the hole could easily result in a serious accident.

INDIAN HEAD (PROFILE) ROCK AND OWL'S WINDOW

These two natural formations are both found at the end of the Natural Bridge ridge on a solitary pinnacle known as the Devil's Pulpit. Both are best viewed in the late afternoon when the sun is behind the ridge. The best viewing place is on Kentucky Route 11 near the turnoff into Whittleton Branch Campground. Start at the campground entrance and walk a few feet north in the direction of Slade alongside Route 11. Stop walking when you can look across both the road and the creek and see the ridge on the other side with a solitary rock promontory standing just beyond it. The side of that sandstone pinnacle facing the ridge contains the profile of a human face whose features suggest an Indian. Just below, right of the face, you can see the small arch or lighthouse known as the Owl's Window.

MILL CREEK LAKE

At the southern end of the park, Kentucky Route 11 goes across a dam that creates this very deep lake. Although it hardly is a fisherman's paradise, the lake

Indian Head (Profile) Rock and the Owl's Window

is stocked with both bass and trout. There are also bluegills by the thousands, and I have seen more than one beautiful string of fish taken from its waters. Although not large, Mill Creek Lake is one of the most attractive man-made lakes I've seen. The forest-covered escarpment down to the lake is both steep and scenic. You can rent a boat in season at the dam. If you have your own boat, There is a good launching ramp by the boat concession. Gasoline motors are not allowed on the lake, so you must row, paddle or use an electric trolling motor. The views on the lake are best in late afternoon not long before sundown. Proceed up the left side of the lake and soon you will see a high red sandstone cliff rising in front of you. A red cliff is most impressive as it reflects the warmer hues of the setting sun. Then turn and look in the other direction toward the dam for another restful and beautiful mixture of water and hazy mountain terrain.

If you intend to fish, a Kentucky fishing license is required. Swimming in the lake is forbidden and so is camping along its shores.

There is an unofficial trail made by bank fishermen that goes around about two thirds of the lake. It starts near the boat concession shed, goes by the corner of an old family cemetery and gives some excellent views of the lake; but its drawback is the tons of empty beer and pop cans, bait containers and other general offal left along the shore by thoughtless bank fishermen which distracts from this otherwise charming walk.

HOE DOWN ISLAND

For those of you who like to participate in or enjoy watching square dancing, there is a caller on the island with appropriate music each Friday and Saturday evening from the spring through the fall. The admission price is low. If you are a novice square dancer, Friday night is usually the best, for it's not so crowded and some of the better dancers often help you with the steps. On Saturday, many of the local residents show up and the dancing is enthusiastically and energetically

Saturday night dancing on Hoe Down Island

performed. Once or twice a year, square dance contests are held here and attract many of the best dancing teams from the Eastern United States. If you are interested in coming during one of the big dance weekends, write Hemlock Lodge at the state park for the exact dates. Use the parking lot next to Middle Fork in the vicinity of the gift shop and the swimming pool for Hoe Down Island.

Walking past the gift shop in the direction of the swimming pool will soon bring you in sight of the little foot bridge that takes you to the island.

Hoe Down Island is interesting for another reason. Just a little over 30 years ago, this man-made island was the loading and unloading point for passengers riding the excursion trains to Natural Bridge. The trains came out of the tunnel that is just the other side of the swimming pool. With all the noise and clamor of those old steam engines, the scene was quite different from the calm of the island that usually prevails there today. When the trains arrived, this area was full of the iron horse's soot, cinders and steam. If you follow the path beyond the swimming pool you can see the tunnel from which these smoke-belching monsters emerged for better than 50 years. How nice it would be if the excursion trains still ran from Cincinnati and Louisville to Natural Bridge. Alas, that day is over and is not likely to return, but the nostalgia of the past still seems to linger here in the vicinity of Hoe Down Island though not a single trace of that romantic age of steam is now evident.

WHITTLETON BRANCH TRAIL #216 AND WHITTLETON ARCH TRAIL #217

Distance from Whittleton Branch Campground to Whittleton Arch: 1 mile
Hike: EASY
Walking Time: 25 to 40 minutes one way Distance from Whittleton Branch Campground to Highway 15: 1.9 miles

Hike: MODERATE
Walking Time: 1 to 1½ hours one way

GENERAL REMARKS: Although Whittleton Branch Trail is not a part of Natural Bridge State Park, I have included it in this chapter because it is the only trail in the Daniel Boone National Forest that touches the boundary of the state park and most walkers will start their hike from the state park campground along Whittleton Branch. Whittleton Arch provides you with a view of one of the longest and most impressive arches in the forest. Its 100 foot front span is the longest of any in the area. It does not seem as spectacular an arch as either Natural Bridge or Gray's Arch, since the opening of the back section of the span is a mere fraction of the front. But this arch was formed quite differently from those ridge top arches and is a beautiful example of a waterfall step arch (see Geology chapter).

For most of its distance the trail follows Whittleton Branch, a beautiful mountain stream which almost always has flowing water. The bottom of this valley also served as the bed for the Mountain Central Railroad, which operated until 1928. When the tracks ran up the valley, the rails crossed the creek no less than 26 times in less than two miles. In certain places the sharp-eyed visitor can still see cuts, crossings and rail ties along the trail. The easiest and quickest way to get to the arch is to start the hike from Whittleton Branch Campground (Old Campground #1) in Natural Bridge State Park.

TRAIL DESCRIPTION. From Whittleton Branch Campground to Whittleton Arch and Highway 15. (For trail description in the opposite direction see page 81).

If you are driving to the trail head, park your car near the guard shack at the entrance to the campground (see Natural Bridge State Park map). Just beyond the guard shack, the campground road forks. Follow the left fork, which has a sign that says:

"TRAILERS ONLY"

At the end of this short road, there is a loop turnaround where the trail begins. If you drive your car back to the loop, do not park it there, for it prevents large motor homes and trailers from using the loop. The trail sign paralleling the trail on the right says:

←——— WHITTLETON ARCH 1
←——— HIGHWAY 15 2

As the trail begins, you can see Whittleton Branch gurgling away on your right. In less than a quarter of a mile, a sturdy wooden footbridge takes you across the creek. Look at the creek bed from the bridge, and you can see that it is a solid slab of limestone exposed in the entire width of the creek bed and running about 50 feet upstream. In another quarter mile, you cross the creek again. This is another section where the stream bed is made of limestone. A short distance further on, you will cross two very short, low wooden bridges that carry you across a couple of small tributaries.

In this area look for some huge slump blocks in the middle of the main creek. If there hasn't been too much rain, you can see that the stream runs freely downstream from under and around the boulders. But when you get upstream beyond the boulders, you will usually find that the stream bed is dry. Down among the boulders, an underground section of Whittleton Branch has resurfaced—something not at all uncommon where layers of limestone are in evidence. The trail follows the dry creek bed; running parallel to the stream is a low wooden walkway that one can use when the water is high.

The next bridge you encounter crosses Whittleton Branch for the third time. Trail #216 does not cross the bridge, but continues on the same side of the creek. By crossing the bridge, you are on the short trail that takes you to Whittleton

Whittleton Arch in Winter

Arch. This trail is #217 and takes you to the arch in just 2/10 mile. There is a sign on the opposite side of the creek that you can read between the two handrails of the bridge which says:

WHITTLETON ARCH TRAIL
DANIEL BOONE NATIONAL FOREST

Even though it is only 2/10 mile to the arch, it is a steady uphill grind which could be a bit much for walkers badly out of shape or with physical handicaps.

Shortly after you leave Whittleton Branch heading toward the arch, there is a large rock on the right side of the trail which you would probably pass by without a second glance, as I have done on several occasions. But the first time I had my four-year-old daughter along, she pointed to the rock and said, "Look, Daddy, at the big face." Sure enough, for those blessed with a little imagination, an eye, nose and mouth were readily suggested in the stone's profile. Since it did not resemble a human face, I asked my daughter whose face she thought it was. After a period of silence while she pondered the question, she replied, "Shamu, the whale." It may not be a perfect resemblance to a killer whale, but it's close enough.

If you're huffing and puffing, a little wooden bridge that you cross should be a welcome sight for although it is still out of view, the arch is found just a short distance beyond.

When first approaching the arch, visitors frequently feel a moment of disappointment, wondering if the walk was really worth it. The arch, set deep in a narrow ravine, is dark and almost foreboding, looking like a gloomy, cavernous, rock shelter. It is not until you are fairly close to this waterfall step arch that you can see the small opening at the rear of the span. It really does have its own magnificence, but this is not visible from the front of the arch. Walk up the steep slope under the arch toward the narrow opening. As the slope brings you almost level with the bottom of the arch, turn around and look back toward the large opening. It is as if you are looking out of the jaws of a hugh cave into the jungle-like density of a primeval forest. It is from high up under the arch that its width and depth take on spectacular proportions, whereas the approaching trail side view too often leaves the feeling of mundane grayness—something nature has forgotten and left incomplete. You can work your way to the top of the arch, but getting there is difficult and dangerous with little scenic reward. The dense vegetation not only blocks your view, but also hides the treacherous sides of the arch. Not too many years ago, a man did fall to his death from atop Whittleton Arch. Don't let this deter you from seeing this arch, for it is one of the prettiest and safest walks in the area.

When you get back to Whittleton Branch and cross the bridge, you can turn left and walk the easy downhill path back to the campground. If you like the scenery along a pretty mountain stream, you might turn right and walk about a half mile further up Whittleton Branch, for the miniature landscapes along the creek are even more charming than they were at the beginning of the trail. You can turn around whenever you tire, knowing that it is a very gentle downhill grade all the way to the campground. As you recross the bridge a sign there facing you says:

TRAIL 216
HIGHWAY 15 1 MI

If you decide to proceed further up the Whittleton Branch Trail, it will not be long before you make three crossings of the creek with the aid of the bridge only on the second crossing. You will then notice that the trail descends steeply down to a main tributary of Whittleton Branch. About half way down this short stretch, you can see the landfill that once led to a trestle across the stream. Although the old railroad bridge has long since disappeared, the landfill on both sides of the stream is still very much in evidence.

After crossing the creek, the trail ascends steeply back to the level of the old rail bed and follows the original course of the railroad for quite a stretch. In a few places along the path, one can still find a few rail ties and cinders dumped there long ago by the little Climax steam locomotives that were used here. As the trail heads up one of the ravines, there are some small rock shelters to the right. You can see that the floors of the shelters are below the level of the trail for fill was added here in the railroad days to maintain an even grade. They end just as a small waterfall becomes visible on the left side of the trail. Just beyond the falls, the path goes into the bottom of a miniature canyon where the trail and stream share the same sandstone floor. Coming out of this small rock enclosure, the trail crosses a wooden bridge that once was in the middle of a small meadow which the forest is rapidly reclaiming.

The rest of the trail is not very interesting from a scenic point of view, and, if you are planning to walk back to the campground, this might be a good place to begin retracing your steps. The trail continues in a more or less straight line along the side of a hollow. At the head of the hollow, the trail crosses the tiny beginnings of Whittleton Branch, then proceeds to go up a steep embankment by using a switchback to the right. After a short climb, you are at the top of the rise at Highway 15.

If you are waiting here for someone to pick you up and you want an interesting view, turn right on the highway and walk a few feet until you see Tunnel Ridge Road across the highway on the left. Walk a few feet down Tunnel Ridge Road, and, from the bridge that crosses the Mountain Parkway, you can see vividly the tremendous road cuts that had to be made and the thousands of cubic yards of material that were removed in the construction of the highway.

WHITTLETON BRANCH TRAIL #216

From Highway 15 to Whittleton Arch and Whittleton Branch Campground

(For General Remarks, see page 79)

Since most of this trail follows the old Mountain Central Railroad bed, it is almost all downhill at a very easy grade. A sign facing Highway 15 says:

A sign on the same post but parallel to the trail says:

←——— WHITTLETON ARCH 1 MI.
←——— NATURAL BRIDGE PARK 2 MI.

As soon as the trail leaves Highway 15, it goes down the only steep descent on the entire trail with a switchback to the left. You cross a tiny stream, then follow in a rather straight line, along the left side of a hollow. In a very short time, you come to an open meadow where two small streams join to form Whittleton Branch. You come to a wooden bridge in the middle of what was a small open area that is rapidly being reclaimed by the forest. The prettiest part of this walk begins where the stream has cut through a large wall of sandstone, with the trail and the stream sharing the same stone floor, surrounded on each side by sandstone walls. The shaping of this narrow section was probably helped by human hands, for you are now on the rail bed of the old Mountain Central and the distance between the walls is just wide enough to accommodate small rail cars.

Just beyond this miniature canyon, the stream goes over an eight foot waterfall on the right side of the trail. Then the water cascades another 20 feet or so below the level of the trail. If you watch the trail floor along this stretch you will see old railroad ties across the trail, as well as cinders dumped there over 50 years ago by the old Climax narrow gauge steam engines. As you walk this section, you will notice some small rock shelters to the left whose floors are much lower than the trail. The rail builders raised this section to maintain an even grade.

As the valley floor widens, the trail drops left of the old rail bed and descends steeply down to the creek. Just before you get to the creek, notice some good sized boulders to the right of the trail. They contain good examples of extreme geologic folding caused by limonite that was once in solution.

After you cross the stream, the trail reascends steeply for a short distance to regain the level of the old rail bed. About half-way up this slope, look to your right, and you can see where the trains once crossed Whittleton Branch. The trestle is gone, but the fill on either side of it is still very much in evidence.

The most charming scenic section of the trail is from here to the turnoff for Whittleton Arch. In this short section, the trail crosses the stream four more times. You will usually find convenient natural stepping stones, and one crossing has the added convenience of a wooden foot bridge.

At the last of these four crossings, there is a large boulder on the right side of the creek. Under it is a delightful pool about three feet deep. Not enough room to practice your crawl stroke, but what an inviting place to take a quick dip on a sultry August day!

Not far beyond this pool, you will come to a bridge on the left side of the trail. This is the beginning of Trail #217, which takes you to Whittleton Arch in a bare 2/10 of a mile and should not be missed. The rest of the walk to Whittleton Branch Campground is less than a mile of easy walking. This lower section of Trail #216 is not as attractive as the upper part, but you do have two bridges to carry you across Whittleton Branch, which has grown appreciably in size.

For awhile, the stream bed seems strangely dry. It has disappeared underground, but soon appears again coming out of some large boulders in the middle of the stream bed. When you cross the two sturdy wooden foot bridges, notice that the bottom of the creek is a solid floor of limestone. Just a short distance beyond the second bridge across the branch, the trail ends at the turning circle in the campground.

VII

NATIONAL FOREST TRAILS ALONG TUNNEL RIDGE ROAD

Tunnel Ridge Road is a narrow dead end gravel road, a little over five miles long, that is maintained by the forest service. It begins at Highway 15 about three and a half miles east of Slade (#11 on large map on page 164). Nada Tunnel was dug through this ridge giving it its name. There are two interesting viewpoints toward the end of the road. The first gives you a nice view of Stargap Arch; the second offers one a good overlook of the lower Gorge at the end of the road turnaround. Because of the increased popularity of several trail and geologic features on or near the road, the forest service has added two new parking areas and two primitive campgrounds in the vicinity of the road since the fist edition of this book was published. A little over a half mile from Highway 15 you will see a sign with a capital P and another with a backpacker below it on the right side of the road with an arrow pointing to the left. This indicates the new parking area for Pinch-Em-Tight Trail. Just 2/10 mile further is the Gray's Arch picnic area with parking for both Gray's Arch and D. Boon Hut Trails. A little further on there is a nice overlook on the right looking down Martin's Branch. Primitive campground #1 is a little over a mile and a half from Highway 15 on the left hand side of the road identified with a sign that is on the right side. If you wish to camp there you must park your car alongside the road and walk back into the primitive campground. Primitive campground #2 is another half mile down on the left hand side of the road, but identified by a sign on the right. It is a big open field with easier access than campground #1. A little less than a mile further you will see another large parking sign on the left side of the road with an arrow pointing to a gravel road on the right. In a short distance this side road ends at the parking lot for Courthouse Rock and Auxier Ridge Trails. You will go almost a mile beyond this junction before you come to a sign on the right side of the road which says: VIEW OF STARGAP ARCH. The view of the arch is to the left and is almost visible from the road. Look through the trees into the valley. On the other side you can see this arch which is one of the larger ones in the area, measuring 72 feet in length with a height of 13 feet. This arch gets its name from the small stream below it. It is said that the people who once lived near the lower part of this stream could look up the branch and see the Morning Star through a small gap in the ridge. Up until recently Star Gap Arch was privately owned, but is now forest service land. There is no official trail to it, but it is not a difficult walk. If you are interested in hiking to it, see the new off-trail hiking section of this book on page 159. About a mile and a half beyond Star Gap view, Tunnel Ridge Road dead ends at a loop turnaround where you have a nice panorama of the lower Gorge. The trail heads and small parking area for the Double Arch and Auxier Branch Trails are to the right just before you reach the end of the road.

TRAILS FROM GRAY'S ARCH PICNIC GROUND PARKING LOT ON TUNNEL RIDGE ROAD

This parking lot is on the right side of Tunnel Ridge Road about a mile from Highway 15. All of the trails listed below begin near this parking lot.

1. Gray's Arch Trail #205 & #221
2. D. Boon Hut Loop Trail #1770 & #236 (page 87)
3. Pinch-Em-Tight Trail #277 (page 89)
4. Rush Ridge Trail #227 (page 91)

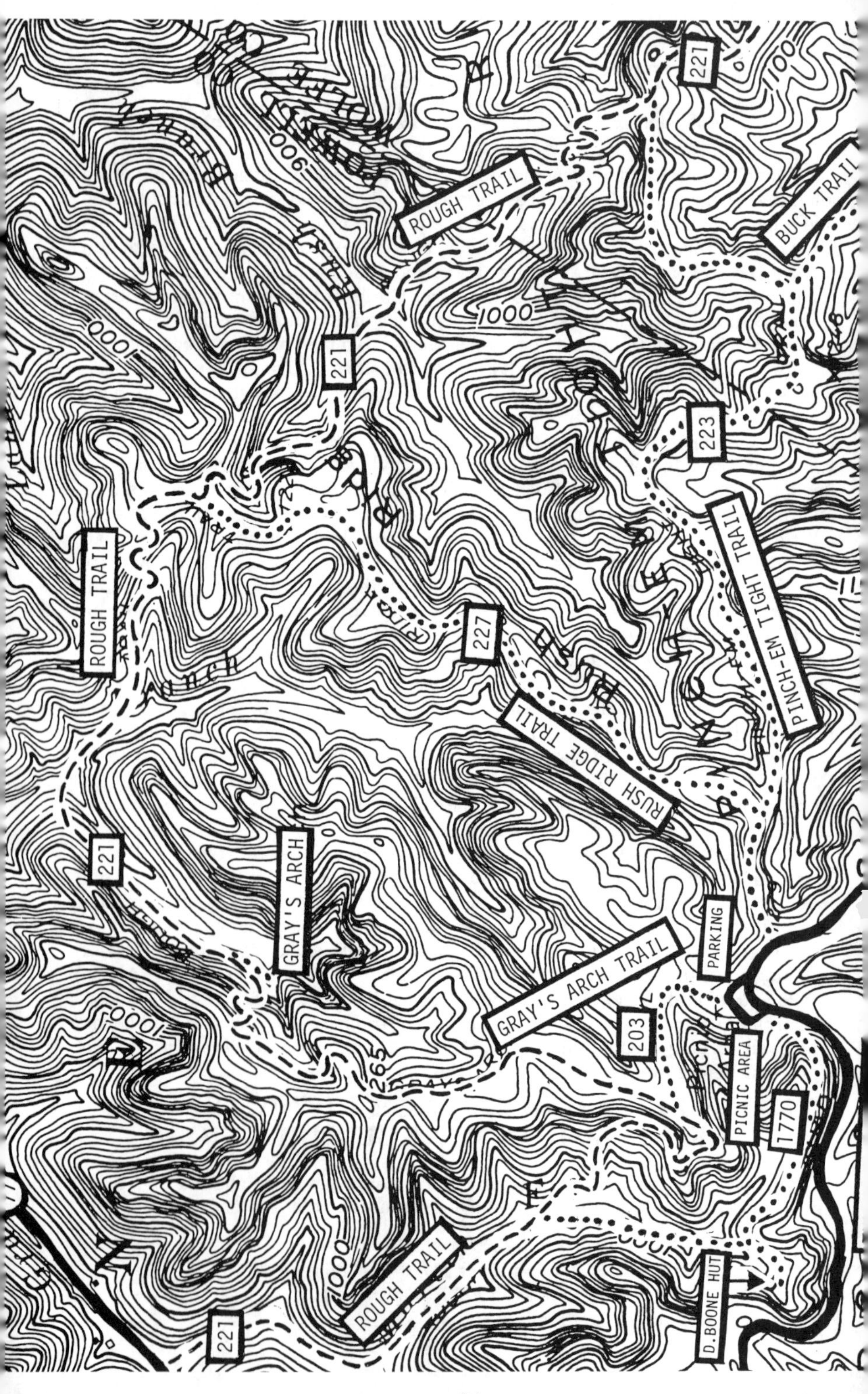
221
ROUGH TRAIL
BUCK TRAIL
900
1000
221
223
ROUGH TRAIL
227
PINCH-EM TIGHT TRAIL
RUSH RIDGE TRAIL
221
GRAY'S ARCH
PARKING
GRAY'S ARCH TRAIL
1000
203
265
PICNIC AREA
1770
1000
ROUGH TRAIL
D.BOONE HUT
221

TRAILS TO GRAY'S ARCH—#205 & #221

Distance: 1.4 miles
Hike: MODERATE
Walking Time: 45 minutes to 1½ hours one way

GENERAL REMARKS: Gray's Arch ranks as one of the most spectacular in the Gorge area. Although not as high as Natural Bridge, its 50 foot rise above its base is still impressive and its 80 foot span is one of the longest in the area, surpassing Natural Bridge by two feet. It is also the only one of the very large ridge top arches that has good sized trees growing on top of its span, and is the largest and possibly the best example of a buttress arch in this geologic area.

There is one big drawback in visiting this area. Its popularity as a sort of gathering place for college age primitive campers has caused an overpopulation problem for a number of years. It was once posted with a sign forbidding camping in the vicinity of the arch, stating "THIS AREA NEEDS A REST". At this writing, the restriction has been lifted, but the dog-eared look of the surroundings, as well as many little unofficial trails running helter-skelter in diverse directions, still indicates the area needs a rest and primitive camping is still prohibited within 200 yards of Gray's Arch. Don't let this deter you from hiking to this spectacular arch, but, for goodness sakes, if you are wilderness camping, go somewhere else for the night. With the great number of people that make this walk annually, it is interesting to note that for many years this was one of the lost arches of the region. Although well remembered by the loggers who timbered out the area at the turn of the century, as they moved on and the forest reclaimed the ground its whereabouts was lost. It was not until the 1930's that Dr. Carl Clark made a concentrated effort to find it and after a frustrating summer of searching, he was finally successful. There are toilet facilities at the picnic area, but no water. The trail head begins at the edge of the parking area. Trail #205 is a short section of trail that takes you to the much longer Rough Trail which takes you to Gray's Arch. Don't let the name frighten you. There are some very difficult sections on Rough Trail but they are not on the stretch going to Gray's Arch. Most of the trail is comparatively easy and safe, but there are two stretches where caution is advised with young children.

TRAIL DESCRIPTION: The sign at the trail head reads:

←GRAY'S ARCH 2 MI.
←TUNNEL RIDGE ROAD 3 MI.

The distance to Tunnel Ridge Road is for the loop trip to Gray's Arch returning on Rush Trail and a very short section of Pinch-Em Tight Trail. The distance, however, is almost a mile longer than the sign indicates while the actual distance to Gray's Arch is about a half mile shorter. This first short stretch of trail that connects up with Rough Trail is wide, fairly level and easy walking. After walking about five minutes, the trail runs into Rough Trail. The Martin's Branch section of Rough Trail goes off to the left and the sign there facing the trail reads:

↑ HIGHWAY 77 2
↑ D BOON HUT 2
TUNNEL RIDGE RD. 3

At this point the Gray's Arch Trail #205 turns right and shares the same path as Rough Trail #221, staying together almost to Gray's Arch. On the right of the trail a sign there reads:

TUNNEL RIDGE ROAD 3 MI.→
GRAY'S ARCH 1 MI.→

After turning right on to Rough Trail, the path narrows somewhat as it heads

Gray's Arch

north but continues a fairly level course along the top of the ridge. After you have walked a few minutes, the trail crosses a clearing that, perhaps was once a homestead or a farmer's field. You can see how nature is busily reclaiming the area for some of the trees are already 15 feet tall. Notice the difference in the plant growth and ground cover in this open section compared with what you see when the path soon returns to the forest. Shortly after returning to the forest, the ridge begins to descend slowly and the trail runs along its right side. You come to a place near the ridge top where one well defined trail goes straight ahead continuing on the ridge, and another turns left and goes over the crest of the ridge. Take the left turn which curves left again dropping you into another hollow and angling down its side in the opposite direction. After curving around the head of that hollow, the trail hangs on its left side gradually angling down to the hollow floor.

It is not long before Gray's Arch is plainly visible across a ravine to the right of the trail. There are two erroneous assumptions that are often made here by people making their first walk to Gray's Arch. Some hikers assume that they have walked the remaining mile and this is as close as the trail gets to the arch. In actuality, only the easiest half of that distance has been covered, and after descending into the ravine, the trail takes you right to the arch. The other far more dangerous assumption is that you can easily cross the ravine and go directly cross country to the arch itself. But the surrounding ground cover gives a completely false illusion. The bottom of the ravine that runs just below and to the right of the trail before you get to this point suddenly disappears into a patch of rhododendron where it drops off unseen for nearly 100 feet to the bottom of a box canyon. So between you and this first viewpoint of the arch, there is a hidden and very precarious drop-off that cannot be seen from the trail. If you have children with you, don't let them get too far off the right side of the trail here. Don't attempt a direct short cut here either for the drop-off is sudden and so severe that surviving such a fall would be unlikely. Don't let this scare you into not making the hike, for the trail is quite safe and not a frightening one as long as you stay on the path.

Continuing on down the trail, the arch disappears in tree cover as the path curves around under a small rock shelter. This is another area to be careful with small children for the drop-off to the right is visibly hazardous. Just beyond the shelter, you rapidly descend three sets of steps to the bottom of the ravine. The first is the shortest with only four steps. After a switchback, you come to the longest section of 37 steps. A couple more switchbacks brings you to the last set of 14 steps. Avoid taking a steep erosion-producing short cut between the two long sets of steps. Beyond this a series of log steps in the ground brings you to a trail junction as the trail T's into another. This is the point where Gray's Arch Trail and Rough Trail separate. Turning left here puts you on the continuation of Rough Trail, while the path to the right takes you under the arch. There used to be a sign here indicating directions and mileage, but it was torn down so many times that the forest service painted the trail numbers on a tree which read like this: ←221 205→. By turning right it is less than a five minute walk to bring you under the arch. Before making the turn, look straight ahead. During the winter months it is plainly visible from this junction. This view always suggests to me the illusion of a huge elephant extending out his trunk until it touches the cliff which forms this buttress arch. Following the trail to the arch, you are soon in the huge box canyon where the heretofore hidden dropoff from the trail above can easily be seen. From here you cross a short wooden bridge, and after a brief but stiff climb up switchbacks, you are under the arch where you can view this magnificent span and its equally fascinating surroundings. For continuation of the King's Branch segment of Rough Trail see page 132.

D. BOON HUT LOOP

TO D. BOON HUT:
Distance: .7 mile one way
Hike: MODERATE
Walking Time: 20 minutes to ½ hour one way

D. BOON HUT LOOP WALK:
Distance: 2 miles
Hike: MODERATE TO STRENUOUS
Walking Time: 1 to 1½ hours

GENERAL REMARKS: This walk has several unusual features that make the hike a rewarding one. In 1959, three men accidentally discovered the huge rock shelter found at the end of this trail. Although it is not the largest one in the area, it is the only monstrous one on public ground that requires considerably less than a mile walk before the hiker is under its stone canopy. The men also discovered the remains of a "niter mine" in the shelter which is protected by a chain link fence today. Potassium nitrate used in making gunpowder was leached out of the sandstone during the War of 1812 and possibly during the Civil War as well. Due to its recent rediscovery, much of the original equipment of the mine is still intact. The other interesting relic discovered in this rock house was a crude shelter with a roof of shingles or shakes supported by piles that are suspended between large rocks at either end of the structure. Inside the shelter, the discoverers found a small fireplace and a board with the words "D BOON" carved on its surface. This led to speculation that the great woodsman had built this hut during one of his many hunting trips. Whether the sign is genuine or placed there to create a hoax similar to the Piltdown Man fraud has never been proven one way or the other. If the hut can hardly be described as spectacular, it is obviously quite old and with the combination of the niter mine and the huge rock shelter, this hike can be an enjoyable, worthwhile experience for many visitors. It also offers the hiker the option of an easy round trip hike of about a mile and a half by returning on the same trail, or for those who want a little more leg stretching, the pleasant longer loop walk which includes the new Martin's Fork Trail as well as part of Rough Trail and Gray's Arch (connector) Trail.

TRAIL DESCRIPTION. To find the beginning of this trail, park your car in the Gray's Arch parking area then walk down the little road that connects one end of the parking area to Tunnel Ridge Road. Just before this short access road rejoins Tunnel Ridge Road, you will see the beginning of the trail on the right side of the road with a small parking lot beside it. A sign at the trail head says: D BOON HUT .7 MI. For a short distance, the trail parallels Tunnel Ridge Road, then a series of 43 wooden steps take you down to a fair sized rock shelter to the left of the trail. You will see a well-defined trail leading away from this recess cave at a 90 degree angle. It is easy to assume this is the right trail. It isn't, but at the end of it there is something you might want to see. In a short distance, this path takes you to another rock shelter where many hikers including the author on his initial walks here, have searched in vain for D. Boon Hut. In the shelter there is a rock that is enclosed in a chain link fence. The rock has some prehistoric Indian petroglyph markings. If you want to see the markings, it is only a couple of minutes walk across the hollow to this shelter with the petroglyph rock to the right.

If you want to go directly to D. Boon Hut and skip the petroglyphs, resist the temptation of turning right and go straight ahead, paralleling the first shelter on your left past its far end. Shortly after going by the shelter, you go down a second and longer wooden stairway with over 60 steps. You do not travel very far before about 15 log steps buried in the ground take you down to a small bridge across a tiny stream. Not too far beyond this branch, the trail makes a decided turn to the left and you soon see that the trail is again paralleling another rock shelter on the left. Moving along the face of the shelter, you will see one trail that follows the cliff face straight ahead and another to the right which immediately goes down 16 log steps. These steps lead to the beginning of the Martin's Fork Trail which you will use if you want to do the complete loop walk; but the way to D. Boon Hut is straight ahead. Soon a large shelter containing the niter mine and hut comes into view below you on the right. You can recognize it by the large chain link fence placed there by the forest service to protect the mine and hut from vandalism. Despite the fence, both the niter mine and the D. Boon Hut are easily seen. Due to the mining activities and natural erosion, there is a substantial amount of sand at the base of this shelter. Many times small children find this huge sand box more interesting than the historical remains. There are two large forest service signs behind the fence that give an excellent explanation of niter mining and the discovery of D. Boon Hut.

For those who do not want to walk the loop, the return trip is a little more difficult than the going, for you have to climb all those wooden steps back to the top of Tunnel Ridge. But as you work your way back on the same trail, you will find most of the climb is fairly gentle, easier and decidedly shorter than the loop. The loop walk, however, is not all that difficult and does cover pleasant new terrain. If you wish to complete the loop, follow the trail back to the log steps. Turn left and read below.

MARTIN'S FORK TRAIL #236

Distance: less than ½ mile
Hike: VERY EASY
Walking Time: 10 to 15 minutes

GENERAL REMARKS: Most of this short trail is an easy downhill stroll. The huffing and puffing part comes on the return to the Gray's Arch parking lot via Rough Trail.

TRAIL DESCRIPTION. After you walk down the log steps you will see a sign on the left side and parallel to the trail which says:

MARTINS FORK TRAIL #236
TO TR. NO 221 1/2 ⟶
HIGHWAY 77 ⟶

Turn left here and a short distance beyond this sign you will come to another set of eight log steps in the ground to help you down the ravine of a small stream. After a switchback to the right, the trail crosses the stream and a smaller tributary. Following the crossing, you have a brief climb out of the ravine followed by an easy downhill stroll until the trail T's into the Martin's Branch section of Rough Trail. On the opposite side and parallel to Rough Trail facing you there is a sign which says:

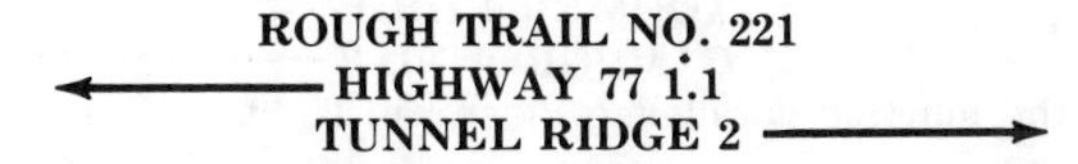

Turn right here for your climb up the ridge. For the trail description of this section of Rough Trail, see page 130.

PINCH-EM-TIGHT TRAIL #223

Distance to Rush Trail: 1/5 mi; to Buck Trail: 1.4 mi; to Rough Trail: 1.8 mi.
Hike: EASY
Walking Time to Rough Trail: 45 minutes to 1 hour

GENERAL REMARKS: This trail is generally used as a beginning or a return section for a variety of loop hikes. Its length covers about half the distance of Pinch-Em-Tight Ridge and has no really difficult sections. The scenery is unexciting but pleasant. If you want an easy stroll on a warm spring or autumn day, this trail may fill the bill. I was curious how the ridge got this unusual name, so I asked Mr. Henson about it. He explained that toward the end of the ridge (not on this trail, but can be seen from Chimney Top Overlook) there is a narrow gap. Children who lived in one hollow used to visit children in the next by squeezing through the gap— hence the name Pinch-Em-Tight. The trail begins at the first parking lot to the left of Tunnel Ridge Road a little over ½ mile from Highway 15. Facing the lot on the right side, a sign indentifies the trail and the trail begins next to it. Paralleling the left side of the trail a sign reads:

GRAYS ARCH 2 ⟶
KOOMER RIDGE 4 ⟶
CHIMNEY TOP ROAD ⟶

TRAIL DESCRIPTION. from parking area to Rough Trail. (for trail description in the opposite direction see page 90). The trail parallels Tunnel Ridge Road for perhaps a three minute walk before turning right and crossing the road diagonally about 100 feet short of the Gray's Arch picnic area. After the road crossing the trail is quite wide. I suspect at one time it was either an old wagon or logging road. You hardly get started before you junction with the Rush Ridge Trail on your left. The Rush Ridge Trail sign reads:

GRAYS ARCH 2 MI
⟵ TUNNEL RIDGE RD 3 MI

On the same post but facing Pinch-Em-Tight Trail there is a sign identifying it as Rush Ridge Trail. The sign at this junction on the right side of and paralleling Pinch-Em-Tight Trail reads:

⟵ KOOMER RIDGE PICNIC AREA 3.8 MI
⟵ CHIMNEY TOP ROAD 3.9 MI
.2 MI TUNNEL RIDGE ROAD ⟶

For description of Rush Ridge Trail, see page 91 . About a quarter mile beyond this junction, the trail bears left, leaving the old road. From here on, the trail is truly a woodland path, much narrower than before but easily followed. As the trail approaches what once had been a field there is a fork in the path. Instead of following the path into the field, turn left and follow the trail that skirts it. Beyond the meadow, the ridge narrows down a bit and you begin to see a gentle slope developing on each side of the trail. The ridge descends gently, then reascends until you have completed the second lap of this gentle walk. Soon you will see where Buck Trail exits from the right. The sign facing you on the right and paralleling Buck Trail says:

BUCK TRAIL NO. 226
KOOMER RIDGE
CAMPGROUND 3 ⟶

A sign at the junction paralleling Pinch-Em-Tight Trail on the left reads:

TRAIL NO. 223
2.5 CHIMNEY TOP ROAD ⟶
⟵ TUNNEL RIDGE ROAD 1.5
2.5 GRAYS ARCH ⟶

From here, it is an easy walk of less than a half mile to the junction of Rough Trail. Twice the trail crosses large floors of smooth sandstone where the topsoil has been eroded away. You will find the junction of Rough Trail just beyond the second sandstone outcropping. If you want to take Rough Trail in the direction of Chimney Top Creek, take the trail to the right and see page 134. If you want to take Rough Trail in the direction of Gray's Arch, take the trail to the left and see page 140. The sign for Rough Trail at this junction reads:

⟵ GRAY'S ARCH 2.0 MI
2.2 MI. CHIMNEY TOP ROAD ⟶
4.0 MI. SKY BRIDGE ROAD ⟶

PINCH-EM-TIGHT TRAIL

From Rough Trail to Tunnel Ridge Road (For General Remarks, see page 89)

TRAIL DESCRIPTION. After the tough up and down sections of Rough Trail, Pinch-Em-Tight Trail is an easy walk. Paralleling Pinch-Em-Tight Trail on the right side is a sign that says:

⟵ TUNNEL RIDGE ROAD 1.8 MI
⟵ KOOMER RIDGE

Attached to the same fence post as the above sign, another sign facing Rough Trail is of some historical interest. It says:

NO. 223
PINCH-EM-TIGHT TRAIL
CUMBERLAND
NATIONAL FOREST

Some confused hiker added a ? behind Cumberland, not knowing that until 1966 this was the Cumberland National Forest and the sign has been left as a reminder of that past name.

If you are using Pinch-Em-Tight Trail to get to Buck Trail, the distance is 4/10 mile. The trail head starts immediately climbing over a small exposed sandstone rise. It soon crosses a second outcropping of sandstone which is about 60 feet long. It is no more than a little stroll before Buck Trail exits from the left. If you are using Buck Trail to complete the loop, you've still got a testy walk ahead, but the area along the right fork of Chimney Top is just downright beautiful. For its trail's description see page 108. A sign to the left of that trail and paralleling it says:

BUCK TRAIL NO. 226
KOOMER RIDGE

CAMPGROUND 3 →

A sign paralleling Pinch-Em-Tight Trail on the right side of this junction reads:

TRAIL 223
2.5 CHIMNEY TOP ROAD →
← TUNNEL RIDGE ROAD 1.5
2.5 GRAYS ARCH

Pinch-Em-Tight Trail continues straight ahead and in about a mile, skirts to the right of a meadow which is rapidly being reclaimed by trees. Once back in the forest, it is only a short walk before the trail joins an old wagon road. In about a quarter mile, Rush Trail exits on the right. The sign which is on the right side of Rush Trail and paralleling it reads:

GRAYS ARCH 2 MI
← TUNNEL RIDGE RD. 3 MI

Another sign at this junction paralleling Pinch-Em-Tight Trail on the left says:

TRAIL NO. 223
← KOOMER RIDGE PICNIC AREA 3.8 MI
← CHIMNEY TOP ROAD 3.9 MI
.2 MI TUNNEL RIDGE ROAD →

When you arrive at Tunnel Ridge Road, a right turn takes you back to the Gray's Arch parking lot in about 100 feet. To return to the Pinch-Em-Tight parking lot, walk across the road and follow the trail to the left for a short walk to the trail head.

RUSH RIDGE TRAIL #227

From Pinch-Em-Tight Trail to Rough Trail

(For trail description in opposite direction, see page 92)

Distance: 1 mile
Hike: EASY
Walking Time: 20 to 30 minutes

GENERAL REMARKS. This untaxing trail is mainly for use in completing loop walks with Rough Trail and Gray's Arch. It is a pleasant hike along the top of a ridge which ends at the junction of Rough Trail. If you are interested in seeing a magnificent two-story rock shelter, a short walk on Rough Trail near the end of Buck Trail will take you to it.

TRAIL DESCRIPTION. To find the trail head, follow Pinch-Em-Tight Trail from Tunnel Ridge Road for 2/10 mile where Rush Ridge Trail begins on the left. The sign alongside Rush Ridge Trail reads:

← GRAYS ARCH 2 MI
TUNNEL RIDGE RD. 3 MI

After turning left onto Rush Ridge Trail, you will find that the path is generally level and the ridge it follows is narrow in several places but not frighteningly so. When this trail dead ends into Rough Trail, the sign to the left of the trail reads:

.8 MI GRAY'S ARCH →
2.2 MI. TUNNEL RIDGE ROAD →
← TUNNEL RIDGE ROAD 1.3 MI.

A sign on the left of Rough Trail and parallel to it reads:

TRAIL 221

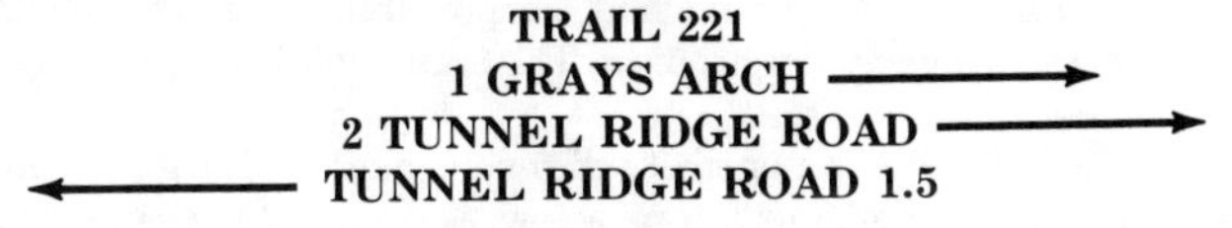

If you want to see the large two-level rock shelter, turn right on Rough Trail and in less than a quarter mile the trail takes you into the shelter.

RUSH RIDGE TRAIL #227

From Rough Trail to Tunnel Ridge Road

For distance signs at this trail junction, see above. If you are using Rush Ridge Trail to complete a loop hike from Gray's Arch, your hard walking is over. You follow along the rather level top of this narrow ridge for about a mile until it dead ends into Pinch-Em-Tight Trail. Turn right here for Tunnel Ridge Road which is an easy 2/10 mile away. If you are looking for the Gray's Arch parking lot, turn right again at the road and you will see it in about 100 feet.

AUXIER RIDGE—COURTHOUSE ROCK TRAILS

From Tunnel Ridge Road

Both trails listed below may be found on the detailed contour map on page 93 . The trail head for both trails is found on the left side of a spacious parking lot found off to the right of Tunnel Ridge Road a little over 4½ miles from Highway 15.

1. Auxier Ridge Trail #204
2. Courthouse Rock Trail #202

Distance—Auxier Ridge Trail: 1.8 miles one way
Hike: MODERATE
Walking Time: 1 to 1½ hours one way

Distance—Courthouse Rock Trail: 2.5 miles one way
Hike: STRENUOUS
Walking Time: 1½ to 2 hours one way

GENERAL REMARKS FOR BOTH TRAILS. Since these two trails run together for the first 7/10 mile and have the same destination, I have combined the comments about them. The description of each trail is treated separately. Until recently, the end of both trails were within a few hundred feet of each other at Courthouse Rock, but they did not connect for one was on the ridge top and the other below. A hiker had to return on the same trail as the walk out. But with the addition of a wooden stairway, the two trails are now connected at Courthouse Rock, making for a dandy loop hike of just under 4½ miles. Auxier Ridge Trail is the easiest, shortest and by far the more scenic route of the two. For those who are short of time or have limited hiking abilities and are not physically up to a couple of demanding uphill sections, following the Auxier Ridge Trail in both directions may be the better choice.

Auxier Ridge Trail is a gentle walk that offers exceptional scenic views. The few grades that the walker must negotiate on this hike are so mild and so few that I would have classified it an easy walk had it not been for the 3.6 miles round trip. For the little physical energy required, this trail pays off in big panoramic dividends. It has several spectacular overlooks where one has the best views of such natural features as Raven's Rock, Double Arch, Haystack Rock and Courthouse Rock. It is also a beautiful area for fall panoramic viewing and photography when the weather and foliage happen to be cooperating. This ridge top trail includes some exciting cliff top areas. Although the trail never comes smack up to the edge of these high cliffs, it comes extremely close in some places. These precipitous drop-offs are an extreme hazard for children who run wildly ahead and refuse to obey their parents. People who suffer from acrophobia may experience some queasy moments on this trail, but for the normal, responsible hiker, this walk is not in the least dangerous nor overly frightening. The trail itself is well marked and easy to follow.

Courthouse Rock Trail is an entirely different matter. Large sections of this trail were torn up for lumber operations a few years ago. It was not maintained

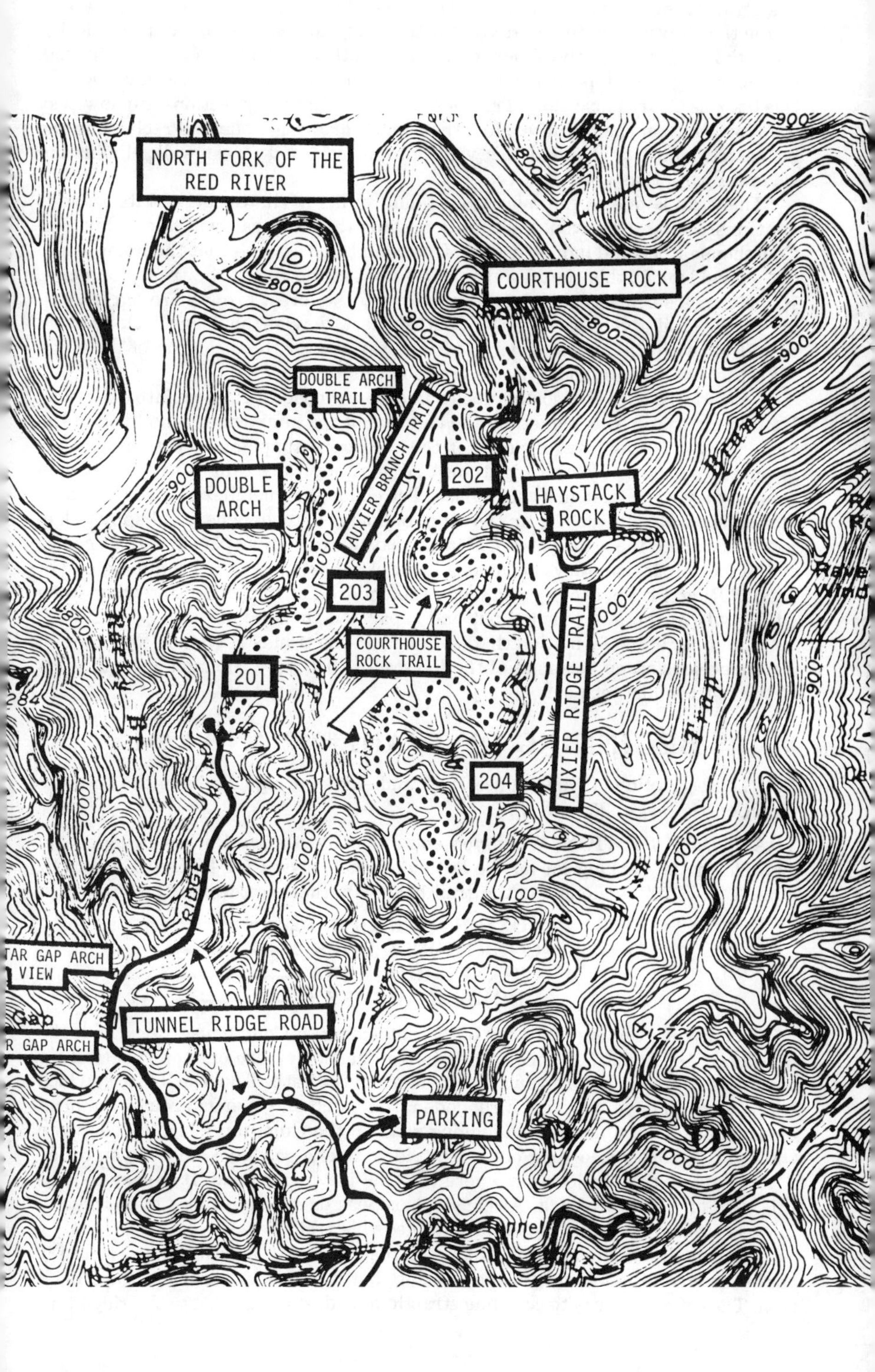
NORTH FORK OF THE RED RIVER
COURTHOUSE ROCK
DOUBLE ARCH TRAIL
AUXIER BRANCH TRAIL
DOUBLE ARCH
202
HAYSTACK ROCK
203
COURTHOUSE ROCK TRAIL
201
AUXIER RIDGE TRAIL
204
TAR GAP ARCH VIEW
TUNNEL RIDGE ROAD
R GAP ARCH
PARKING
800
900
1000
1100

as a trail for a number of years and wasn't reopened until the spring of 1973. Since the trail both utilizes and crosses many sections of old logging roads, it was a very easy trail to lose. When it was first reopened there were stretches that were so vague that it was easy to go astray, but that situation has improved dramatically. Even though it follows the almost exact same path as it did when it was reopened, no trail changed in appearence as much between the first and revised editions of this book as Courthouse Rock Trail has. The once confusing sections are now easy to follow, but, on the negative side, the rapidly growing woodland reclaiming the harvested land has changed this walk into an enclosed forest walk eliminating several open areas and vistas.

This trail is one of the more demanding walks in the Gorge and its name is a bit misleading. One would naturally assume that the trail will take a hiker to Courthouse Rock and indeed it does. One would also assume that the hiker would get a good look at this significant rock sentinel at the end of the trail. You don't. Its bold rock surfaces are hidden from view by the forest growth around it. Auxier Ridge Trail gives the hiker by far the finest view of this large rock promontory. But, with the new stairway, it is an easy matter to get on top of the ridge from the lower Courthouse Rock Trail for this better view.

I asked Clarence Henson how the name Courthouse Rock came into existence. He told me that it was named by the children of the lumbermen who lived in the vicinity over 50 years ago. Some of these loggers supplemented their meager incomes by making "White Lightning". When they were caught by the revenue agents, they were tried in a courthouse. The children remembered the large stone edifice, separate and aloof from the other buildings in town, where unhappy judgements disrupted the usual pattern of family existence. As they played various games at the foot of this solitary monstrous hunk of sandstone at the crumbling end of Auxier Ridge, it apparently reminded the children of that other enduring stone edifice where the law reached out and separated their families.

The other stone formation that is seen from the trail is Haystack Rock, which is a marvelous stone facsimile of the haystacks that were common around farms of the not too distant past.

BEGINNING OF TRAIL #202 AND #204

For the description of Courthouse Rock and Auxier Ridge Trails in the opposite direction see page 96 and 98

TRAIL DESCRIPTION. When you enter the Courthouse Rock parking area a sign facing the parking lot on the left side which says: COURTHOUSE ROCK TRAIL NO. 202 is alongside the trail head. Another sign facing the trail says:

AUXIER RIDGE TR. 1/2 ⟶
COURTHOUSE ROCK 2 ⟶
TUNNEL RIDGE RD 3 ⟶
DOUBLE ARCHES 4 ⟶

This is the starting point for both trails going to Courthouse Rock with the division of the trails 7/10 mile from this trail head. You are only on this trail for a couple of minutes before you come to a fork in the path. Take the left fork which will soon drop down through a rhododendron patch and swings around the head of a hollow. It then hits an old logging road on the ridge top which it follows to the right. Before proceeding out on the ridge, take a good look behind you to see if you can identify the location where the trail leaves the road. It is easy to miss this turn on your way back. Although there was once a sign there to aid hikers, it was missing the last two times I walked this trail.

In about five minutes of walking, the road comes to a cleared area where it angles down on the left side of the clearing, but it no longer serves as the official trail. The correct way is to continue straight ahead, staying close to the ridge top.

Auxier Ridge and Courthouse Rock as seen from Raven's Rock

From the clearing, the trail generally follows the crest of the ridge and climbs up two short switchbacks. Then, after a gradual descent where the ridge makes a dip, the trail comes to a second and smaller cleared area. The trail that branches off to the left is Courthouse Rock Trail and the sign to the left of that trail and facing you reads:

COURTHOUSE ROCK TRAIL NO. 202
←—— COURTHOUSE ROCK 2
←—— TUNNEL RIDGE RD 3

For the continued description of Courthouse Rock Trail, see page 97. The trail that goes straight ahead is Auxier Ridge Trail and a sign on the right side of that trail reads:

AUXIER RIDGE TRAIL NO. 204
↑ COURTHOUSE ROCK 1
TUNNEL RIDGE RD 3

Since more hikers will probably follow the Auxier Ridge Trail than the one to the base of Courthouse Rock, I include its description first. After walking along the ridge top for about ten minutes, Auxier Ridge Trail cuts sharply to the right, declines slightly and goes around the head of a ravine. This right turn takes you over to the longest finger of Auxier Ridge. Just after the trail goes around the ravine and levels off, a good view of Haystack Rock can be seen from a small cleared area on the left side of the trail. From this clearing, look in the same direction as the trail and through a break in the trees you can see Haystack Rock about a quarter of a mile away. If you miss this viewpoint, and it is easy to do, you will get a much closer look at it later on. The trail continues to follow the easy up and down variations of the ridge top as it gradually begins to narrow. You will then arrive at the first high cliff area where the foliage on the left side of the trail gives way to the bare sandstone of the cliff. From this point on, keep a close watch on any young children accompanying you, for the cliff edge on both sides of the trail is close and is usually sheer.

From this first cliff edge the panorama is outstanding. As you face the valley from this bare sandstone area, look left for an excellent view of Haystack Rock. By looking directly across the valley cut by Auxier Branch, you can easily see Double Arch near the top of the ridge on the other side. Looking down and slightly to the right, you can see part of the lower Red River Gorge complete with farmhouses, barns and cultivated fields.

As you proceed further on the trail, the right side of the ridge also becomes bare sandstone. This opens the panorama on both sides and Raven's Rock dominates the view to the right. The visible cliff face on Raven's Rock marks the location where in 1976 two hang glider pilots sailed off to their deaths.

At this point the trail comes closest to the edge and it is quite an edge. Almost immediately beyond this point, the trail again returns to the forest. Just before you reach the end of the trail, you must climb up an abrupt three-foot elevation in the sandstone ridge. If you look left, you will see a small tree close to the rise and indentations in the sandstone which can serve as steps to help you up this final ledge. Walk a few feet more and you have an excellent view of Courthouse Rock directly ahead of you. Enjoy the scenery, but remember the drop-off is severe on three sides.

If you wish to explore around the edges of Courthouse Rock or find the connection with the Courthouse Rock Trail, continue out the ridge and go down a substantial wooden stairway with 29 steps. To find the Courthouse Rock Traill, continue out this lower section of the ridge for about 40 feet beyond the stairway. Then look left and slightly to your rear. There you will see the beginning of Courthouse Rock Trail angling down the side of the ridge. If you are going to follow this trail to complete the loop, walk to Double Arch or try the proposed Raven's Rock Trail, see below.

COURTHOUSE ROCK TRAIL #202

From Courthouse Rock to the Courthouse Rock Parking Lot

Distance: 2½ miles
Hike: Mostly MODERATE. One short uphill stretch is VERY STRENUOUS
Walking Time: 1 hour 15 minutes to 2 hours

TRAIL DESCRIPTION. Once you are on the descending trail below the stairway at the end of Auxier Ridge (see above) you will see the trail soon switches back to the bottom of a small cliff face. Walk a short distance along this rock wall until you see a trail that angles down the escarpment to the left. When it levels off follow it back in the direction of Tunnel Ridge.

Here is the junction for the proposed Raven's Rock Trail. At this intersection this new trail goes to the right. A sign there will say:

RAVEN'S ROCK TRAIL #2

Trail not completed at this writing

For the trail description of this trail see page 163.

After you are past this junction you have an easy downhill walk of about a quarter mile before arriving at the junction with the Auxier Branch Trail. A sign to the left and paralleling Courthouse Rock Trail at that junction reads:

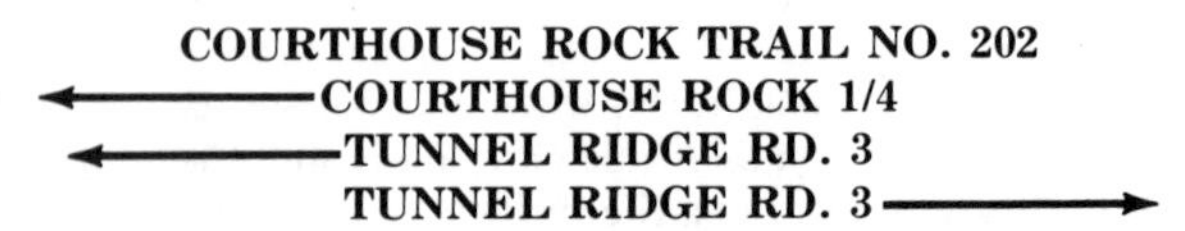

As you look down the trail to the right you can see a sign alongside the trail facing you which reads:

TRAIL #203
.9 MI TUNNEL RIDGE ROAD ↑
1.6 MI DOUBLE ARCH

For the trail description of the Auxier Branch Trail see page 101

The distance back to the parking lot is a half mile shorter than the above sign indicates. You now have a pleasant forest walk of about a mile and a half, crossing a few small streams along the way before you get to the only real difficult part of the trail. That is the climb back up to the ridge top where the two trails from Courthouse Rock join. Despite the six switchbacks the gradient is very steep in places and will be a real struggle for many walkers. But it doesn't last long and once you make a right turn on the ridge top you will find only a few gentle rises. After a couple of switchbacks the trail joins an old logging road and follows it for perhaps a quarter of a mile. If the sign is down it is easy to miss the point where the trail drops off this old road to the left. If you miss the turn you can follow the road back to Tunnel Ridge Road and turn left until you see the side road that takes you back to the Courthouse Rock parking lot. If you make the turn, the trail swings around the head of a hollow and up to the parking lot.

COURTHOUSE ROCK TRAIL #202

From Trail Junction #202—#204 on Auxier Ridge to Courthouse Rock

Distance: 1.8 miles
Hike: STRENUOUS
Walking Time: 1 to 1½ hours

For the trail description of the first part of this trail, see page 94 . The sign at the trail junction is on page 95

TRAIL DESCRIPTION. After turning left at the junction of Trails #202 and #204, the trail almost immediately goes down six steep switchbacks. Parts of this descent are very steep, and, especially in wet weather, it can be downright treacherous. Brief as it is, the stretch is only for the agile and it is much easier to go up than down. After the switchbacks, the trail begins a more gradual decline down to the bottom of a ravine where it joins an old logging road. Once down you now have a much easier forest walk of approximately 1¼ miles to the Auxier Branch junction with a few easy stream crossings along the way. When arriving at the junction you will see a sign to the right of the trail and paralleling it which says:

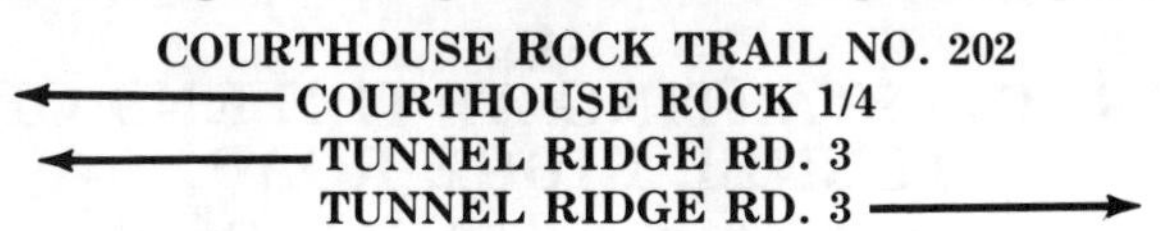

You will be able to see the Auxier Branch Trail going off to the left. A sign alongside that trail and facing the trail you are on says:

TRAIL #203
.9 MI TUNNEL RIDGE ROAD ↑
1.6 MI DOUBLE ARCH

Proceeding straight ahead from this junction, you have a fairly steady moderate to moderately steep climb angling up the ridge. In this area the new proposed Raven's Rock Trail will come in from the left. A sign there will reads:

RAVEN'S ROCK TRAIL NO. 2

Trail not completed at this writing

For the description of this trail see page 163

Beyond this junction the Courthouse Rock Trail turns right and climbs up a steep escarpment to a rock wall in the side of the ridge. You will be able to see where many hikers have scrambled up some rather steep breaks in the wall, not knowing there is a much easier way to get up the ridge. I made the same mistake and found it a tough struggle up before I discovered the official and much less demanding way to the top. When you reach this low cliff face, turn right and walk along its base until you can see the trail switching back to the left. There you have a moderate gradient up to a lower plane of Auxier Ridge with Courthouse Rock to your left. To gain a better view of Courthouse Rock and the beginning of the Auxier Ridge Trail, follow the narrow ridge top to your right which will bring you to a stairway with 26 wooden steps. This takes you to a higher level of Auxier Ridge with a better view of Courthouse Rock to the left and the Auxier Ridge return trail ahead of you. (For the trail description of that trail see below.)

AUXIER RIDGE TRAIL #204

From Courthouse Rock to the Courthouse Parking Lot

Distance: 1.8 miles
Hike: MODERATE
Walking Time: 1 to 1½ hours

TRAIL DESCRIPTION. From the stairway at the end of Auxier Ridge, the trail takes you through a narrow section of the ridge top with exposed sandstone rim rock on both sides. You will see Raven's Rock on the left and a little further on, Haystack Rock on the right. Be careful getting close to the edges here for, in places, the drop-offs on both sides of the ridge are sheer and long. By looking right across the valley you will be able to see Double Arch in the next ridge.

As you get closer to Tunnel Ridge, the forest becomes heavier. Arriving at the junction of Courthouse Rock Trail you will see that trail going sharply off the ridge on the right and a sign next to the path that identifies it. Passing this junction and continuing straight ahead you will soon have a couple a short switchbacks before the trail joins an old logging road. You are on this narrow old trace road for about a quarter mile before the trail turns left dropping off the ridge top and away from the road. This turn is easy to miss and since the sign to identify it has been torn down, you might walk right by it. If that is the case, just stay on this old road until you hit Tunnel Ridge Road. Turn left and then left again on the first gravel side road which will take you to the Courthouse Rock parking lot. If you successfully make the left turn away from the old road, you will find the trail takes you around the head of a hollow through a rhodendendron patch and up to the parking lot.

TRAILS STARTING AT THE END OF TUNNEL RIDGE ROAD

Just before you get to the turnaround at the end of Tunnel Ridge Road, you will see a small parking area to the right of the road where the trail head is located. Before you begin your hike, you may want to walk to the end of the road to enjoy a wonderful panoramic view of the valley below. There is a very short path leading off from the left of the road which goes down to a rock outcropping that offers an especially nice view of the valley and farms below.

1. Double Arch Trail #201
2. Auxier Branch Trail #203 (page 100)

DOUBLE ARCH TRAIL #201

Distance: 1 mile one way
Hike: MODERATE
Walking Time: 45 minutes to 1 hour one way

GENERAL REMARKS. This gentle hike is well worth it even for those with limited time. After walking a relatively easy mile, one sees the only ridge top arch of any appreciable size in the area that has another smaller one directly above it.

Haystack Rock as seen from Auxier Ridge Trail

Most of the well defined trail is level. The only difficult section is the last .1 mile on your return trip when you climb back to the top of Tunnel Ridge. This is a particularly good family trail. Caution is urged at the arch itself for the drop-off on the other side of the arch is sudden and long.

There is now a good scenic loop hike possible from this trail head. After a visit to Double Arch, the hiker can follow the Auxier Branch Trail to the Courthouse Rock Trail, then out to Courthouse Rock. Climb up the stairs to the top of Auxier Ridge and follow that ridge back to Tunnel Ridge Road, then hike the road back to this trail head. The distance covered is about 6½ miles and the route can easily be seen on the area map found on page 93 .

TRAIL DESCRIPTION. Starting at the parking lot, the sign at the beginning of the trail reads:

←——— DOUBLE ARCH 1.0 MI.
←——— COURTHOUSE ROCK 1.6 MI.

There is a forest service toilet here but no water. Just a few yards down the trail you descend 45 wooden steps which take you through a long narrow crack in a large outcropping of sandstone. You can see excellent samples of Rockcastle Conglomerate on the walls that rise on either side as you go down the stairway. At the bottom of the wooden steps there are a series of swtichbacks that take you down to a lower level. From here the trail has no more serious uphill or downhill sections. You proceed in a northerly direction with Tunnel Ridge above you on the left. In 1/10 mile, Auxier Branch Trail exits to the right. Double Arch Trail continues straight ahead with the Tunnel Ridge cliffs above you to the left. A sign paralleling the trail to the left says:

TRAIL NO. 201
←——— TUNNEL RIDGE ROAD
.8 MI. DOUBLE ARCH ———→

A sign to the left of the Auxier Branch Trail reads:

AUXIER BRANCH TRAIL #203
COURTHOUSE ROCK 1 ⟶
TUNNEL RIDGE RD. 3 ⟶

For the trail description of the Auxier Branch Trail see page 100

If you are hiking the trail during the months when the foliage is off the trees, keep an eye on the cliff wall to your left. You will be able to see Double Arch high above you in the sandstone ridge, about a quarter mile beyond the intersection of Auxier Branch Trail. This view is blotted out in the spring and summer months, but remember that the arch is best seen at the end of the trail. The path begins winding its way across a sloping hill filled with man-sized sandstone boulders. The trail now rounds the end of Tunnel Ridge and starts along the other side of this ridge finger. Along this section of the trail, there is a large rock just to the left of the path with some interesting natural marks on its surface which divide up roughly into a series of imperfect rectangles. Less than 100 yards beyond the rock, you go up about 30 wooden steps where the trail then brings you to the bottom of the arch. The span of the lower arch is 30 feet long and 11 feet high. Above it there is a slit of light showing an opening about 1 1/2 feet high and approximately 25 feet long. This little horizontal crack gives Double Arch its name. Be careful when going under the arch for the drop-off on the other side of the arch is abrupt and extreme. To the right of the arch on the trail side, there are 28 steps that take you to the top of this ridge top arch. From there, you get a nice view of Auxier Branch Valley. On the far side, you can see some rather formidable cliffs along Auxier Ridge. Auxier Ridge Trail makes its way along the top of those cliffs and gives one an excellent distant view of the arch you are standing on. Looking left, you can see Courthouse Rock which caps the end of Auxier Ridge.

Returning to the base of the arch, one has a nice place to take a short rest, doze, daydream a little and, perhaps, have lunch. On many days there is a cool breeze passing through the arch furnishing a sort of natural air conditioning. Once you have had your fill of the arch and its view, you go back the way you came. Fortunately, such wooded trails as this often look surprisingly different when walking them in the opposite direction.

If you decide that you wish to walk to Courthouse Rock when you arrive at the Auxier Branch intersection, remember it is a far tougher walk than the one to Double Arch. If you are returning to the parking lot, you only have 2/10 mile to go, but the last half of this is the testiest part of the trip. When you return to the first wooden fence, you are ready for the switchback climb to the top of Tunnel Ridge. You can look right up the cliff from here which shows you how much you have to climb. It is mercifully short and really isn't as bad as it looks. Almost before you know it, you're back at the parking area, short of breath perhaps, but with pleasant memories of Trail #201.

AUXIER BRANCH TRAIL #203

From Double Arch Trail to Courthouse Rock Trail

Distance: 8/10 mile
Hike: MODERATE
Walking Time: 25 to 40 minutes one way

GENERAL REMARKS. This trail crosses the valley cut by Auxier Branch. Except for the loop hike using Courthouse Rock Trail, this trail offers little in the way of unusual scenery for never in its entire length does it ever furnish a good view of Courthouse Rock. Although the distance of the actual trail is only 8/10 mile, the total distance from the beginning of Double Arch Trail to the base of Courthouse Rock is 1.3 miles. The walk down to Auxier Branch is often steep and the climb out of the valley on the other side is a stiff one.

TRAIL DESCRIPTION. (For description in the opposite direction, (see below). After a distance of 2/10 mile on Double Arch Trail, Auxier Branch Trail exits to the right. The sign there to the left of the trail reads:

1.0 MI. COURTHOUSE ROCK →
3.0 MI TUNNEL RIDGE ROAD →

This trail goes steadily down hill for about a quarter of a mile until it hits Auxier Branch. The trail immediately crosses the creek, turns left and parallels the stream for about another quarter of a mile. Then it turns away from the stream and begins a steady but not difficult climb up the ridge. Sometimes the first section of this climb can be very damp for this part becomes a small stream in rainy weather. After quite a bit of climbing, the trail crosses a well defined old logging road. Cross the road and proceed up the trail. A very short walk takes you to the official junction of the two trails. The sign in front of you reads:

TRAIL #202
← .9 MI. TUNNEL RIDGE ROAD
← 1.6 MI. DOUBLE ARCH

You turn left here for the short walk to the base of Courthouse Rock. (For trail description, see page 97 .)

AUXIER BRANCH TRAIL #203

From Courthouse Rock Trail to Double Arch Trail

For signs of this trail, see paragraph immediately above. Starting at the junction of Courthouse Rock and Auxier Branch Trails, it is only a very short walk until you come to an old logging road. Cross the road and continue on the trail that begins a steady descent down to Auxier Branch. Just before you get to the stream, the going often gets quite soggy for the trail at this point becomes an active runoff stream during and just after any appreciable rain. Once the creek is reached, the trail levels off and follows the creek upstream. With the stream on your right, follow its course for about a quarter mile before crossing it. From here on your work is cut out for you, for in slightly over a half mile, this trail climbs about 400 feet.

After a short climb from the branch, the trail levels off on what was an old wagon road many years before. You are only on this level stretch for a short distance before the trail cuts right, leaving the road and going up the slope. The trail continues to climb until it joins with Double Arch Trail. If you want to go to Tunnel Ridge Road, turn left here and you will climb up Tunnel Ridge and arrive at the road in just 2/10 mile. If you want to go to Double arch, turn here and in 8/10 mile this easy walk will take you to the base of that arch.

VIII

TRAILS FROM THE KOOMER RIDGE RECREATION AREA

To get to the Koomer Ridge Recreation Area, exit the Mountain Parkway at Slade and take Kentucky 15 east in the direction of Pine Ridge and Campton. About 5.5 miles from Slade, a large forest service sign on the south side of the road identifies the location of the recreation area and campground with its entrance just across the road. (#11 on area map found on page 166).

Once you have made the turn into the campground area the road forks. A sign between the two roads and facing you says:

←——— TENT CAMPING
TENT OR TRAILER CAMPING ———→

To find the trail heads take the left fork and, almost immediately you will see another road to the left. This is the entrance to the parking lot for day hikers and backpackers. Before turning into the parking lot, look right where you will see a brown mobile home-type structure which is used for various purposes by the forest service. Beside this building is the trail head for all the Koomer Ridge Trails except Cliff Trail, with a sign there telling you that it is TRAIL #220 KOOMER RIDGE TRAIL. But it is also the official starting point for Hidden Arch and Silvermine Arch Trails. A sign next to the first one and paralleling the trail head on the right side says:

←——— TUNNEL RIDGE ROAD 4
←——— GRAY'S ARCH 5
←——— CHIMNEY TOP ROAD 3

During the camping seasons you can follow either fork of the camp roads in your vehicle to fill your water bottles and/or use the pit toilets before your hike. During the winter months the water is shut off and the campground is closed. The closing and opening dates vary from time to time due to federal regulations and budget considerations. This need not worry the hiker for the trail head and the parking lot for hikers are always open and accessible.

KOOMER RIDGE TRAIL #220 AND BUCK TRAIL

Distance: Koomer Ridge Trail to Rough Trail: 2 miles
Hike: MODERATE to STRENUOUS
Walking Time: 1 hour 15 minutes to 1 hour 30 minutes
Distance: Buck Trail from Koomer Ridge Trail to Pinch-Em-Tight Trail: 1.5 miles
Hike: STRENUOUS
Walking Time: 45 minutes to 1 hour 15 minutes

GENERAL REMARKS FOR BOTH TRAILS. Since both trails share a common beginning section before they go their separate ways and are used in a good loop walk, I have combined their general descriptions. These trails go down separate forks of the same creek and end at junction points of other trails so they can be used in several different loop hikes. Both trails also go to the ends of different fingers of Koomer Ridge then descend. Buck Trail goes down to the right fork of Chimney Top Creek, then climbs out to the top of Pinch-Em-Tight Ridge. The areas along Chimney Top Creek are among the most attractive sections of moun-

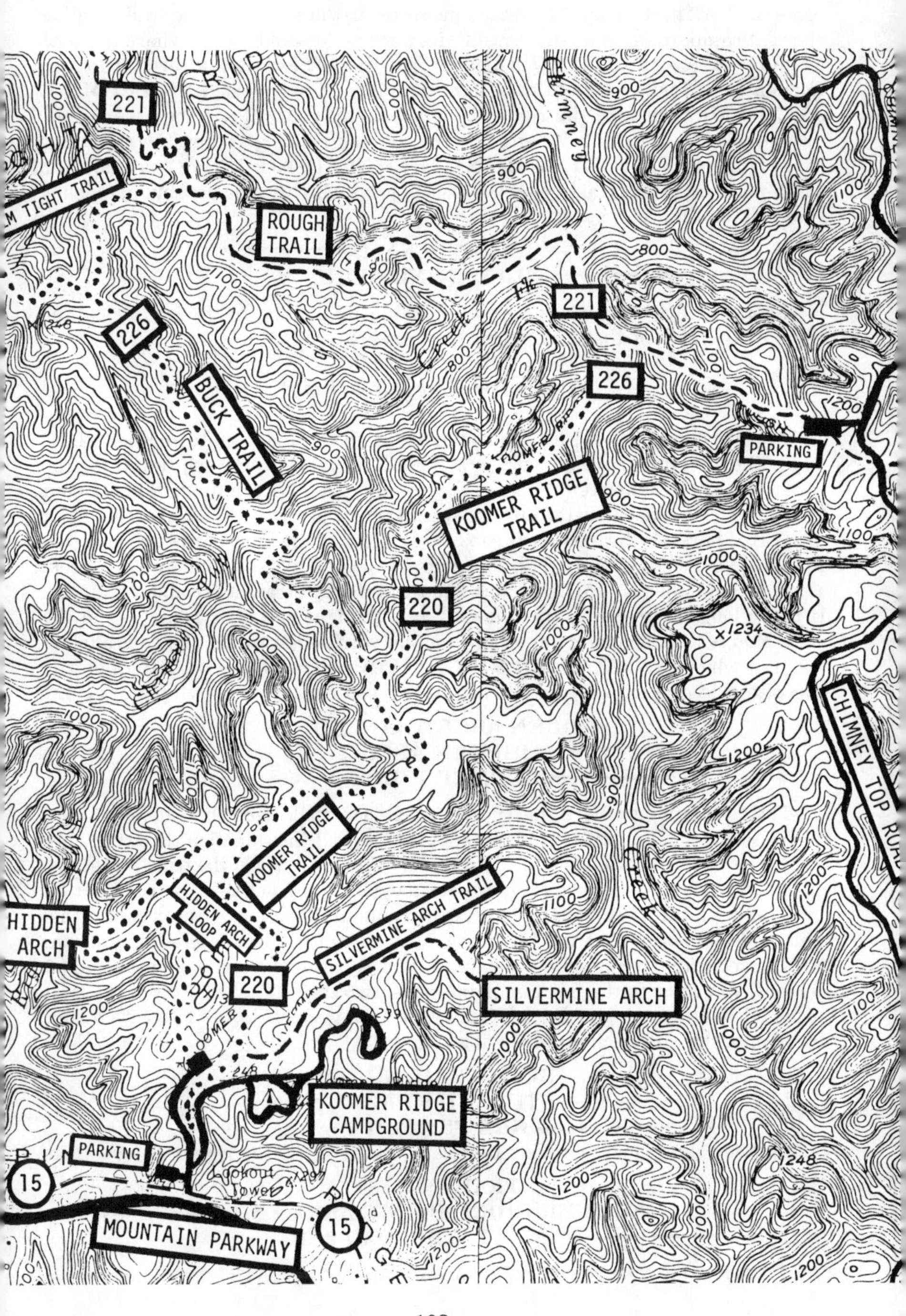
221
TIGHT TRAIL
ROUGH TRAIL
226
BUCK TRAIL
221
226
PARKING
KOOMER RIDGE TRAIL
220
KOOMER RIDGE TRAIL
HIDDEN ARCH
HIDDEN ARCH LOOP
220
SILVERMINE ARCH TRAIL
SILVERMINE ARCH
CHIMNEY TOP ROAD
KOOMER RIDGE CAMPGROUND
PARKING
15
15
MOUNTAIN PARKWAY
Chimney
Creek
Lookout Tower
900
800
1000
1100
1200
1234
1248

tain streams in the area.

Koomer Ridge Trail goes down the main fork of Chimney Top Creek junctioning with Rough Trail not far from the point where the two forks of Chimney Top Creek join.

TRAIL DESCRIPTION. From the trail head you go about 100 feet before you come to a fork in the trail. Follow the narrower path to the left. The trail parallels the tent campground road briefly until its parking lot can be seen where the path again forks. A sign to the left indicates that the left fork is the turn off for the Hidden Arch Trail. A sign to your right paralleling the trail says **SILVERMINE ARCH 1 MI.** You take the right fork and shortly you will see the other campground road to the right. When you come to a sign facing you on the right side of the trail which says: **SILVERMINE ARCH TRAIL NO. 225,** you have arrived at the point where the trails go their separate ways. On the same post but paralleling the trail another sign says:

KENTUCKY 15 ⟶
⟵ SILVERMINE ARCH

From here you can see the Koomer Ridge Trail going to the left. A sign on the opposite side of that trail facing you reads:

(sign missing at this writing)

After making the left turn the trail crosses a wash and T's into another where you make a right turn. The path now follows alongside the wash downstream.

In just about a quarter of a mile, the stream takes a precipitous drop of about 30 feet which makes a pretty but not spectacular waterfall when the creek is not dry. From here, the branch stays considerably below the level of the trail and you won't be alongside running water again until you get down to Chimney Top Creek.

A little further on, the trail runs almost perfectly straight for about 200 feet. It is the longest stretch of trail running in a straight line, that I know of in the area. You will soon come to another junction with a sign to the right paralleling the trail which says: **KOOMER RIDGE CAMPGROUND½ ⟶**. A sign on the opposite side of a trail to the left and facing you says:

HIDDEN ARCH TRAIL NO. 208
⟵ HIDDEN ARCH 1
⟵ KOOMER RIDGE 2

This is the point where the Hidden Arch loop walk joins the Koomer Ridge Trail. By proceeding straight ahead, not far beyond this junction, the trail cuts away from the little branch, which is now far below the level of the trail, and starts up another hollow. The trail then crosses a well defined path. If you turn left on this trail it ends up back at the tent campground parking lot. After crossing this trail, you will notice that the terrain on each side of you slopes gradually down, for Koomer Ridge is beginning to narrow. Shortly after the trail makes a gradual descent, you come to the junction point of the two trails. The left fork of the trail is the official beginning of Buck Trail. Buck Trail goes off to the left with a sign on its opposite side facing you saying:

BUCK TRAIL NO. 226
⟵ TUNNEL RIDGE 3
⟵ GRAY'S ARCH 4

Another sign which parallels the trail you are on to the right reads:

TRAIL NO. 220
KOOMER RIDGE PICNIC AREA 1 MI ⟶
⟵ CHIMNEY TOP ROAD 2 MI

If it seemed to take you longer than you thought to get here, the distance back to the trail head in the Koomer Ridge Campground is about 1/4 mile longer than the sign indicates and you are now one half way to this trail's terminus at Rough Trail.

Continuing on Koomer Ridge Trail, the walk descends gradually staying on a finger of the ridge for another half mile. The trail then drops off the top of the ridge and starts down in earnest. In the next quarter mile, you drop about 300 feet with two switchbacks near the top of the drop and two more switchbacks near the bottom to keep the grade from becoming too steep. There is a large sandstone boulder in this section on the left side of the trail that has a beautiful miniature arch in its surface. Just beyond the boulder, Chimney Top Creek can easily be heard if not seen. After crossing a couple of tiny streams, the trail goes down a steep grade to Chimney Top Creek. At the creek, the trail turns left and follows the creek downstream until it reaches the junction of Rough Trail. At this junction, there is a sign paralleling the trail to your left which says **←KOOMER RIDGE PICNIC AREA 2.2 MI.** As the trail T's into Rough Trail you can see a sign on its opposite side facing you reading:

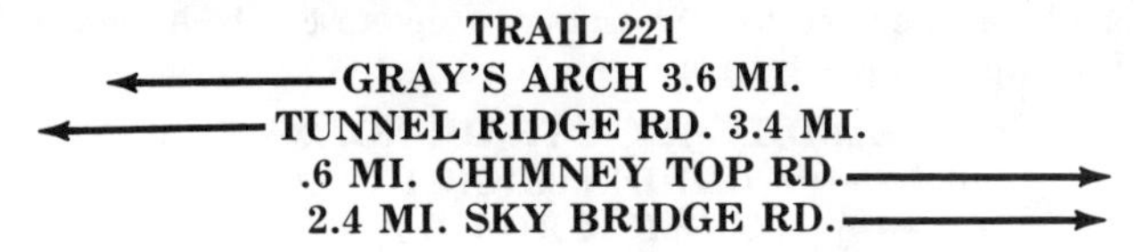

For the Chimney Top Creek section of Rough Trail to the left, see page139; for the Chimney Top Ridge section to the right see page 135.

KOOMER RIDGE TRAIL #220

From the Rough Trail Junction to the Koomer Ridge Recreation Area

Distance: 2.2 miles
Hike: STRENUOUS
Walking Time: 1 hour 15 minutes to 1 hour 30 minutes

TRAIL DESCRIPTION: A sign to the right of the Koomer Ridge Trail and paralleling it says: **←KOOMER RIDGE PICNIC AREA 2.2 MI.**

In less than half a mile, this trail climbs over 300 feet so the first part is quite strenuous. The rest of the trail is either level or has a gentle uphill grade. As the trail begins, Chimney Top Creek is on your left. The trail parallels the creek in the upstream direction. About 65 feet from the the trail head, the trail seems to fork, the left fork proceeding along the creek bank, the right fork going up a short, very steep embankment. The right fork up the embankment is the correct one. The trail continues to follow the creek for awhile, then abruptly cuts right and leaves the creek for good. Here the stiff climb begins. After two switchbacks the trail crosses two tiny streams. It is not any distance before a large sandstone boulder crops up on the right side of the trail. The first time I saw it in the wooded distance, it vividly reminded me of a derelict Japanese warship I had seen gutted and partially sunk in the shallow waters off the island of Guam in World War II. When the trail passes close to the rock my illusion faded, but on closer inspection, one can see it has an excellent miniature arch in one of its corners.

Once the boulder is behind you, there are two more switchbacks on the trail just before you are on the top of the ridge. Your serious climbing is over, but you still have over 1½ miles to go. From here, the trail follows the ups and downs of the ridge top. You will pass over one narrow section that is quite similar to the top side of an arch.

When you reach the Buck Trail junction, Buck Trail goes off to the right. The sign on the right side of Buck Trail reads:

BUCK TRAIL NO. 226

←TUNNEL RIDGE 3
←GRAY'S ARCH 4

The Koomer Ridge Trail continues, more or less straight from this junction and the trail sign to the left of the trail paralleling it reads:

TRAIL NO. 220
KOOMER RIDGE PICNIC AREA 1 MI→
←CHIMNEY TOP ROAD 2 MI

Despite what the sign says, you still have 1¼ miles to go to arrive at the Koomer Ridge Campground. Continue on this until it crosses a wide trail. If you want the quickest way to the Koomer Ridge parking area, turn right on this trail and an easy walk will bring you to the tent campground parking lot. The official trail is a bit longer, often mucky in places, but more scenic. If you wish to stay on the official trail, don't turn but cross this wide trail and continue on. You will soon come to the junction of the Hidden Arch Trail which exits to the right. If you have the time and are not tired, you can take the Hidden Arch Trail back to Koomer Ridge. It is a bit longer and has two sets of steps to climb. A sign to the right of that trail and parallel to it says:

HIDDEN ARCH TRAIL NO. 208
←HIDDEN ARCH 1
←KOOMER RIDGE 2

A sign to your left paralleling the Koomer Ridge Trail says: **KOOMER RIDGE CAMPGROUND 1/2.** As you continue you will see a good sized ravine developing to the left of the trail with a small stream at its bottom. Finally, the branch catches up to the level of the trail where the stream has about a 30-foot waterfall. Since the stream is seldom more than a trickle, it is hardly an awe-producing wonder, but it is interesting from a geologic standpoint. Below the hard top layer of sandstone, there are softer layers that are eroding faster leaving an overhanging lip. If the water could find a crack further back and begin undermining the lip, the conditions would exist for creating a natural arch in the same manner as Rock Bridge.

Beyond the falls, there are lots of little trails going off to the left. Keep the little stream bed on your left and you will be on the right trail. Finally the official trail does cut left and crosses the wash, then T's into the Silvermine Arch Trail. A right turn will soon lead you to the trail head. Since there is a well used trail that does not cross the wash, it is easy to miss the left turn. But if you miss it, there is little difference for the straight ahead trail brings you to the tent campground parking lot.

BUCK TRAIL #226

From Koomer Ridge Trail Junction to Pinch-Em-Tight Trail

(For the General Description of this trail and the route to the trail head, see page 102. For the description of the trail in the opposite direction, see page 108).

TRAIL DESCRIPTION. Almost immediately after leaving Koomer Ridge Trail, Buck Trail starts down the left side of the ridge. After the first switchback, the grade is steep, but not dangerously so. After the second switchback, the trail levels off and it is an easy descent down to the right fork of Chimney Top Creek. After two more switchbacks, you come into a thick rhododendron patch. Another couple of switchbacks and you may hear the mountain stream gurgling below you just out of sight. Soon the creek comes into view and the trail descends down to its banks.

The trail follows the right bank of the creek for perhaps a quarter of a mile. There is one section where the trail is actually in the creek for about 40 feet when the water is up. It looks inviting to cross to the other bank here, but you plod down the creek bed until you see a flat limestone rock about a yard long that is well

View from the top of Sky Bridge

above the water level. Before you get to this rock you might get wet feet, but this section along Chimney Top Creek is one of the most beautiful natural settings in the entire forest. After jumping up on the flat rock, you can see the trail goes through a grove of small hemlocks where the bottom of the trail has been dug out to make a level passage in the side of a small rise. This is part of the old rail bed where better than 80 years ago, the Swan & Day Lumber Company had its narrow gauge steam railroad that hauled logs up to the top of the ridge, then down Whittleton Branch joining the main line at Campton Junction near Natural Bridge.

This whole section, once totally cut over, has returned to the wild and only an occasional cut of an old railroad bed reminds us that we are in a secondary forest. Not far beyond this little hemlock grove, the trail does cross the creek. This crossing is easily seen for the creek begins cutting into a steep bank on the right side and there is no room for a trail, however, there is a nice flat area on the other side. Once across the creek, the trail follows along the bank for about 40 feet. There is a fork in the trail. One follows the creek, the other cuts abruptly left and goes up a short but steep embankment. The left fork up the embankment is the correct way which quickly leaves the stream behind. This is the last place where you will be close to any sizeable amount of flowing water on Buck Trail.

Now the climb begins up to Pinch-Em-Tight Ridge. After a couple of switchbacks, you pass a low but dry rock shelter with evidences of old campfires. After two more switchbacks you can see the top of the ridge not far above you. Although you've still got a bit of distance to travel to Pinch-Em-Tight Trail, all the difficult climbing of Buck Trail is behind you. The trail now goes gently up and down as it traverses one of the fingers of Pinch-Em-Tight Ridge and it is rather easy walking to the trail junction. When you reach the junction with Pinch-Em-Tight Trail a left turn will take you to Tunnel Ridge Road. A right turn will take you to Rough Trail. The sign paralleling Buck Trail on the right reads: **BUCK TRAIL NO. 226 KOOMER RIDGE CAMPGROUND 3 ➔**. A sign facing you on the opposite side of Pinch-Em-Tight Trail reads:

TRAIL NO. 223
2.5 CHIMNEY TOP ROAD ⟶
⟵ TUNNEL RIDGE ROAD 1.5
2.5 GRAY'S ARCH ⟶

If you wish to take the loop hike back to Koomer Ridge you turn right here. If you wish to go to the Gray's Arch parking lot, you turn left.

BUCK TRAIL #226

From Pinch-Em-Tight Trail to Koomer Ridge Trail

Distance to Koomer Ridge Trail: 1.5 miles
Hike: STRENUOUS
Walking Time: 50 minutes to 1 hour 15 minutes
Distance to Koomer Ridge Campground: 2.7 miles
Hike: STRENUOUS Walking Time: 1 hour 40 minutes to 2 hours

A sign alongside the beginning of Buck Trail paralleling the trail on the left hand side reads: **KOOMER RIDGE CAMPGROUND⟶**

TRAIL DESCRIPTION. This trail goes down the valley cut by the right fork of Chimney Top Creek, then climbs up to Koomer Ridge on the other side. It's a fairly rugged and tiring trip and the distance back to the campground is a quarter mile longer than the sign says it is, but the view along Chimney Top Creek is among the best in the area and will make the walk worthwhile for many hikers. The trail begins by following the undulation of a ridge finger for about a third of a mile, then makes a gentle sweeping curve to the left as it starts down the side of the ridge. A little further down, there are two short switchbacks then the trail curves right over and around the beginning of a small hollow. The trail curves left as this little hollow hits the larger valley of the right fork of Chimney Top Creek. As you swing around this corner, the creek can often be heard although it is out of sight some distance below you. After a rather straight gentle downhill stretch, there are two rather long switchbacks. Not long after the second one, the trail curves to the right directly in front of a small rock shelter. There are evidences of campfires in the shelter and if you look to the right part of the shelter, you can see a tiny hole or lighthouse. Although a trail passes the entire length of the recess cave's opening, the official trail turns right and moves directly away from it in about half its length. The path then switches back and goes down to the bank of Chimney Top Creek. In this very lovely section of mountain stream, it appears as if the trail turns left and goes downstream, but it doesn't. Turn right and walk about 40 feet upstream and cross to the other bank. The water is usually several inches deep here so a dry crossing is not always possible. Proceed upstream on the trail through a beautiful grove of small hemlocks. You will notice there is a cut in the slope of the hill here making a level path for the trail. This is an old cut for the logging railroad that ran through here better than 70 years ago.

The trail now comes to a large flat limestone rock about three to four feet across. It lies next to and above the stream bed. It looks as if you should cross the stream here, but you don't. After jumping down to the level of the stream bed from the flat rock, stay on the same side of the stream and walk upstream over the rock strewn bottom parallel to the creek until it again rises above the creek bed. The stream is usually not so high as to cover this part of this rock section, but if the water is up, you may have about a 40 foot walk upstream wading through the water.

Shortly beyond the point where the trail rises above the streambed, the path sharply rises and leaves the stream behind for good. The trail then has two gentle upgrade switchbacks then climbs slowly with no serious turns for a rather long stretch. After encountering four more switchbacks, there is just a short pull uphill

Silvermine Arch

to the junction of the Koomer Ridge Trail. A sign facing you at the junction reads:

KOOMER RIDGE PICNIC AREA 1 MI
←——— CHIMNEY TOP ROAD 2 MI

Turn right here if you wish to go on to Koomer Ridge Campground. It may take you a little longer than you expect to get there, for the distance is 1/4 mile longer than the sign says it is. If you need a trail description back see page 106.

SILVERMINE ARCH TRAIL #225

Distance: 1 mile one way
Hike: MODERATE
Walking Time: 30 to 45 minutes one way

GENERAL REMARKS: From its name, many people believe there is an abandoned silver mine near this arch. The name is all tied up with the legend of John Swift's lost silver mine discussed in the history section of this book. If there are no shafts and heavy mining equipment to behold, many attempts to rediscover these legendary and probably non-existent mines have been made close to this arch, hence the name. But don't let the lack of old mining digs deter you from seeing this most unusual arch. Most of the walk is baby simple with only the last quarter mile becoming a bit testy. Although not large, this arch is most unusual in character. First of all, it was formed in a different way from the ridge top arches (see Waterfall Step Arches in the geology section). It also has a steep escarpment cutting close to one side of the arch which makes the underneath section somewhat dark. It reminded me of the grotto that Leonardo daVinci created in his famous painting, "The Virgin of the Rocks". It doesn't physically appear the same as Leonardo's grotto, but it can leave one with a similar emotional feeling especially if it happens to be a somewhat misty day. There is a small rock shelter on the other side of the arch that tends to enhance the grotto effect. It also has another oddity that

I have never seen in any other arch.

The arch extends out from the steep bank and curves in the normal way that most arches do. But when the curve starts down and should, by normal respectable arch standards, return to the ground, it doesn't. Erosion has eaten out the bottom of the wall for quite a few yards leaving a large cliff-like section of rock hanging from above before the sandstone wall returns to the earth. You might call it a suspended cliff, complete with arch.

TRAIL DESCRIPTION. The trail head is the same as the Koomer Ridge Trail. Since they run concurrently for about 1/4 mile (see page 104 for directions).

Shortly beyond the junction you will pass a sign which tells you the amphitheater is 1/2 mile away. It is not long before the trail takes you to the amphitheater. Walk along the left side of the amphitheater to its far corner. Turn left on the trail here.

Continue in the same general direction until the trail T's into another. There is a #225 trail sign indicating a left turn. Once on this segment the number of unofficial paths decline and the correct trail is easier to follow. There is one more fork before you reach the rimstone. Take either fork for they soon join up again.

It is not long after the reconverging of the forks that you come to the steep slope that goes down to the headwaters of Chimney Top Creek. You do not have to go down that far, but here is where the fun begins for those who are out of shape. There are two sets of sturdy wooden steps that one must go down to reach the arch. Several years ago, my wife and I went down this section before the steps were built. The slipping and sliding were something and the trip back up was even worse. Now, with this solid set of steps all such agonizing is a thing of the past and no alpine experience is necessary.

After walking to the bottom of the second stairway, the arch is almost in front of you. Take a good look at the arch and its suspended cliff, allowing yourself a good rest before the return journey. The only official way back to Koomer Ridge is up the side of the slope the way you came. The first quarter mile back up to the top of the ridge is a lung buster but think how much tougher it used to be before the steps were built. Once back on top, the going couldn't be easier.

HIDDEN ARCH LOOP TRAIL #208

Distance: to arch—.8 mile; complete loop—2 miles
Hike: to arch view—VERY EASY; complete loop—EASY to MODERATE
Walking Time: to arch view—20 to 30 minutes; complete loop—1 to 1½ hours.

GENERAL REMARKS: Being only about four feet high and six feet long, this arch hardly competes with the larger more spectacular arches. But its unique, tucked-away location in a small side spine of a ridge gives this arch its name and adds an interesting contrast to the better known Gorge arches. Since it is less than a mile from the tent area parking lot over fairly level ground, the trail to this arch was originally envisioned as a paved ambulatory trail. Those in wheelchairs could propel themselves to a location where an overlook view was possible. Although these plans were laid aside, a path was cleared to this overlook from where a person could climb down to the arch through a steep and narrow gap in the ridge. Later a wooden stairway was added, making access to the arch itself far easier. Finally another stairway was constructed below the arch and from there a trail was cut through to the Koomer Ridge Trail which added another pleasant short loop hike. For those rushed for time or whose physical limitation restrict them to easier trails, they will find that returning from the arch by the same trail they walked out on, this round trip walk of a little over a mile and a half is far easier than the complete loop trip and may be a reasonable short hike for them to consider.

TRAIL DESCRIPTION. The beginning of this trail is the same as the Koomer Ridge Trail. There soon is a V in the trail where you follow the smaller path to

Hidden Arch

the left which runs near the tent campground road. When you are in view of that campground's parking lot, there is a second fork in the trail where the Hidden Arch and Koomer Ridge Trails part company. There is a sign that tells you that the left fork is the Hidden Arch Trail and the distance to the arch is one mile. The trail then crosses the campground parking lot over to the drinking fountain. Follow the path to the pit toilets, but just before you get to them the trail turns left. A sign to the right of the trail says:

← HIDDEN ARCH 1
← TRAIL NO. 220–2
← LOOP 3

All of the mileage numbers on the sign are considerably longer than the actual distances. You will not go very far down the trail before you run into a fork. The branch of the fork that goes straight ahead soon links up with an old logging road, which is the wrong way. Take the fork to the left which sweeps around until the trail has formed a large "U". Not far beyond the "U" it turns right onto a little projection of a ridge from where the arch can be seen. From this point there is a stairway of 26 wooden steps that take you down to the arch.

Turning left, the trail immediately comes to a second wooden stairway descending 35 steps. The trail now hangs on the side of the ridge with a few easy up and down sections. Then there is a gradually moderately steep climb up to the ridge top. When you come to a well defined old logging road, a sign there indicates that you do not turn onto this road, but continue straight across it. About 100 feet beyond it this trail T's into the Koomer Ridge Trail where a sign facing you paralleling the opposite side of Koomer Ridge Trail reads:

KOOMER RIDGE
CAMPGROUND 1/2 →

The Mountain Central's "Dinkey" which once ran alongside Koomer Ridge

If you wish to complete these short loop hikes, turn right here. Directions from this point on the Koomer Ridge Trail are found on page 106.

CLIFF TRAIL

Distance: less than ½ mile
Hike: VERY EASY
Walking Time: a few minutes

GENERAL REMARKS & TRAIL DESCRIPTION. Cliff Trail follows close to the edge of a Chimney Top Creek side hollow. The easiest of the two shortest trails described in this book, Cliff Trail is more of a stroll than a hike. Skirting the top edge of a rather formidable cliff face, the walk meanders pleasantly with no real uphill or downhill sections. There is a split rail fence between the path and the precipice that is broken only by three stone overlooks. As long as you stay on the trail side of the fence, there is no danger of going over the edge. The pleasant, if not spectacular views are fairly restricted due to the natural timber in the hollow below. There are two places where one may begin the Cliff Trail walk. Alongside Koomer Ridge Campground site #35 and across the road at campsite #13 signs say:

CLIFF TRAIL NO. 206
CLIFF TRAIL

If you follow the trail keeping the cliff face to your left, you will eventually come to a place where the split rail fence crosses the trail indicating its end. If you follow the continuing trail beyond the fence, it soon leads to the head of the hollow. There are several little unofficial trails leading away from the cliff which all lead to various points along the campground road.

IX

TRAILS IN THE VICINITY OF ROCK BRIDGE RECREATION AREA

Rock Bridge Recreation Area is located at the end of Rock Bridge Road (see IV on large map). This three mile, one-lane gravel road with turnouts for passing is located just one half mile north of Pine Ridge, Kentucky on Kentucky Route #715. At the loop turnaround, this recreation area has parking space, picnic tables, toilet facilities and, during the summer months, drinking water. Overnight camping is prohibited in the picnic area, although primitive camping area #5 is located on the left side of Rock Bridge Road about two miles from Route 715. All of the trails in the vicinity of the Rock Bridge Recreation Area are shown on the detailed contour map found on page 114.

ROCK BRIDGE LOOP TRAIL #207

Distance: 1.4 miles
Hike: MODERATE
Walking Time: 1 to 1½ hours

GENERAL REMARKS: Rock Bridge is one of the scenic geologic highlights of the area, and if at all possible, affords a hike that should be included in everybody's agenda. If you are physically able to walk about a mile and a half with some moderate climbing on well defined and maintained steps and trails, the loop hike is within your limits. I've seen people in their 70's and anemic three year olds do the loop without undue difficulty. The trail descends approximately 250 feet in altitude down to Rock Bridge and then climbs back up the ridge.

Rock Bridge is the only natural span in the area and one of the few in the world that does cross over a stream, and a good sized stream at that. Set in a deep forest, its natural setting is uniquely beautiful and strikingly different from any other arch in the area.

Many tales abound about its past. Its geologic formation, which involved an ancient waterfall, is quite different from the more common ridge top arches (see geology section). Swift Creek, whose waters flow under the arch, was used during the lumbering days to float thousands of logs down to the Red River. Up until 1984 there were remains of one of the old log splash dams used in the logging operation alongside trail #219 less than a quarter mile from the loop trail that could easily be seen.

Rock Bridge was dynamited once, but fortunately, the blast failed to destroy the span. For years it was believed that the attempted destruction was done by lumbermen because it hindered and sometimes blocked the flow of logs during high water periods. It is now generally believed that the lumbermen did not do the dynamiting, for they possessed more than enough skill in explosive techniques to blow the bridge to Kingdom Come. Furthermore, even in very high water, there is still sufficient space to permit a steady flow of logs under the span without their getting hung up on the bridge. No one is sure who made the attempt, but the bridge has served as a natural crossing point for centuries.

Indian petroglyphs, unfortunately now obliterated, were once visible on the arch, indicating that aboriginal Indians used the bridge thousands of years ago to cross Swift Camp Creek. Early white settlers also used Rock Bridge. There are legends about feuds between the early settlers over boundary rights during

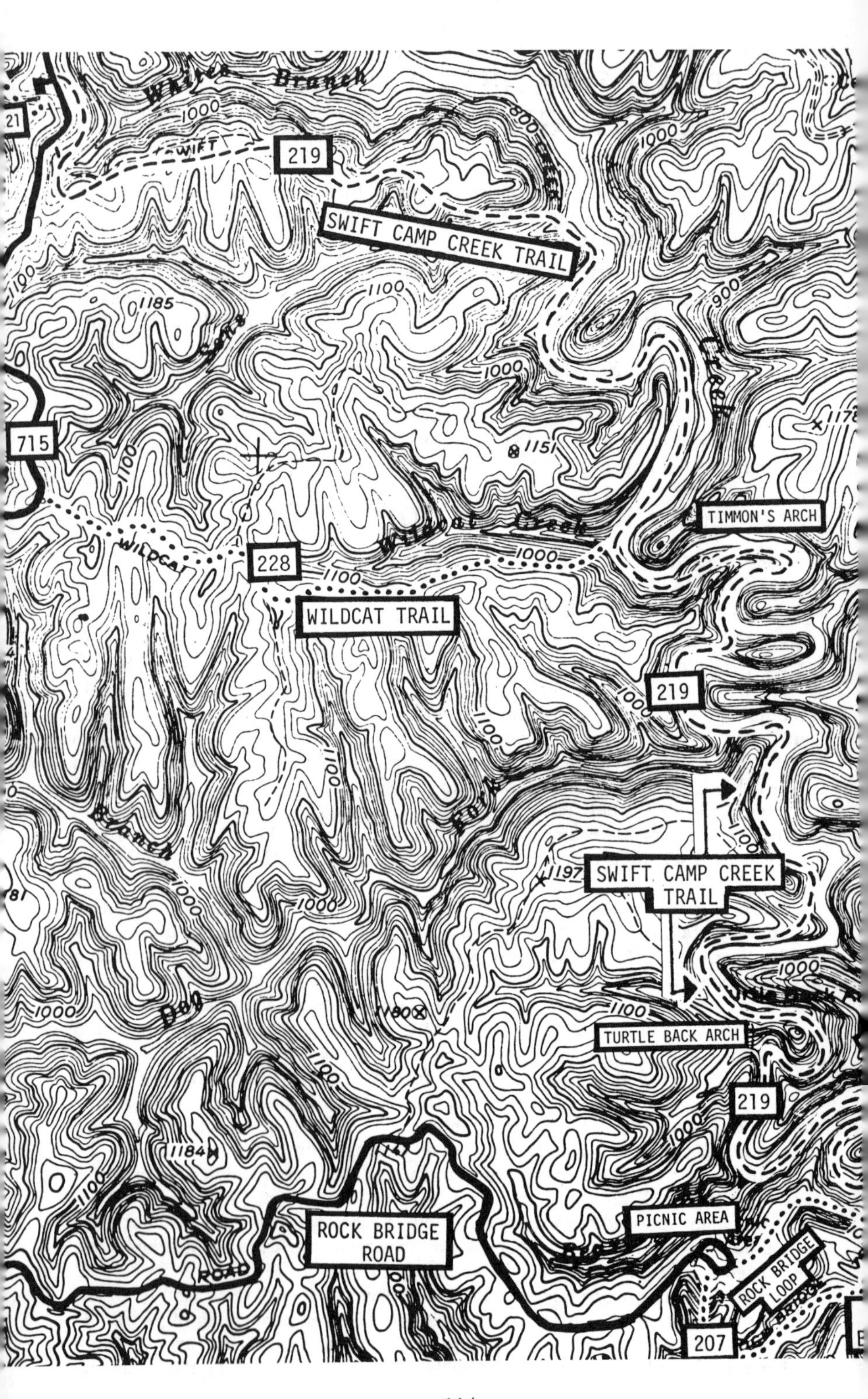
219
SWIFT CAMP CREEK TRAIL
715
TIMMON'S ARCH
228
WILDCAT TRAIL
219
SWIFT CAMP CREEK
TRAIL
TURTLE BACK ARCH
219
PICNIC AREA
ROCK BRIDGE
ROAD
ROCK BRIDGE
LOOP
207

the time that lumbering firms began buying up timber rights. Possibly a disappointed claimant attempted to blow up the bridge as revenge.

There once was a small settlement near Rock Bridge in the nineteenth century. It contained a grist mill, complete with dam and a small cording factory, whose builder was probably one James Drake. The mill and the village that grew up around it, however, were wiped out in a catastrophic stroke called the June Tide. There was a huge log jam upstream which began backing up the waters of the stream. An unusually heavy cloudburst during the month of June rapidly flooded the creek far above its banks. Suddenly, the tremendous water pressure broke the log dam, bringing a holocaust of logs and water that swept all before it. All standing structures of the village were destroyed. The village was never rebuilt and there is no trace of it to be found today.

Swift Camp Creek itself was named after the famous legend of the lost silver mines (see history section). Because of similarities in the terrain, many felt the stream flowing under Rock Bridge to be the same creek the John Swift journals described as running alongside his base camp.

The Rock Bridge Loop Trail had been set up by the U.S. Forest Service as a self guiding nature trail. Many trees along this walk are identified by the attached metal tags.

TRAIL DESCRIPTION. As you enter the one-way loop at the end of Rock Bridge Road, you will come to a parking area to the left of the road. There is a forest service bulletin board there as well as a drinking fountain. Two pit toilets are located directly across the road from the parking area. The Rock Bridge Trail begins just to the left of the toilets on the opposite side of the road from the parking area. A sign alongside the edge of the asphalt trail head and paralleling it to the left says:

ROCK BRIDGE NATURE TRAIL NO. 207
ROCK BRIDGE 1/2 ⟶
SWIFT CREEK TRAIL 3/4 ⟶
NATURE TRAIL LOOP 1 ⟶

The paved surface of the trail lasts only to the first set of steps that start the descent. It is only about 300 feet before you come to an overlook with a protective wall.

From this point the trail starts its descent down to Swift Creek with 25 steps cut in the surface of the sandstone. Soon there is another set of 47 steps with wooden guardrails and a third later on with 11 steps. There, the trail switches back then crosses two small wooden bridges. Just beyond the second bridge, the trail looks like it goes in two directions. The one to the right dead ends in about 50 feet at a moderate sized rock shelter. If you are new to the area and not in a hurry, take a look at it, although there are far more spectacular ones in other nearby parts of the forest.

When you take the left turn you will notice a small trickle of a stream developing which finally gets large enough to be called Rock Bridge Branch. The foliage in this part of the trail is green even in the winter months because it has so many pines and rhododendron bushes. A small wooden bridge takes you across the branch which is often dry at this point. For the rest of the distance to Rock Bridge, the developing stream stays on your right. Shortly after this, you come to another wooden bridge about 25 feet long that parallels the branch and helps you across a soggy spot of ground. Not far beyond this, you can see that Rock Bridge Branch has grown from its original trickle to a respectable creek. The trail then climbs above the stream and comes alongside what was once an easily seen open meadow. This location, which is being rapidly reclaimed by the forest, is the site of the last settler's dwelling in this area. A man named Sam Duff and his family lived and farmed here until 1906. Since the nearest school was then three miles away, his children had a six mile walk every day. Sometime around 1906 Sam built a home up on the ridge because he wanted the convenience of having a house on the road.

Although he did some farming, his major work was with the Broadhead & Garret Lum-

Views from each side of Rock Bridge

ber Company. Sam's job was to maintain a series of wooden dams along Swift Creek. Known as splash dams, they helped control the water level of the creek and held back logs until conditions were right for floating them out. In 1910 Mr. Duff let the last logs pass the splash dam and maintenance of them was discontinued. The remains of one of the old splash dams was still visible along Swift Creek Trail, just a quarter mile from the loop walk, until 1984.

From this old homesite, you can hear a little waterfall in Rock Bridge Branch below. The trail then descends easily to the falls. One geologic explanation for the formation of Rock Bridge is that it was created by a waterfall, so this small one has beome known as Creation Falls (see geology section). When you reach the falls, look across its upper side near the opposite bank of the creek and you can see a miniature Rock Bridge.

After passing the falls, the trail runs above a beautiful pool of water. Since the drop-off from the edge of the trail to the pool is abrupt and sheer, the forest service has built a long guardrail along the right side of the trail to keep you from getting an unwanted dunking. If you wish to get a striking view of this charming area, when you reach the end of this guardrail, turn right and go down nine sandstone steps. Walk a few feet further and you arrive at a rock overlook that gives you the best view of the falls and the pool below.

When you return to the trail, you will soon come to eight more sandstone steps. Look straight ahead and through the trees you have your first view of Rock Bridge. As you approach a little wooden footbridge on the trail, Rock Bridge becomes more clearly visible on the right. Follow the trail across the wooden bridge and through a six foot gap in a natural sandstone ridge. When this ridge reaches Swift Camp Creek, it forms Rock Bridge. This gap affords views on each side of this large natural arch. The gap is also the easiest place from which to walk out on the span if you desire to do so. Climbing to the top of the bridge isn't difficult if you are used to climbing a small rock wall, but it isn't for everybody. If you don't feel like climbing that wall, don't give it a second thought for your best view of the arch is yet to come. When you pass through the gap, look directly ahead of you. There is a large open area alongside the creek, complete with a bench. From there you get the best view of Rock Bridge.

When you are ready to press on, return to the gap but don't go through it. Keep that ridge of sandstone on your left and follow the trail that parallels it. Move away from the bridge for about 75 feet. The official trail then cuts sharp right, away from the sandstone outcropping. A false trail continues on paralleling the sandstone and many people have mistakenly taken it. The forest service has placed a sign there which says: ← **PARKING AREA** → to help you make the turn, but I have seen signs torn down by vandals at this locatiion more than once. About 100 feet after making the right turn, look back to your right and you will be able to see Rock Bridge through the trees. In another 1/10 mile, the loop trail junctions with Swift Camp Creek Trail. The sign to the right of the trail reads:

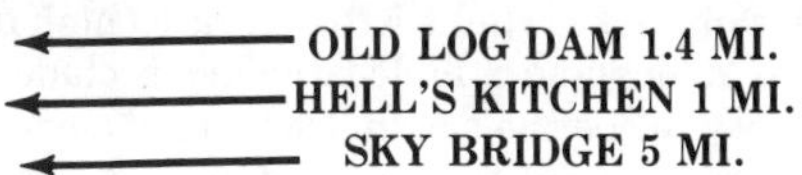

← OLD LOG DAM 1.4 MI.
← HELL'S KITCHEN 1 MI.
← SKY BRIDGE 5 MI.

If you don't want to hike all of that very tough trail, you might consider doing part of it. Another mile takes you to the still on Bear Pen Branch. If you feel up to it, the walk makes a nice appendage to the Rock Bridge trip. (see description of the Swift Camp Creek Trail below). If, however, you feel that you have done all the walking you care to do and wish only to complete the loop hike, turn left at this intersection and start up the ridge. There is a sign there that says:

← PICNIC AREA

This is where your climb back to the ridge top really begins. It is only a half mile to the parking lot with the last quarter of a mile being fairly level. This means that most of your climb is in the first quarter mile. There are several small trails that parallel each other up the ridge. Since they all join up again, it is relatively unimportant which one you follow. You will also encounter a few small groups of well worn steps cut into the sandstone on your way up. When you come to another man-made overlook with a sandstone wall, you are almost at the top of the ridge. Once on top, you come to a nice open area that follows a hogback

Splash dam log which remained anchored to the bottom of Swift Creek near Rock Bridge until 1984

ridge. This open space was made by the forest service as a helicopter landing site for fighting forest fires and other emergencies. After passing back into the forest you hit the loop road with a drinking fountain on the left. Cross the road and walk through the picnic area to arrive back at the parking lot.

SWIFT CAMP CREEK TRAIL #219

GENERAL REMARKS. If you are beginning this trail from the Rock Bridge loop, there are numerous things of interest to be seen in about a mile of walking. If you begin the trail at its north end at Parched Corn Overlook, you will have over five miles of walking to get to the same area. Hell's Kitchen rates high both scenically and historically. The Bear Pen Moonshine Still, located in a secluded rock shelter, gives you the unique opportunity to see the original setting of a once active mountain still with equipment used to turn out the corn squeezin's. Turtle Back Arch is a marvelous text book example of how two rock shelters on opposite sides of a narrow ridge join together to form an arch.

Although the walk from Rock Bridge to Turtle Back Arch is moderate, the section of Trail #219 between Turtle Back Arch and Wildcat Trail is the most physically demanding trail in the Red River Gorge area. I always think of that stretch as the mountain goat section, not because it is particularly high, but it goes up and down so many times that only a mountain goat would feel comfortable on it. Those up and down sections are usually not very long, often going down across a tiny stream at the foot of a small rock shelter, then immediately back up again. Sometimes the slopes are quite steep and the bottoms are often a quagmire of black ooze. No fun unless you have a good pair of hiking boots and a strong back. There is also one sloping sandstone wall on the off trail walk to Turtle Back Arch which some hikers might find too difficult or risky.

Be careful about hiking time on this trail, especially if you are carrying any kind of pack. Any experienced hiker should have no serious difficulty beyond a slower hiking pace, and I have seen ten and eleven year olds leaping up and down the difficult stretches like gazelles. I have also seen inexperienced backpackers on the point of serious exhaustion before they reached the halfway point of this trail.

Swift Camp Creek Trail is often referred to as the trail of the three arches since there are three good sized arches in this valley. The name, however, is somewhat misleading for only Rock Bridge can be seen from the trail. The little unofficial trail to Turtle Back Arch is not long and I have included a description of how to find the arch. The third one, known as Timmons Arch, is a different matter. It is on the other side of the creek and is almost never visible from the trail. There is also no easy path to follow to it. It is a tough climb and hard to find. The arch bears the name of its discoverer who was looking for John Swift's lost silver mine. This is an appropriate combination because Timmon's Arch, for most of us, remains about as hard to find as the legendary mine.

SWIFT CAMP CREEK TRAIL #219

North from Rock Bridge Loop Trail to Parched Corn Overlook

(For trail in opposite direction see page 123)

Distance to Hell's Kitchen: 1/2 mile
Hike: EASY
Walking Time: 20 to 30 minutes one way

Distance to Moonshine Still: 1.1 miles
Hike: MODERATE
Walking Time: 40 to 50 minutes one way

Distance to Wildcat Trail: 3.8 miles
Hike: STRENUOUS
Walking Time: 3 to 4 hours one way

Distance to Parched Corn Overlook: 6.7 miles
Hike: VERY STRENUOUS
Walking Time: 4 to 5 hours one way

TRAIL DESCRIPTION. To get to this trail head, follow the Rock Bridge Loop Trail until you reach the sign at the beginning of the trail that reads:

←—— OLD LOG DAM ¼ MI.
←—— HELL'S KITCHEN 1 MI.
←—— SKY BRIDGE 5 MI.

This mileage sign is a bit misleading, but not intentionally so. The splash dam is much less than a quarter of a mile, but it fits the old forest service policy of marking trail lengths to the nearest quarter mile. The distance to Hell's Kitchen shows the usual misinterpretation of thinking Bear Pen Branch Narrows is the original Hell's Kitchen. Sky Bridge is actually about 9 miles from here, but the 5 miles indicated on the sign represents the distance from the trail head to Sky Bridge Road using Wildcat Trail. There is another little sign on the right side of the trail that says, **"AVERAGE WALKING TIME TO SKY BRIDGE ROAD 4 HOURS."** If you are walking to the junction of Rough Trail at the parking lot on Route #715 or the Parched Corn Overlook, take the sign seriously for much of the trail is slow going.

From the Rock Bridge Loop Trail, Swift Camp Creek Trail has a deceptively easy start and it is not more than an effortless stroll to the former site of the old splash dam which used to be just a few feet to the right. A hand-hewn log once was anchored to the bottom of Swift Creek across the entire width of the stream bed. This log formed the lower part of the original logging splash dam. The first builders must have anchored it well, for it was last used in 1910 and the section remaining defied many a violent flooding of Swift Creek. When the water was moderately high, this remaining log of the old splash dam created a little waterfall. But in 1984 stump branches from a huge snag of fallen trees, pushed by relentless flood waters, finally gouged the log from the bottom and it was finally swept away.

Swift Creek's "Hell's Kitchen"

If the water in Swift Camp Creek is very low, the weather is warm and you don't mind getting your feet wet you might consider an off trail side trip by walking a few hundred yards down the stream bed from this point. This will take you to the bottom of the area known as Hell's Kitchen. Here the creek runs for quite a distance through a sandstone gorge with solid rock faces on each side of the creek. The space between these solid sandstone walls is usually no wider than the creek. There is one stretch of the creek where this narrow gorge runs for over a 100 feet with no breaks in the 30 to 40 foot high walls.

The timbermen often had a tough time keeping the logs moving through this narrow section of river and log jams were frequent. They often had to spend hours working in wet clothes but usually kept a pot of hot coffee going to keep them from getting chilled—hence the name Hell's Kitchen or the Devil's Kitchen.

If there is a moderate to high level of water in the creek, do not attempt this walk for this little canyon becomes a death trap when the flow is strong. You will be able to see part of this area from above a little later on the official trail.

There is a sign at the location of the old dam, but since the hewn log is gone, it is anybody's guess how long a sign will remain. In case it is missing, look for the first small footbridge that takes you over a little trickle of a steam. At that point, walk down the short distance to Swift Camp Creek and you will be in the vicinity of the old dam. Although the trail follows Swift Creek for approximately five miles with the stream often in sight or sound, this is the last place for the next five miles where the trail is in sight of the creek, at about the same level, and a walk between them is easy.

After following the official trail about a half mile beyond the old dam site you can see that the creek is below you in a sheer drop-off of about 40 feet. You now have a restricted view of Hell's Kitchen from above. If you have young children along, watch them on this stretch of trail for there is little on the right side of the path except the drop to the creek.

Beyond Hell's Kitchen, the trail loses sight of the creek, descends and crosses a large wooden foot bridge quite close to the water of a small branch below it. Beyond the bridge, the trail and the small stream cut through a small gorge of sandstone. For about 100 feet, there are sandstone walls on both sides of the trail and you share the sandstone bottom with the stream. Many visitors think this rock enclosed section of the trail is Hell's Kitchen, as I did the first time I walked this trail. But Hell's Kitchen is on Swift Camp Creek, and this stream is Bear Pen Branch. I call this section Bear Pen Narrows. The excellent water in this little stream was used by previous unknown mountain men in the manufacture of a corn by-product, known as White Lightning. You can't see the location of the still from the creek, but it's not far away.

Immediately after the trail passes through the narrows, it leaves the creek bed and switches back to the right, climbing above the creek quite rapidly. Shortly thereafter, the trail passes between two sandstone boulders. Just before you get to the boulders, there is a little trail that goes off to the left. The sign to the right of the trail facing you reads:

BEAR BRANCH STILL 1/4

If the sign is down, you can still locate this little side trail by the two large rocks close to each side of the trail. This short trail goes up and around the left side of the largest boulder and in less than 500 feet it ends at a small rock shelter with a chain link fence across the opening. In this rockhouse a moonshiner once had his still. Although the original still has long since disappeared, there are six wooden barrels buried in the ground that are part of the original operation. The forest service obtained another genuine mountain copper still that was confiscated by revenue agents in another part of the state. It is set up in the rock shelter just the way it was originally used. But to keep anyone from making a midnight requisition for the further manufacture of corn squeezin's, the copper still has been filled with cement. A forest service sign erected alongside of the still gives an excellent description of how the still operated. It is easy to see how such a secluded rock shelter made an ideal location for making clear firey liquid. The close proximity to Bear Pen Branch meant that a good and steady supply of water was nearby. The overhang of the rock shelter allowed no clue from the air, for no buildings could be seen and the shelter is far enough down the ridge that tell-tale smoke would be largely dissipated before it reached ridge top levels.

When you return to the main trail and wish to continue on, turn left and pass between the two boulders. The trail begins ascending, then passes over a small stream whose bed at the crossing point is a floor of dark solid rock. If you want to find Turtle Back Arch, the little side trail is about 120 feet beyond this small branch. This unofficial trail branches off to the left of the main trail. Although narrow, it is easy to find and to follow. The path to Turtle Back Arch soon leads you up to the top of a small ridge. You will turn left on the ridge top, but before proceeding, look back at the section of trail you have just covered and memorize this turn, for this one is an easy place to miss on your way back. As you go up the ridge, you will come to a small stone ledge about four feet high. This first one is easy to climb, but the second ledge immediately beyond is a steep rock slope about 20 feet high which you must negotiate to arrive at the arch. If you are a little unsteady on your feet or are wearing slippery, smooth-soled shoes, it might be better to miss this climb, but any good hiker wearing sneakers or vibram-type soled shoes should have little difficulty. Once you have topped this ledge, you come to another easy one about four feet high. About 25 feet beyond this ledge you encounter another stone outcropping about ten feet high.

Work your way around the left side of it and keep the ledge on your right. Walk parallel to the ledge and in about 30 feet more, you'll be under Turtle Back Arch. There are actually two arches here, but the larger one has an upper span with the silhouette in the shape of a giant turtle. The main opening is 12 feet long and four feet high. Since the openings on the ridge walls on either side are much higher and wider than the center of the arch, this is an excellent example of how two rock shelters on each side of a ridge finally join together forming first a lighthouse, then an arch.

Back on the main trail, you will shortly go up a steep ascent following along a sandsone wall on your left. Then the trail rapidly descends again and skirts a rock promontory on the right side of the trail. This rock hangs out from the ridge. From its edge you can see Swift Camp Creek quite a bit below threading its way through some very large boulders. This is one of the prettiest views along this trail, but use caution when going out on the rock. There is no guardrail and the dropoff is sheer.

You are now commencing the toughest part of this trail which takes you up and down over a series of branches and ravines. It is pretty slow going especially if you are carrying a pack, but you do get some excellent views of Swift Creek below you. When the trail runs along the edge of the first rock shelter of any appreciable size, you will notice that the sandstone floor gives way to layers of shale. About the middle of the shelter, the trail turns away from the shelter, dropping down towards a good sized stream. A combination of water dripping on the shale from the underside of the shelter and the foot action of many hikers has turned the trail into a muck similar to the ooze of the Great Dismal swamp, about as gooey as chicken fat. But after you fight your way through this gray-black bog, you are on the very pretty banks of Dog Fork. Since Dog Fork is the largest tributary of Swift Creek, it is big enough to make many hikers think it is Swift Creek. Indeed, Swift Creek is less than 50 yards from here, and if you don't mind wading through the water of Dog Fork, a short walk downstream will take you to the confluence of the two.

There are many little trails going in several directions along the banks of this creek, but for the correct one, go directly to the creek, immediately cross it, go up a short steep bank directly on the other side and follow the trail that moves directly away from the creek. There is a #219 trail sign on the top of this little rise making it a little easier to find.

The first time I walked this trail, the sign at Dog Fork was missing. I hit this crossing of Dog Fork about the same time that a backpacking couple and a troop of 27 Boy Scouts and leaders arrived. With all of us searching, it took almost a half hour until the right trail was discovered. Before you leave this area, if the weather is pleasant and you want a nice spot for lunch or a rest, walk just a few yards upstream where there are several lovely flat areas just made for lunch stops or afternoon cat naps.

Once across Dog Fork, the trail passes between two large boulders and begins the toughest up and down section of all. Many of these short ascent-descent sections are very steep, mucky at the bottom with greasy-like slippery slopes; especially if the weather has been wet. You finally come to an obvious trail junction with a trail coming downhill joining Swift Creek Trail from the left. That is Wildcat Trail and the sign alongside it facing you reads:

← SKY BRIDGE ROAD 1.3 MI.

For Wildcat Trail description see page 128)

The trail that starts descending to the right of Wildcat Trail is the continuation of Swift Creek Trail, and the sign to the right of the trail reads:

← SKY BRIDGE ROAD 2.9 MI.
3.8 MI. ROCK BRIDGE →

The trail immediately begins descending down to Wildcat Branch. Although the rest of the trail is not quite as demanding as the last stretch from Dog Fork, it still has plenty of up and down sections to further exhaust the unconditioned. There is usually a good supply of water in Wildcat Branch. After crossing the stream, the trail turns right and follows the left bank of the stream until it drops rapidly below you and joins Swift Creek out of sight of the trail.

For about a mile and a half, the trail hangs well above Swift Creek, which you can occasionally see below you on the right. Then the trail starts downward until it reaches the banks of Swift Creek. The trail follows alongside the creek until it comes to a small rock shelter on the left side of the trail. At the far end of this shelter, you will see 20 stone steps that move up and away from the trail and the stream. This is where the trail leaves the sight of Swift Camp Creek for good. There is a #219 trail sign painted on the rock with a white arrow pointing to the steps. It is still easy to miss this turnoff since a well-defined trail continues alongside the creek and the 20 steps aren't too obvious if you are not looking for them. If you cross a little stream just before it enters Swift Creek, you have missed the turnoff. Turn back and in just a few feet of retracing your steps, you'll see the stone steps on the right side of the trail.

After you walk up those well worn sandstone steps, the trail rapidly drops down to a little stream. Here the trail and the stream pass between two huge slump blocks which enclose the trail in a quasi-grotto.

After you have crossed the stream, you begin your climb up to the ridge top. It is about 1.4 miles to Sky Bridge Road and most of the climbing takes place in the first quarter mile which gains over 300 in altitude. The grade is steep, but not treacherously so—just enough to make you huff and puff a little. After this last uphill section is behind you, there is only one mile of easy walking to the trail head parking lot.

You will come to a point where the trail forks. A sign between the two trails facing you reads: **TRAIL #219 ⟶**. If you take the right fork in the direction of the arrow the trail will soon parallel Route 715, then crosses it over to the parking lot and the trail head for Rough Trail. The left fork will also take you to Sky Bridge Road, but at the Parched Corn Overlook and the beginning of the short Angel Windows Trail.

SWIFT CAMP CREEK TRAIL #219

South, from the Rough Trail, Swift Creek Trail Parking lot to the Rock Bridge Recreation Area.

Distance to Rock Bridge Recreation Area (via Rock Bridge): 7.6 miles
Hike: VERY STRENUOUS
Walking Time: 4 to 5 hours one way
(For General Remarks, see page 118)

TRAIL DESCRIPTION: When driving into the parking lot, which is just 2/10 mile south of the Parched Corn Overlook on Sky Bridge Road, the trail head for both Swift Creek and Rough Trails is in the far left corner. Signs at the trail heads read:

⟵ SWIFT CREEK 1 1/2
CHIMNEY TOP RD. 2 ⟶
KOOMER RIDGE
CAMPGROUND 5 ⟶

There is also a branch of this trail that begins at the Parched Corn Overlook but if you are hiking for any extended length of time it is better to park your car in the parking lot south of the overlook because it is off the highway and has more room. The trail turns left from the parking lot, crosses Highway 715, turns right paralleling the road briefly, then goes deeper into the forest.

If you have read the general remarks, you are aware you have quite a walk ahead of you both from the standpoint of stamina and scenery. The only really easy part of this trail is the first mile which undulates along the top of the forest covered ridge. Then for a third of a mile, the trail descends steeply toward Swift Camp Creek, losing over 300 feet in altitude. Almost at the bottom of this descent, there is one extra steep stretch which is very straight and about 40 feet long. At the bottom of this short section, the trail looks like it proceeds straight ahead, but it actually cuts abruptly right and heads down towards a small stream. A #219 trail sign is painted on a tree with a white arrow indicating the right turn. If you miss this cut off, it is no real problem for you will soon junction with Swift Camp Creek. Turn right at the creek and shortly you will pass over a small stream just before it enters Swift Creek. Just beyond this point you are on the official trail again simply by continuing on the path that parallels the creek.

If you managed to find the right turn on the official trail before reaching Swift Camp Creek, you will descend to a small stream. Here the trail and the branch share a common floor between two good sized boulders that enclose the trail in a kind of grotto. After crossing the stream, the trail turns abruptly right for a short distance, then left around a large boulder.

You will then encounter about 20 steps carved into the sandstone which take you down to the banks of Swift Camp Creek. The trail looks like it might go along the banks in both directions here, but the official trail turns right and heads upstream. For a short distance the trail follows along the banks of Swift Camp Creek before climbing up and away from it. Although this trail follows the same side of Swift Camp Creek for the entire length of the path, this is the only section of Swift Camp Creek Trail which runs close to the bank of the creek until you reach the former location of the old log splash dam some six miles away.

The trail climbs about half way up the ridge, then hangs on the side of it for a good distance. Eventually the trail makes a decided right turn when it temporarily leaves the main valley and turns up the tributary ravine cut by Wildcat Branch. You will soon be able to see that stream below you on your left. After a short walk, you cross Wildcat Branch and begin a short, stiff climb up to Wildcat Junction. Wildcat Trail exits on the right and immediately begins going uphill. The sign for Wildcat Trail which parallels that trail on the right reads:

← SKY BRIDGE ROAD 1.3 MI.

If this much of Swift Camp Creek Trail has exhausted you, it might be wise to consider taking Wildcat Trail back to Sky Bridge Road, as the next three miles of Swift Camp Creek Trail are the most physically demanding in the area. If you are still game and off to Rock Bridge, the sign to the left of the trail paralleling it reads:

TRAIL NO. 219
← SKY BRIDGE ROAD 2.9 MI.
3.8 MI. ROCK BRIDGE →

Remember that the distance to Rock Bridge is correctly marked at 3.8 miles, but it is about 5 miles to the Rock Bridge parking lot. Timmon's Arch is somewhere across Swift Camp Creek in the ridge on the other side and is not visible from here. Since I've never seen it, trying to tell you how to find it would be a good example of the blind leading the blind.

From here the trail gets a bit rough. It goes repeatedly down short steep slopes crossing gooey bottoms, then climbs steeply up again. You have a slow mile of such fun before reaching Dog Fork. When the trail takes you to the foot of a large boulder, you are almost at Dog Fork. At the end of the boulder, the trail cuts right and takes you down to Dog Fork, the largest tributary of Swift Camp Creek and the largest stream you will cross on this trail. Many hikers mistakenly believe it is Swift Camp Creek which isn't very far away, but this trail never crosses that stream. If you wish to see Swift Camp Creek and don't mind getting your feet wet, walk downstream along (and in) Dog Fork and in less than 50 yards you will arrive at the junction point of these two streams.

The area around Dog Fork is a marvelously scenic spot. If you have time, it is fun to explore the creek banks as many people have done, leaving a confusion of little trails on the stream's banks. As you look across the creek before crossing, it seems that the trail turns right on the other bank and follows the creek upstream. This path does lead to some lovely places to rest, have lunch or possibly spend the night, but it isn't the official trail. To find the correct continuation of the trail, before you cross Dog Fork, look directly across the stream and you will see a slope of gray goo under a rock shelter. It is an exposed section of shale that has been turned into muck by water dripping from the ceiling of the rock shelter and stirred into a quagmire by the waffle stompers of many hikers. The trail goes up through this muck until you are well into the shelter. It then turns left and gradually the shale gives way to sandstone and you have firm footing again.

The next stretch of the trail has some more of those short up and down sections, but the most difficult ones are behind you. Occasionally this section offers attractive glimpses of Swift Camp Creek through the trees on the left and a good distance below you. The best of these is a rock promontory on the left side of the trail that overhangs Swift Camp Creek. You shouldn't have any trouble finding it, since Swift Camp Creek threads its way through a narrow gorge made by a series of gigantic boulders. The waters make an appropriately audible roar as they tumble and fight through this narrow section. The drop-off of this overlook is sudden and severe. Just beyond this viewpoint the trail cuts away from the creek. To the right of the trail, there is a large sandstone outcropping that rises above it about 50 feet. Because of peculiar erosion patterns, it resembles a giant brown candy jar. The trail goes up and along the base of this rock formation before going down again. This is quite close to the turnoff for Turtle Back Arch.

If you would like to follow the short unofficial trail to this arch,go to where the trail crosses a little stream whose bottom at the crossing point is solid gray-black rock. Turn around and retrace your steps for about 120 feet where the turnoff begins. Then follow the directions to the arch given on page 121.

When back on Trail #219 after crossing over the little branch with the stone bottom, you will soon pass between two boulders right up against each side of the path. Just beyond the boulders, there is a little trail to the right. It is the very short trail that takes you to the original site of a mooshiner's still. The sign there reads:

← **BEAR BRANCH STILL 1/4**

For a description of the still area, see page 121. After returning to the main trail, you descend down to Bear Pen Branch. The stream has cut a waterway through solid sandstone for about 100 feet, leaving a small stone gorge about 15 feet wide. The trail and the creek share the rock bottom of this sandstone cut. Many think this is Hell's Kitchen, which is actually a half mile further up the trail from here. I call this the Bear Pen Branch Narrows to avoid the confusion. Immediately after passing through the narrows, the trail crosses over a substantial wooden bridge and moves away from the branch. It will not be long before you will see Swift Camp Creek on your left below you in a sheer drop of about 40 feet. Here Swift Camp Creek flows through an area where the sandstone walls come almost vertically down to the edge of both sides of the stream. It is similar to the kind of cut you just walked through at Bear Pen Branch, but on a far larger scale. This is known as Hell's Kitchen.

About a half mile beyond this point, you will approach the former location of the old splash dam. A sign along the trail indicates the place where you can walk the short distance to the creek bank to the old dam site. If the sign is down, find a place along the trail where the space between the creek and the trail is rather open and only a few yards separate the two. Walk toward the creek and look downstream. When the water is low the off trail walk through Hell's Kitchen begins here. For details see page 120. From this point it is only 800 feet to the Rock Bridge Loop Trail. At this junction, there is a sign on the left side of the trail that tells the distance to the area from whence you have just come. If you have previously seen Rock Bridge and want the quickest way to the Rock Bridge parking lot, take the trail to the right that goes up the hill. There is a sign alongside this trail that reads:

PICNIC AREA

If you want to see Rock Bridge, do not turn right at this junction, but continue straight ahead. In less than an easy three minute walk you will be able to see Rock Bridge through the tress on your left if you are hiking during the months when the leaves are off the trees. The trail soon comes to a small stone ridge where it cuts left and follows alongside this ridge heading towards Swift Camp Creek. This ridge forms Rock Bridge when it gets to the creek. To the left of the ridge alongside the creek bank, there is a nice flat area, complete with a bench which is excellent for viewing the span of the bridge. When you wish to view the bridge from the other side of the arch and to continue on the Rock Bridge Loop Trail, look for a very conspicuous gap in the ridge quite close to the bridge. Pass through the gap, then go down some stone steps and cross a little foot bridge. In this vicinity you get a good view of the upstream side of this natural arch.

If you wish to continue on the Rock Bridge Loop Trail, do not return to the other side of the bridge, but walk away from it keeping Swift Camp Creek on your left. In just a few feet you will see eight well worn sandstone steps. When you are on top of them, look left and you can see where Rock Bridge Branch runs into Swift Camp Creek. Here the trail leaves Swift Camp Creek for good and begins to follow the branch. A little over 60 feet beyond the steps, you will see a wooden guardrail on the left side of the trail, and almost in front of the guardrail there is a set of stone steps that go down from the left side of the trail. In a few feet, this takes you to an overlook with a very pretty view of a waterfall with a pool beneath it. Since one geologic explanation has Rock Bridge created by a waterfal, this one has become known as Creation Falls.

When you get back to the trail, you will find that the wooden guardrail runs about 90 feet to keep you from falling into the pool you have just been viewing. As the trail takes you by the waterfall, if the water isn't too high you might see a mini rock bridge on the top far side of the waterfall.

From here, the trail begins to climb and soon passes a meadow on the right side of the trail which is rapidly being reclaimed by the forest. This was the homesite of the last settler in the area, employed to keep the splash dams in repair.

As the trail keeps climbing, Rock Bridge Branch gets smaller and smaller. You come to a low wooden bridge about 25 feet long that parallels the stream, and not too far beyond it, you cross a second small bridge that takes you over that small trickle of a stream. Because of a heavy concentration of evergreens and rhododendron, this part of the trail has much greenery the year around. When you come to a fork in the trail, the left fork soon dead ends in a fair-sized rock shelter. The right fork is the continuation of the Rock Bridge Loop Trail. It then crosses two very small wooden bridges and begins the climb up the ridge in earnest. There are three goups of steps cut into the sandstone. The second one is the longest with 47 steps; the last, with 25, brings you to the level of an overlook with a man-made sandstone wall. The trail from this overlook is paved with asphalt, and in 300 feet, it takes you to the Rock Bridge parking area.

WILDCAT TRAIL #228

Distance to Swift Camp Creek Trail: 1.3 miles one way
Hike: EASY
Walking Time: 40 minutes to 1 hour one way

GENERAL REMARKS: Wildcat Trail gets its name not from an abundance of those shy and seldom seen kitties, but from a small stream that runs below and out of sight of the trail. The bobcats native to this area are so few and secretive by nature that your chances of seeing one are about as good as catching a ten pound trout in Wildcat Creek. Which is all probably very well for the faint of heart, for the cacophonic shriek of a wildcat in the middle of the night can turn a 250 pound linebacker into an incoherent blob of fear.

Wildcat Trail ends at about the halfway point of Swift Camp Creek Trail, so it is frequently used to begin or complete various loop hikes. If you are planning to use this trail in conjunction with the longer hike on Swift Camp Creek Trail, you are in for an arduous walk, for although Wildcat Trail is not strenuous, both directions on Swift Camp Creek Trail involve rugged going. The distance from this trail head to Rock Bridge parking lot is about six miles. The distance north to Parched Corn Overlook is about 4.5 miles.

TRAIL DESCRIPTION. (From Sky Bridge Road to Swift Camp Creek Trail. For Trail Description in the opposite direction, see page 128)

When you come from Pine Ridge, the trail head is on the right side of Highway 715, about 2.9 miles past the Rock Bridge Road. Parking space at the trail head is limited. The sign at the beginning of the trail reads:

SWIFT CREEK 1¼ MI.
ROCK BRIDGE 5 MI.

The trail starts out on an old farm and logging road which forks in about 100 yards. Wildcat Trail follows the left fork. If you have the time and are interested, the right fork, which has a wooden barrier across it, leads to a private family cemetery. A few of the graves here are indicated by badly weathered sandstone surfaces or by iron pipes protruding a few inches above the ground. These family cemeteries are quite common in this area, and if an original homestead is purchased by the government for added acreage of the National Forest, the family retains ownership of these cemeteries and has the right to continue to bury members of the family there. This one is still in active use as a family plot for a new stone was recently placed there for a deceaseds member who lived to be 95 and died in 1981. If you visit this small family plot, remember you are trespassing on private property. Treat the area with the respect it deserves.

Continuing on the left fork of the road, the trail leaves the road only to join it again so it makes little difference if you follow the road or the trail at this point. When the trail drops off to the left of the road and leaves it for good, it ambles nicely along a gradually declining ridge. Then two quick switchbacks lower you to the bottom of an exposed sandstone outcropping on the right side of the trail. Following along the base of this sandstone wall, the trail, passes a series of small rock shelters where the footing can be a bit mucky. In this vicinity two large trees have fallen across the trail in which the forest service has cut huge notches to make it easier for hikers to cross over them.

Just beyond the second of these fallen trees, there is a small wooden bridge which takes you over a minute sandstone wash then goes quickly down four more switchbacks. The intersection with Swift Camp Creek Trail comes shortly after the last switchback where a sign to the left of you paralleling the trail read:

←——— SKY BRIDGE ROAD 1.3 MI.

The trail to the right is the southern part of Swift Camp Creek Trail going in the direction of Rock Bridge. The trail to the left that goes downhill rather quickly to Wildcat Creek is the northbound section of Swift Camp Creek Trail that takes you to Parched Corn Overlook on Sky Bridge Road. The sign on the opposite side facing you reads:

TRAIL NO. 219
←——— SKY BRIDGE ROAD 2.9 MI.
3.8 MI. ROCK BRIDGE ———→

For trail description to Rock Bridge see page 124; to Rough Trail, page 122.

WILDCAT TRAIL #228

From Swift Camp Creek Trail to Sky Bridge Road

Distance: 1.3 miles
Hike: MODERATE
Walking Time: 40 minutes to 1 hour

The sign at the trail head reads:

←——— **SKY BRIDGE ROAD 1.3 MI.**

If you are using Wildcat Trail as a way back to Sky Bridge Road after walking either the upper or lower sections of Swift Camp Creek Trail, the most scenic and the most difficult part of your hike is behind you. Most of the 200 foot climb of this trail comes in the first half mile of the walk. The rest of the trail is an easy walk.

When the trail commences from Swift Camp Creek Trail, it immediately begins to climb. After the trail goes up four switchbacks, you will see a sandstone outcropping appearing on your left. The trail follows the base of this wall which contains a few small rock shelters. The trail then goes over a small wooden bridge that carries you over a slick sandstone wash. Just beyond this point, two large trees have fallen across the trail. The forest service has cut away the top portions of these trunks to help hikers cross them. You will soon come to two more switchbacks which quickly take you above and beyond the sandstone wall.

There is now a very gentle climb until the trail runs into an old logging road. Turn right on the road. This old logging road will take you right back to Sky Bridge Road. There is one stretch where the trail cuts off from the right side of the road, but the trail only parallels the old road and joins it again after a few yards. When you are about 100 yards from the end of the trail, another well defined dirt road comes in from the left with a wooden barricade across it. To reach Sky Bridge Road, continue in the same direction you have been traveling and very shortly the trail dead ends at the paved road.

If you have time, you might want to turn left up the barricaded road, for in less than another 100 yards, it takes you to a small private family cemetery. Such burial plots are quite common in this area and are owned by the family that once lived here and farmed the surrounding land. Some of the grave markers are made from badly weathered sandstone or simply from iron pipes sticking up a short distance above the ground. If original homesteads are purchased by the government for added acreage of the National Forest, the federal government allows the families to retain ownership of these cemeteries. They have the right to continue to bury members of the family there. In 1981 a new grave was added here for an old gentleman who died at the age of 95. If you decide to take this short side trip, remember that this is private property and that you are trespassing. Treat it with the respect that it is due.

X

ROUGH TRAIL #221

The usual distance, hiking level and walking time will be given for the individual sections of the trail.

GENERAL REMARKS: Rough Trail is the longest continuous trail in the Red River Gorge, measuring 8.5 miles from Highway 77 to Sky Bridge Road. At its Sky Bridge terminus, one can easily continue on Swift Camp Creek Trail to the Rock Bridge Recreation Area for an additional 7.6 miles without repeating a step or doing more than crossing a road; a total of 16 miles of fairly tough trail walking. With the completion of the new Raven's Rock Trail, which forms a link between Rough Trail and the trails at the end of Tunnel Ridge Road, a super hike of 21+ continuous miles from Double Arch Trail to Rock Bridge will soon be possible.

Shorter sections of this trail can be used for less demanding hikes and for many loop hike possibilities. Although Rough Trail approximately parallels the lower Red River Gorge and is less than a mile from it, never once in its 8.5 mile course does Rough Trail give the hiker a view of the Gorge itself. But it does drop into the valleys of Gorge tributaries no less than four times before climbing up to the ridge tops again. Although very little of the trail would be considered easy walking, its name makes it sound harder than it really is. There are even stretches that would be considered easy walking and suitable for the non-conditioned Sunday Stroller, but not many. For the sturdier hiker, Rough Trail with its five trail junctions, gives an infinite variety of walks and loop hikes that can vary in length from a short afternoon hike to a backpack trip with a couple of overnight stays.

Scenically, there are several sections with interesting and very large rock shelters, but the only arch visible along the entire trail is Gray's Arch. The trail follows and crosses several attractive mountain streams which offer plentiful supplys of cool water in numerous locations (chemical treatment is advisable) and appropriate mellifluous gurgling noises. Although these streams are too small for any type of boating, Chimney Top Creek does have a few trout for the expert angler. There are also some pools in this creek that are large enough to make nice summer swimming holes for perspiring hikers.

Since trails look very different when walked in opposite directions, Rough Trail is described in both its easterly and westerly directions. To find any particular section of this trail in the easterly direction, check the page numbers below. For the westerly directiion, check page 137. These individual sections are also listed in the Table of Contents. The entire length of Rough Trail is shown on the large maps found on pages 164 and 166. All of Rough Trail except the Parched Corn Creek section is also included on the two detailed contour maps found on pages 84 and 103.

EASTERLY DIRECTION OF ROUGH TRAIL #221

MARTIN'S BRANCH SECTION OF TRAIL #221

from Highway 77 to Gray's Arch Junction

Distance: 1.2 miles
Hike: MODERATE
Walking Time: 40 minutes to 1 hour one way

GENERAL REMARKS. This trail follows along Martin's Fork for about half of its length then begins the climb of about 400 feet to the top of Tunnel Ridge. If you don't like or can't climb even moderate trail elevations and are looking for an easy walk on a little used trail that crosses a tiny attractive stream several times (without bridges) you might find the first 3/4 mile on this trail to your liking. Once the trail starts up, however, the climb is a bit more demanding.

TRAIL DESCRIPTION. To find the trail head, take Kentucky Routes 11 and 15 west from Slade towards Stanton. In about two miles you will hit Route 77. Turn right on 77, go through the town of Nada and the Nada Tunnel. As soon as you have driven through the tunnel, check your mileage indicator. Go about 8/10 of a mile further and look for the trail beginning on your right. There is a small parking lot on that side with room for only two or three autos. At the trail head, there is a sign facing you which reads: **MARTINS BRANCH TRAIL #221.** On the same post but parallel to the trail on the right hand side another sign says:

TUNNEL RIDGE ROAD 2
GRAY'S ARCH 2

The distance to Tunnel Ridge Road is actually 3/10 of a mile shorter than the sign indicates while the Gray's Arch distance is 3/10 of a mile longer. There is a sturdy wooden bridge to take you across Gray's Branch, an amenity which will not occur again until the Parched Corn segment of Rough Trail. The trail then makes the first of 12 stream crossings of Martin's Branch, a tributary of Gray's Branch, in less than half a mile. Just before the last crossing the trail junctions with Martin's Fork Trail which leaves Rough Trail to the right. A sign facing you paralleling the left side of Martins Fork Trail says:

MARTINS FORK TR. NO. 236
D. BOONE HUT 1/2
TUNNEL RIDGE ROAD 2

Distances given on this sign are misleading as well as mispelled for D. Boon Hut is about 3/10 mile while tunnel Ridge Road is just over a mile from this point.

The Martin's Fork Trail is part of the D. Boon Hut loop walk. If you would like to see D. Boon Hut and the old niter mine, you can follow this trail to the recess cave that contains them, then follow the D. Boon Hut Trail back to the Gray's Arch parking lot. From there you follow the Gray's Arch Trail back to Rough Trail. This will increase your distance to Gray's Arch by about a half a mile. For General Remarks see page 87. A sign to the left on Rough Trail and paralleling it says:

ROUGH TRAIL NO. 221
HIGHWAY 77 1.1
TUNNEL RIDGE 2

If you wish to proceed on Rough Trail, you have one more stream crossing

Author looking at an Indian "Hominy Hole"

before the tough part begins. The trail suddenly leaves the stream and climbs the steep valley side. After two switchbacks, the trail becomes less steep and goes through a large rhododendron patch. You soon see a fairly prominent cliff face above you on the left side of the trail. Gradually, the trail curves around the bottom of this cliff. If you keep a lookout to the right, you may find an opening in the foliage which permits a view of the valley below. This view will convince you that you have climbed quite a bit and are now on a Snuffy Smith type ledge between two cliffs. The trail curves around the finger of this ridge cliff, revealing scars of old campfires along indentations in the sandstone cliff face.

When you come to a rock outcropping directly in front of you, the trail forks. So many hikers followed the incorrect right fork that the forest service built a wooden barricade across it. In about 25 feet after taking the left fork you will come to a set of seven wooden steps. Going up the steps, the trail turns and goes about 40 feet, then switches back right and onto a small open flat ridge. Directly to your left are a series of rock outcroppings above you. The trail goes up and over them, but they are neither steep nor high. After negotiating these rock caps, you are on top of Tunnel Ridge and a short walk takes you to the Gray's Arch Trail junction. The trail to the left is the continuation of Rough Trail and a sign on its left side paralleling it says:

TRAIL NO. 205
TUNNEL RIDGE RD. 3 MI.
GRAYS ARCH 1 MI.

The trail to the right takes you to the Gray's Arch parking area. Since so many visitors use only this section of Rough Trail to Gray's Arch, I have included its description with the trails that begin at the Gray's Arch parking lot on Tunnel Ridge Road. For the Gray's Arch section of Rough Trail, see page 85.

KING'S BRANCH SECTION OF ROUGH TRAIL

from Gray's Arch to Rush Ridge Trail

Distance: 8/10 mile
Hike: MODERATE
Walking Time: 30 to 45 minutes

TRAIL DESCRIPTION. There used to be a sign at this junction which said:

GRAYS ARCH 50 YARDS
TUNNEL RIDGE ROAD 2.1 MI
KOOMER RIDGE 4.9 MI

But because it was torn down so many times, the trail markings are painted on a tree and say ←221 205→

The distance to Tunnel Ridge Road indicated on the old sign is by way of the Rush Ridge Trail. A longer loop walk can be made by using the Pinch-Em-Tight Trail. Shortly after you start out on this section of Rough Trail, there is an unusual rock shelter on the left with beautiful orange colored markings over most of its surface. The trail continues with a very moderate downhill grade. Watch for a good sized boulder to the right of the trail with some interesting geologic formations covering much of its trail side surface.

After a rather straight course, the trail makes a decided right turn and begins to drop down to King's Branch. You first cross a little tributary of King's Branch just a few feet before it enters the branch which you then cross three times. There are many nice flat cleared areas along the stream with evidence of campfires. It is a pleasant place to have lunch, with a handy natural water supply, or to just sit awhile and cogitate while you spell yourself.

After the third crossing of King's Branch, the trail parallels the stream for a short distance then begins to climb above it. After a few walking minutes of a mild upgrade, the trail cuts sharply left and begins a steep climb with a couple of switchbacks. You hardly have time to catch your breath when you hit the most difficult section of this part of the trail. The path goes up through a very steep and slippery gap in a rock ledge. It is a place to make strong men weep if they are carrying a heavy backpack on a rainy day. When this slope was very wet you used to step up one foot and slide back three. Now a series of 17 log steps help you up the lower part of the slope and a second set of 20 takes you right through the gap. Once you have negotiated them, you will soon be on top of Rush Ridge. A short walk on the ridge top brings you to the Rush Ridge Trail junction. Rush Ridge is the trail to the right and the sign there reads:

TRAIL 221
1 GRAY'S ARCH
2 TUNNEL RIDGE ROAD
TUNNEL RIDGE ROAD 1.5

If you want to walk the shortest Gray's Arch loop, you proceed straight ahead here on Rush Ridge Trail (see description on page 92). If you are continuing on Rough Trail, take the path to the left.

RUSH BRANCH SECTION OF ROUGH TRAIL

from Rush Trail to Pinch-Em-Tight Trail

Distance: 1.2 miles
Hike: MODERATE to STRENUOUS
Walking Time: 40 minutes to 1 hour

The sign at the trail head reads:

3.4 MI. CHIMNEY TOP ROAD
4.1 MI. KOOMER RIDGE PICNIC AREA
5.2 MI. SKY BRIDGE ROAD

TRAIL DESCRIPTION. This section of Rough Trail has one very large rock shelter and some interesting rock formations as it works its way through a narrow sandstone gap. In less than five minutes walking, the trail makes a U turn to the right and begins dropping down off the ridge into a large shelter which has a unique shelf which makes it look like a two-story aboriginal apartment. One almost expects Fred Flintstone to peer over the upper shelf and shout at you that this is his private property that you are invading.

The trail goes almost up to the double shelf shelter before turning left and heads toward a narrow gap in the sandstone wall. Dropping through this cut, the path shares the bottom with a small stream. In its very narrowest section, there is a large tree with its roots partially exposed, the lower section of its trunk leaning definitely to the left. It looks very much like the trail goes to the left of the tree and out along a ledge, however, the correct way is around the right side of the tree through the muck. The trail continues through this narrow gap for about 40 feet with high stone walls on each side. When you get to the end, turn around and look back. To me, the gap has an unusual brand of eerie charm not unlike a jungle fantasy of Henri Rousseau.

As you leave the narrow enclosed section, you will notice a rock shelter on your left. The trail parallels the shelter for about half its distance, then turns abruptly right and moves away. As the trail leads away from the shelter you can look to your left and see that this is a large box canyon with a deep ravine below it. The trail descends on the right slope of the ravine with some sandstone outcroppings on the right. The trail levels out for awhile, then descends a steep section of about 100 feet with two switchbacks taking you down to Rush Branch.

Two small streams join here and the trail goes directly across the one to the right arriving at an inviting large cleared area where many previous hikers have stopped to rest for lunch. Several fire rings are found here indicating illegal camping because overnighters should be out of sight of the official trail. There are unofficial trails here running in every direction making it dificult to know which is the official trail. To find the continution of Rough Trail, make a right turn after crossing the stream and go a few feet upstream towards the flat open area. Look to the left and you will see the trail going uphill quite steeply. There is a 221 marker on a tree to assure you that this is the right path. Since you left the top of the ridge you have lost about 350 feet of altitude. The rest of this section of Rough Trail is spent gaining the 350 feet back again. Although the trail is now well above the stream level, it follows the same side of the same hollow almost to the junction of Pinch-Em-Tight Ridge.

You will pass a small rock shelter to your left on your way up. Notice about 100 feet beyond it the trail forks. Although the left fork is the correct one, if you have time, take the right one for a short distance because it almost immediately leads you into a charming isolated box canyon with various sized rock shelters. Although it is far from the top of the ridge, one can see how streams here have run into an erosion resistant ledge of sandstone leaving this secluded little step area about half way up the ridge.

Returning to the left fork of the trail, you will find that beyond this point the trail is more or less on the bottom of the hollow. As you approach the end of the hollow, the trail continues to climb doing a big U turn around its head. There is one place where the trail looks like it goes straight ahead but actually makes a sharp switchback to the left and keeps climbing. Another curve to the right puts you on top of Pinch-Em-Tight Ridge. In a very short walk you arrive at the trail junction. Pinch-Em-Tight Trail is to your right and the sign on the right side of

Attractive trailside view in the Gorge area

that trail and paralleling it reads:

TUNNEL RIDGE ROAD 1.8 MI.
KOOMER RIDGE PICNIC AREA 2.9 MI.

If you are taking the longer Gray's Arch loop, you turn right here. (For Trail Description see page 105) The continution of the Chimney Top Creek section of Rough Trail is to the left.

CHIMNEY TOP CREEK SECTION OF ROUGH TRAIL

To Koomer Ridge Trail

Distance: 1.6 miles
Hike: EASY
Walking Time: 50 minutes to 1 hour 15 minutes one way

TRAIL DESCRIPTION. The sign for Rough Trail at this intersection reads:

GRAY'S ARCH 2.0 MI.
2.2 MI. CHIMNEY TOP ROAD
4.0 MI. SKY BRIDGE ROAD

This section of Rough Trail starts out rather gently following the undulations of one of the fingers of Pinch-Em-Tight Ridge. Once it begins to descend in earnest down the right side of the ridge, you are on the section known as Pure Misery Hill. But the misery is for those going in the opposite direction. For you it is just an easy stroll down a long gentle descent. You will reach a little wash that is usually dry at the bottom of a ravine. This ravine hits an exposed ledge of sandstone and water action has eroded a cut in the ledge. The trail follows the wash through this little gap in the sandstone and from here you can usually hear, but not see, the right fork of Chimney Top Creek. A few feet beyond the break in the ledge, the trail cuts left and parallels Chimney Top Creek some 60 to 70 feet below. After a gradual descent to the creek, you reach the right fork and cross it. There are no helpful stepping stones here and making a successful crossing with dry feet isn't easy. Once across the right fork, the trail turns left and takes you to the confluence of the right and left forks of Chimney Top Creek. Keeping the fork you just crossed on your left, walk downstream and immediately cross the larger fork. Again, a dry crossing here is difficult. Once across the creek you will notice evidence of camping in a pleasant thicket of small evergreens with many little trails diverging in all directions. The correct trail turns right and follows Chimney Top Creek upstream. The trail climbs rather sharply up and around a huge boulder. Once around this gargantuan hunk of sandstone, the trail is well above the level of the creek. Looking down to where the creek sweeps the underside of the boulder, you can see a nice size pool that might be a good place to cool off on a hot summer day. You don't have to go down that steep slope to get there for the trail soon returns to the level of the stream at a much gentler angle. Back down on the creek level, Rough Trail crosses the creek again. The bottom here is solid limestone and can be very slippery, so ford the stream with caution. A few more yards and you arrive at Koomer Ridge Trail junction. Koomer Ridge Trail is the one on the right and the sign to the right of that trail reads:

KOOMER RIDGE PICNIC AREA 2.2 MI.

Rough Trail continues to the left where it immediately crosses Chimney Top Creek.

CHIMNEY TOP RIDGE SECTION OF ROUGH TRAIL

from Koomer Ridge Trail Junction to the Rough Trail parking lot on Chimney Top Road

Distance: 6/10 mile
Hike: STRENUOUS
Walking Time: 30 to 40 minutes one way

The sign for Rough Trail at this junction paralleling it on the right reads:

GREY'S ARCH 3.6 MI.
TUNNEL RIDGE RD. 3.4 MI.
.6 MI. CHIMNEY TOP RD.
2.4 MI. SKY BRIDGE RD.

TRAIL DESCRIPTION. Although it is just a little over a half mile to Chimney Top Road, the trail climbs over 450 feet to the top of the ridge. You start out by crossing Chimney Top Creek for the last time. Once across the creek, the trail turns right and climbs briefly up to a higher level. An unofficial trail continues straight ahead, but Rough Trail turns left and begins proceeding up the hollow. There are many little paths wandering around but the official trail goes up the right side of the hollow in a steady climb with huge slump blocks visible from both sides of the trail above and below you. The painted trail numbers on the trees help to keep you from wandering off on one of the little side trails.

When you start noticing an overhanging ledge above you on the right, you are approaching a climb that used to be almost impossible to go up during or after a heavy rain. It was like trying to climb the sides of a greased bowl. Fortunately some recent trail engineering, which included adding some stratigically placed switchbacks, has made this climb far easier than it used to be. It is still a bit of a lung buster but far easier to negotiate than it was a few years back. You will encounter the first two of these switchbacks, and a little later on, four more gets you through the worst of it. Beyond this series the climb moderates considerably

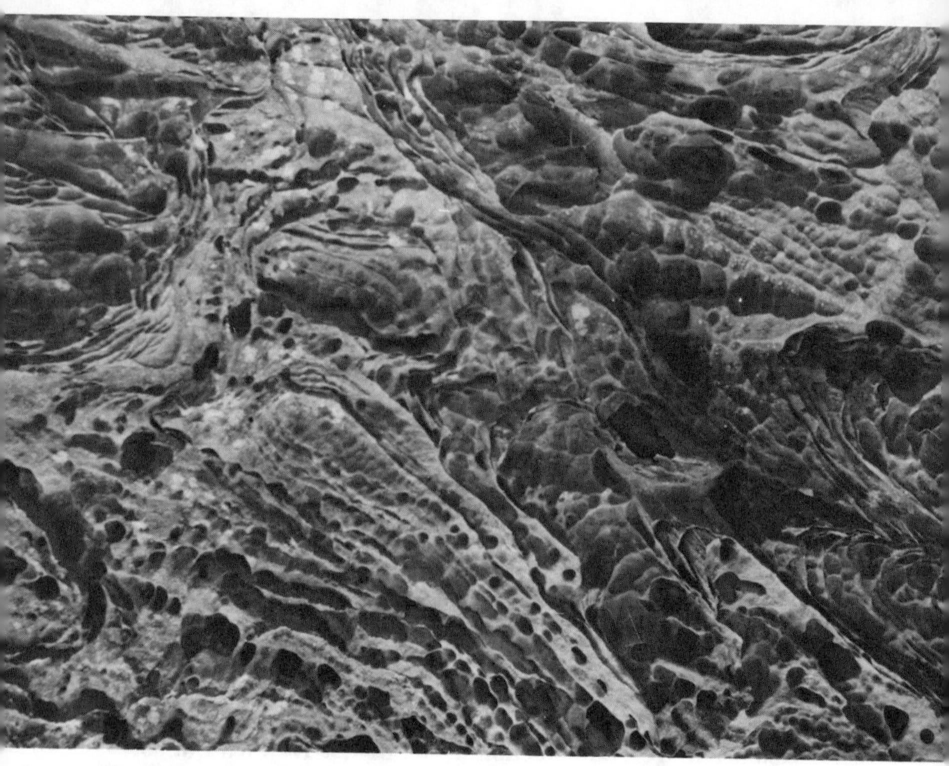

Sandstone conglomerate formation on rock surface along Rough Trail

with two more rounding switchbacks before the top. The open meadow with a visible privy that you pass to your right is Primitive Campground #3. Not far beyond it, the trail enters the Rough Trail parking lot on Chimney Top Road. The Parched Corn section of Rough Trail begins directly across the parking lot.

PARCHED CORN CREEK SECTION OF ROUGH TRAIL

from Chimney Top Road to Sky Bridge Road

Distance: 1.8 miles
Hike: MODERATE to STRENUOUS
Walking Time: 50 minutes to 1 hour 15 minutes

GENERAL REMARKS. This section of Rough Trail can be a nice hike all by itself. Beginning from the Rough Trail parking lot on Chimney Top Road about 1.6 miles from Route 715, it descends about 300 feet into the valley of Parched Corn Creek then up again to Sky Bridge Road. This trail takes you by one of the largest rock shelters in the forest and follows the banks of Parched Corn Creek with numerous pretty places for woodland peace and relaxation.

TRAIL DESCRIPTION. When entering the parking lot from Chimney Top Road, the trail begins on the left hand side. A sign to the right of the trail head reads:

SKY BRIDGE ROAD 1.8 MI.
ROCK BRIDGE 8.5 MI

You are only on the trail about a minute before it crosses Chimney Top Road. It then works its way along a finger of the ridge and T's into another trail just before it begins dropping into the hollow. Turn left at the T where the trail starts gently down and passes a beautiful miniature lighthouse (small arch) in the rock outcropping to the left of the trail. As the trail continues down, the wall on the left is beginning to develop into a sizable cliff above you. The trail then takes a sweeping curve along the bottom of this rock wall in front of a large curving rock shelter. Just beyond this point, the trail begins to parallel the opening of one of the largest rock shelters in the area. The trail goes along the opening of this rock shelter, which is well over 200 feet long, then curves to the right and starts down with the rock shelter now paralleling the trail on the right. The official trail soon crosses a very small wooden bridge going over a branch that is often dry. The trail has a series of short steep zigzags which take you to a stream that usually contains water. There is a bridge across the branch where the trail turns right putting a rock shelter on your left. The trail now gradually descends on the left side of the hollow alongside the creek. The stream wanders along a beautiful forest floor which is usually wide and flat in this section. It used to be that the trail only crossed the stream once but a landslide caused a trail rerouting across the creek rounding a large slump block on the opposite bank before recrossing the stream. When it crosses Parched Corn Creek for the last time it is easy to miss the turn since a well established trail continues along the bank. Watch for a large flat open space on the opposite bank with fire rings. There is a 221 trail sign painted on the tree to aid you.

Moving directly away from the creek the trail follows alongside a tributary of the creek on the right then turns left following another fork of the same stream. After passing a rock shelter on the left, the trail has a series of four switchbacks to get up one steep section followed a little later on by two rounding switchbacks before the trail splits. Turn left here and up some stone steps cut on the surface of a rock. Not far beyond this, the trail brings you to the parking lot alongside Sky Bridge Road. If you wish to continue your hike on Swift Camp Creek Trail, see page 123.

WESTERLY DIRECTION OF ROUGH TRAIL #221

(for General Remarks, see page 129)

PARCHED CORN CREEK SECTION

from Sky Bridge Road to the Rough Trail parking lot on Chimney Top Road

Distance: 1.8 miles
Hike: MODERATE to STRENUOUS
Walking Time: 50 minutes to 1 hour 15 minutes

GENERAL REMARKS. This section of Trail 221 has two particularly pleasing features that make it worthwhile for a short hike in itself. The first is a pleasant forest glen running alongside a crystal clear mountain stream which seems to be remote and isolated enough to be many more miles away from any road or other signs of civilization than it actually is. The second feature is seen as you climb out the other side of the valley as you make your way up to Chimney Top Road. There the trail parallels one of the largest rock shelters in the area. Since the trail descends about 300 feet into the Parched Corn Valley and up the ridge on the other side, the real work comes at the end of the walk. This trail begins at the Rough Trail—Swift Camp Creek Trail parking lot on Sky Bridge Road about 2/10 mile north of the Parched Corn Overlook. When entering the lot, you will find the trail heads in the extreme left corner. A sign at the trail head reads:

SWIFT CREEK 1 1/2
CHIMNEY TOP RD. 2
KOOMER RIDGE
CAMPGROUND 5

TRAIL DESCRIPTION. From the trail head Rough Trail turns right. When you see a rock wall developing on your left and the trail goes down some stone steps, you will see a trail going straight ahead and another going off to the right. Make the right turn. Immediately the trail descends toward the bottom of a sandstone cliff. The trail switches back several times to and from this wall which contains several small rock shelters. Then the trail follows the right side of a little ravine until you reach Parched Corn Creek. There are some very pleasant clearings in this area that are good for lunch stops or just plain loafing.

The trail crosses the stream immediately, then turns left and follows the branch upstream. This stretch seems to have an almost Garden of Eden quality about it. The trail used to stay on this side of the creek until its end, but a necessary trail rerouting caused by a landslide returns you briefly to the opposite bank. The path curves to the right around a bend in the creek that skirts a large slump block on the opposite bank. The trail then recrosses the stream. As soon as the trail cuts away from the stream, it begins a steep climb up a side ravine. This ravine is narrow and deep enough that you can see some good sized sandstone cliffs and tall straight poplar trees on the opposite side. This climb out can wind you but it isn't really a steep grade. When you come to a rock shelter on the right side of the trail, you can see from this point you are walking into a box canyon with a rather formidable curving sandstone cliff at its end. After passing this first rock shelter, the trail completes a horse shoe curve to the left which crosses a small stream and zig zags rather steeply uphill towards the huge recess cave at the end of this hollow.

It then crosses just a trickle of a stream with a rather delapidated tiny bridge. A few more feet and the trail curves left taking you under the overhang of the huge rock shelter. It is well over 200 feet long, at least 50 feet deep and quite high. The trail follows along the opening of this enormous shelter for almost its entire length. Although camping is not allowed in the shelter because it is within sight of the trail, it is a nice place to rest or hole up during a rainstorm.

Rough Trail then passes by another large rock house that is so close to the first one they are almost connected. After passing this second large shelter, the trail skirts a rock outcropping that has a beautiful miniature arch or lighthouse that is only about two feet high. Just beyond this little arch and about 50 feet beyond the point where the rock wall on your right disappears, take the first switchback to the right, leaving the well established trail that continues straight ahead. From here you have less than a mile of easy walking through the small trees of the ridge top forest before the trail hits Chimney Top Road. Once across the road it is only about a minute's walk to the Rough Trail parking lot. The Chimney Top Ridge segment of Rough Trail begins directly across the parking lot.

CHIMNEY TOP RIDGE SECTION OF ROUGH TRAIL

from the Rough Trail parking lot on Chimney Top Road to the Koomer Ridge Trail junction

Distance: 6/10 mile
Hike: MODERATE to STRENUOUS
Walking Time: 25 to 40 minutes

GENERAL REMARKS. This section of Rough Trail is usually used for a variety of longer hikes from this point. The distance indicated on the sign for Tunnel Ridge Road is for using Pinch-Em-Tight Ridge Trail. If you are planning to hike to the end of this trail, the distance to Highway 77 at the end of the Martin's Branch section is 6.5 miles. All of the longer hikes from this point are strenuous. The scenery along Chimney Top Creek is quite attractive. This stream also has a few elusive trout that might be caught by an expert fly fisherman as well as a couple of large pools suitable for cooling off on a hot summer's day. Since there are no bridges across this creek, it is hard to make dry crossings.

TRAIL DESCRIPTION. The trail head is on the right side of the Rough Trail parking lot which is found on the left side of Chimney Top Road about 1.6 miles from Route 715. A sign on the right side of the trail head reads:

KOOMER RIDGE PICNIC AREA 3 MI.
TUNNEL RIDGE ROAD 4 MI.
GRAY'S ARCH 4 MI.

From the trail head, the path is fairly level for about a quarter of a mile before it hits the rather steep escarpment down to Chimney Top Creek. While still on top of the ridge you will see an open field to the left with a privy. This is Primitive Campground #3. When you get to the descending section, the first part is very steep for you drop better than 400 feet in less than a half mile. This used to be one of the most treacherous stretches of trail in the whole Gorge area, but it has been considerably improved recently with some first class trail enginering. After a couple of rounding switchbacks you come to the very steep part which is now traversed by four well placed switchbacks. Shortly thereafter, two more switchbacks help you negotiate down through the last of the steep sections. Soon you will pass an enormous slump block to the right of the trail. If you look to the left, you can see the cliff from which it broke loose some time in the recent geologic past.

From this point, the trail gets less steep and it is a steady easy grade downhill. When you can see Chimney Top Creek straight ahead below you, there is a trail both to the left and right. Take the path to the right which drops down and crosses Chimney Top Creek. In just a few feet after the crossing, you will see Koomer Ridge Trail coming in from the left. A sign on the opposite side of that trail facing you says: **←KOOMER RIDGE PICNIC AREA 2 MI.** The continuation of Rough Trail is to the right.

CHIMNEY TOP CREEK SECTION OF ROUGH TRAIL

from Koomer Ridge Trail to Pinch-Em-Tight Trail

Distance: 1.6 miles
Hike: STRENUOUS
Walking Time: 1 to 1½ hours one way

TRAIL DESCRIPTION. A sign to the right of Rough Trail and paralleling it says:

GRAY'S ARCH 3.6 MI.
TUNNEL RIDGE ROAD 3.4 MI.
.6 MI. CHIMNEY TOP ROAD
2.4 MI. SKY BRIDGE ROAD

From the intersection, Rough Trail follows Chimney Top Creek downstream. In a very short distance, it crosses over to the right bank of the stream. There is a trail that goes straight ahead along the bank at this crossing. To find the right crossing point, look to the opposite shore where the correct trail can be seen going up the small embankment. Notice that the bottom of the creek is a solid bed of limestone and can be quite slippery so cross it cautiously. As soon as you are across the creek, the trail turns left and climbs about 30 feet above the creek level. On the left side of the trail, there is an enormous sandstone boulder with the creek running smack into its lower section. The water is deflected left around the boulder, leaving a pleasant pool at its base. Once around the boulder, the trail descends again to creek level and enters a dense thicket of small evergreens. As you come down from that rise you arrive at a fork in the trail. The correct left fork leads you back to Chimney Top Creek which you immediately cross. There are lots of little trails heading in many directions here. The best way to tell if you are crossing the stream in the right place is to look across the creek and see if there is a large tributary joining the creek on the opposite side just down from the trail crossing. That is the right fork of Chimney Top Creek and indicates the correct place to ford the creek. If you should cross the creek and find yourself in the middle of a big field, you have gone past the correct crossing and should backtrack until you see the confluence of the two forks and cross over directly above them.

After crossing the biggest fork of Chimney Top Creek, Trail #221 heads directly away from it with the right fork of the creek on the right. In a very short distance the trail crosses this fork. This is the last time you will be near a large stream for quite a distance for, after a couple of rounding switchbcks, the trail immediately begins a long climb. This lengthy stretch up Pinch-Em-Tight Ridge is known as "Pure Misery Hill". But don't let the name scare you since the sizable climb of over 400 feet is spread over 3/4th of a mile and the slope is gentle. When my youngest daughter was four years old, she was a notorious hater of long walks. She hiked this hill with me one day and I purposely did not tell her the name of the hill for I knew I would immediately hear cries of "Daddy, carry me, I'm tired." In her blissful ignorance of this awesome name, she bounced up to the top as if there were no hill there at all.

After the serious climbing is over, the trail crosses two treeless sections where the topsoil has been eroded away leaving floors of sandstone. Soon you will arrive at the junction of Pinch-Em-Tight Trail. At this junction, the continuation of Rough Trail curves to the right while Pinch-Em-Tight Trail goes straight ahead. The sign to the right of PinchEm-Tight Trail reads:

TUNNEL RIDGE ROAD 1.8 MI.
KOOMER RIDGE PICNIC AREA 2.9 MI.

RUSH BRANCH SECTION OF ROUGH TRAIL

from Pinch-Em-Tight Trail to Rush Branch Trail

Distance: 1.2 miles
Hike: MODERATE to STRENUOUS
Walking Time: 40 minutes to 1 hour one way

The sign at this trail junction reads:

GRAY'S ARCH 2.0 MI.
2.2 MI. CHIMNEY TOP ROAD
4.0 MI. SKY BRIDGE ROAD

TRAIL DESCRIPTION. This section of Rough Trail quickly drops about 350 feet in altitude down to Rush Branch then climbs back up that 350 feet to the top of Rush Ridge. Starting from the Pinch-Em-Tight Trail junction, the trail heads north following the top of a short finger of Pinch-Em-Tight Ridge. In a very short distance, the trail cuts left away from the extension of the ridge top with a rounding switchback and begins dropping into the hollow. Although there is a trail of sorts that continues straight ahead, there is a needlepoint switchback to the right which is the correct way to go. The trail curves around the head of a hollow with the sandstone bluff of Pinch-Em-Tight Ridge on the left. This section is thick with rhododendron. After you have rounded the curve of the hollow, the trail hangs on the right side of the hollow. You continue on this easy downgrade section for almost a half mile. The trail drops quite steeply into a fairly large flat cleared area under a canopy of trees.

Two hollows join together here, each with its own stream and between them there is much evidence of man-made fires in little hastily constructed stone circles. There are many little trails going in many directions around this illegal camping area. To follow the official trail, as you drop down into this hollow, head directly toward the nearest stream and follow it downstream for a short distance and cross the stream. You are now at the lowest elevation of this stretch of Rough Trail and you are about to commence the climb up to Rush Ridge. Once across the stream the trail turns left. After two switchbacks, there is a very steep straight section of trail where slipping and sliding is the order of the day if the trail is wet. Beyond this brief section, the upgrade becomes more gradual as you are walking up into what will become a box canyon. As you go up this hollow, a good sized sandstone cliff develops above you on the left. When the trail follows the base of this cliff, it passes several small rock shelters. A very unusual stretch of trail is just ahead.

The trail heads directly toward the wall of the box canyon leading to a fair sized rock shelter. At the foot of the rock shelter, the trail turns left and soon is enclosed in a narrow ravine. The trail shares the cramped bottom of this gap with the stream that made it. Because of its narrowness, much of this little gorge is in shadows. With the combination of being tightly encompassed between high moss and lichen covered walls and the murky atmosphere, one can experience an ominous feeling when passing through. But it is one of visionary enchantment rather than fear.

After climbing up through this cut, the trail arrives at a more spacious area with a large rock shelter on the left. The trail curves around to the right skirting this large double-storied shelter, which is one of the largest and more attractive ones on the trail. After walking to the opposite end of this shelter, the trail turns right and climbs alongside a rock wall to the left. When you climb above this wall the trail switches back to the left and you are on top of Rush Ridge. From here, it is a very short walk to the junction with Rush Ridge Trail which comes in from the left. A sign paralleling that trail on its opposite side and facing you reads:

TRAIL NO. 221
1 MI. GRAY'S ARCH
2 MI. TUNNEL RIDGE ROAD
TUNNEL RIDGE ROAD 1.5 MI.

KING'S BRANCH SECTION OF ROUGH TRAIL

from Rush Ridge Trail to Gray's Arch

Distance: 8/10 mile
Hike: EASY
Walking Time: 25 to 35 minutes one way

TRAIL DESCRIPTION. This section is often used as part of a loop trip to Gray's Arch. The trail goes down the escarpment of Rush Ridge to King's Branch with an elevation loss of about 300 feet. Around this pleasant little stream, there are some delightful places to lunch or rest on pleasant days. There are also some quite unusual geologic formations alongside the trail near Gray's Arch. From the trail head, the path follows a finger of Rush Ridge before starting down to King's Branch.

After a couple of switchbacks, the trail has a very steep short section downward through a gap which used to be hard to negotiate and treacherously slippery in wet weather. The descent of this steep grade has been made easier by the addition of 20 log steps in one series and 17 in a second. Although still not a cakewalk, it is far less difficult than it once was.

The trail then cuts right and the grade is decidedly easier. King's Branch appears below the trail on the left. The stream and the trail parallel each other for a short distance. Then the trail goes down to the branch and crosses it three times. This area is clear of underbrush and has much evidence of campfires. After the third crossing of King's Branch, the trail crosses a smaller tributary of the branch just about a yard way from the point where it empties into the larger stream.

From here the trail leaves the branch and begins to climb above it. After a brief uphill section, the trail cuts left and the grade becomes easier. For a long stretch, the trail goes in more or less a straight path. Along this stretch, look for a good sized boulder on the left side of the path partially covered by interesting geologic formations. Not far beyond this boulder, a rock shelter on the right side of the trail has an unusual orange colored surface.

From this shelter it is just a few yards to the short trail to Gray's Arch. At this point Rough Trail starts a steep climb to the right while the short Gray's Arch Trail is straight ahead. There used to be a sign at this junction paralleling the left side which said:

GRAY'S ARCH 50 YARDS
SKY BRIDGE ROAD 6.0 MI.
TUNNEL RIDGE ROAD 2.1 MI.
KOOMER RIDGE 4.9 MI.

Hoodlums tore it down so many times that the forest service had to revert to painting the trail numbers on a tree at the junction. They say:

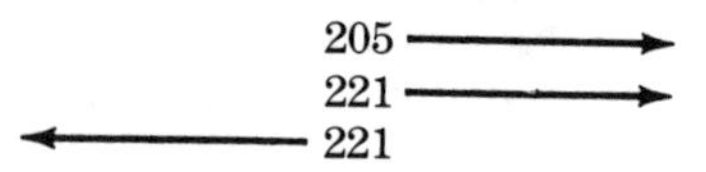

The short walk to Gray's Arch should not be missed for it is one of the largest and most interesting arches in the area.

GRAY'S ARCH SECTION OF ROUGH TRAIL

from Gray's Arch to the beginning of the Martin's Branch Section

Distance: 1.1 miles
Hike: MODERATE
Walking Time: 35 to 45 minutes one way

TRAIL DESCRIPTION. From this point, there is about a 200 foot elevation climb to get to the top of Tunnel Ridge and most of the climb happens in the first quarter mile. You start up a few log steps which then lead to the first of three groups of wooden steps with hand rails. Don't take the steep trail to the left but follow straight ahead to the steps. The first series with railings has 14 steps. A couple of switchbacks bring you to the longest set with 37 steps. The last set has only four steps.

The trail soon curves around and under a small rock shelter on the right. After you have passed this shelter, keep a lookout to the left, for Gray's Arch will come into view again. This time you are higher than the arch so you can see what it looks like from above. You can also see how deceptive this area is, for it appears that one might easily descend from here directly to the arch, not realizing the tremendous drop-off that this section of ridge takes between this viewing place and the arch.

From this point, the trail angles up the right side of a hollow. There are so many paths going in so many different directions here it is difficult to tell which one is the right trail. The official path stays above the bottom of the hollow then U curves to the left around its head and angles up the opposite side to the ridge top. The trail then follows a curving switchback to the right across the top of the ridge and heads in the opposite direction, staying close to the top. From here the walk is very easy.

You will cross a large meadow that is rapidly being reclaimed by small trees. A short walk beyond the meadow brings you to the Gray's Arch, Martin's Branch Trail junction. A sign at this junction paralleling the trail on the right says:

TUNNEL RIDGE ROAD 3. MI.
GRAY'S ARCH 1. MI.

The trail going straight ahead of you is the beginning of the Martin's Branch section of Rough Trail. See below for the sign at this trail head. The trail to the left is the path that takes you to the Gray's Arch parking lot. This short trail to the parking area is wide and easy and in a very few minutes you will see the picnic tables that surround the parking area.

MARTIN'S BRANCH SECTION OF TRAIL #221

from Gray's Arch Trail junction to Highway 7

Distance: 1.2 miles
Hike: EASY
Walking Time: 30 to 40 minutes one way

GENERAL REMARKS. A sign on the right side of the trail facing you reads:

HIGHWAY 77 2
D. BOONE HUT 2
TUNNEL RIDGE RD. 3

For those people who would like a delightful walk with only mild downhill slopes and then follow the course of a very pleasurable mountain stream, the walk to the Highway nicely fits the bill. But if you do not have someone to pick you up at the highway, the return trip is far more demanding. A loop trip to D. Boon Hut is also possible from here in the reverse direction. For the description of that walk, see page 87 .

TRAIL DESCRIPTION. The trail starts out on a fairly level section of ground on top of the ridge, then begins a gradual descent over the face of various sandstone outcroppings. After the trail has dropped about 50 feet in altitude, it leads to a flat open section on the edge of a small ridge. It is a little difficult to see where the trail goes from here. Look for the continuation of the trail well back on the right side of this little flat open area and not out toward the edge where one might expect it to be. After the trail takes you down on the right side of this open space, the trail switches back to the left and goes for about 40 feet. It then goes down eight wooden steps with a railing. Just beyond the steps, it appears the trail goes in two directions. The one to the right is the correct trail. There is now a wooden barricade there to keep you from making the wrong left turn.

Shortly, a large sandstone bluff appears above the trail on the right which gives you some idea of how much altitude you have already lost since leaving the ridge top. Continuing along the base of the cliff, there are the scars of old campfires among the small indentations in the cliff. The trail then curves right around the base of a high finger of the ridge. As you walk around this cliff face, keep an eye to the left. There is a break in the trees that gives you a good view of the valley below and also some idea of the altitude you have yet to lose. This area of the trail is on a ledge with cliffs above and below you.

Soon, the trail cuts its way through a large rhododendron patch. With a gentle downward slope, the trail descends until it reaches Martin's Branch. From here

The Bear Pen Narrows on Swift Creek Trail

on there is little difficulty in following the trail, for it continues on the valley floor to the road. The trail crosses this little stream no less than 12 times before Highway 77 is in sight. There are no bridges to aid you on these stream crossings, but since Martin's Branch is tiny, you can usually ford it without getting wet feet. Just after the first crossing, the trail comes to the Martin's Fork junction with that trail coming in from the left. A sign that parallels Rough Trail to the right says:

ROUGH TRAIL NO. 221
HIGHWAY 77 1.1
TUNNEL RIDGE

There is a sign paralleling the left side of Martin's Fork Trail which says:

D BOONE HUT 1/2
TUNNEL RIDGE RD. 2

In both cases, the distances are shorter than indicated. There is one quite mucky section of the trail where a sizable amount of dirt has been removed to make this stretch level. It was probably done in the days when once a little tram railway, as pictured in the history section, passed this way.

After your last crossing of Martin's Branch, another stream called Gray's Branch comes in from the left. After you have made this stream crossing with the luxury of a sturdy wooden bridge, you will find the junction with Route 77 just beyond.

Just across this paved road there will eventually be the beginning of the proposed Raven's Rock Trail which will take you to Courthouse Rock. Although the route of this trail has been laid out, the trail itself did not exist at this writing.

XI

CANOEING IN THE GORGE AREA

By using the North Fork of the Red River through the Gorge, two entirely different canoe adventures await those who enjoy this increasingly popular sport. This river course is almost evenly divided between the upper and lower Gorge areas. The lower is for novices; the upper is for experts. Of course, all river trips are conditioned by the amount of water flow which can change quite rapidly with varying weather conditions. After long dry spells, the river is so slow and sluggish that you will end up pulling your canoe or kayak much more than riding in it. Generally speaking, the higher the water, the more the fun and the greater the danger, especially for the novice. Since the water level of this stream can change drastically in a matter of hours, it is not easy to forecast what kind of canoe trip you are going to have before you arrive.

LOWER GORGE CANOE TRIP

The easier course through the lower Gorge begins where the cement bridge on Highway 715 crosses over the North Fork of the Red River about 6.2 miles north of Pine Ridge. A convenient place to end this trip is where the steel bridge on Route 77 crosses the same stream about 9.8 road miles downstream from the cement bridge. Both the cement bridge and the steel bridge are marked on the area map found on pages 164 and 166 at the back of this book and are also mentioned in the chapter covering the automobile loop trip through the lower Gorge. Since the road and the stream follow pretty much the same course, you have about a ten mile float trip with no serious hazards for the novice. Unless the water level is treacherously high, this trip offers a gentle non-taxing ride through the scenic lower Gorge with just a whiff of white water.

Twisting through the lower Gorge, you will pass Sky Bridge to the left, Tower Rock to the right and Chimney Top Rock on the left high above you. Of these three, Chimney Top is the only one easily seen. If the scenery is not as spectacular as the run through the upper Gorge, it is more than pleasant as you thread your way around many bends often next to huge slump blocks. The only annoying distraction is the sound of automobiles. Although the road is usually out of sight, it is close enough that every passing auto is an intrusion on your water and woodland privacy. There is a river gauge giving the current stream level on the cement foundation on the north side of the steel bridge with appropriate suggestions for good running levels. Much below one foot becomes more of a bottom bouncer than a float through. One to three feet is ideal. Three to six feet is marked with a question mark. If you are not a skilled river runner, it's a good time to go hiking. Above six feet the sign spells it out in a single word "NO".

If you are a beginner at this exciting river sport, this is a nice easy stream to try if the water isn't too high. It is not a taxing challenge for advanced white water boaters, but the beauty makes it worthwhile for anyone with some paddling experience. Using the international rating for level of difficulty (the lower the number, the easier the river) the lower Gorge trip is rated as a Class 1 to 1+ stream at acceptable running water levels.

THE UPPER GORGE CANOE TRIP

This magnificent stretch of cliffs and white water has recently been appropriately designated by the state of Kentucky as a "Wild River". Kentucky's U.S. Senator Wendell Ford has also been active in trying to get the federal government to declare the upper Gorge as a Wilderness Area, a move that would go a long way in protecting what is one of the most scenic wilderness canoe runs in the eastern United States. So far, he has had no luck. Fortunately, the state "Wild River" designation states that those sections of the river bank that are privately

Upset in the Roughs of the Red

Successfully running a drop on the North Fork of the Upper Red River Gorge

owned may not be developed commercially within sight of the river.

Beginning at Spraddlin Bridge, the Red River worms its often treacherous way for the nine mile upper Gorge trip, ending where the lower Gorge trip begins at the cement bridge. Although this exciting ride offers some of the most spectacular scenery to be found in the eastern United States, it should only be attempted by advanced canoers and kayakers. Rated as a Class III or III½ river when the flow is good, it is definitely not a stream for novices. Each year the river batters beyond salvation several canoes of those who thought they could make it through without advanced white water techniques. Well over 100 canoes have been wrecked beyond repair on this stretch of the Red River and each year a dozen or more are added to the list. I haven't seen any bleached human bones alongside the twisted and torn aluminum and plastic hulls, but imagination sometimes fills up the void. I know of no drownings yet in either the upper or lower Gorge, but it is a distinct possibility, especially for the unskilled and the unprepared. There have been several mishaps that have resulted in serious injury. Because of the seclusion and general inaccessibility of the upper Gorge, there is no easy in or out until the end of the trip. This makes outside help and medical treatment many hours away.

If you are a beginning canoer, stay out of the upper Gorge unless you go with an expert or until you have experience doing white water at a Class II level and know something about how to "read a river". Use only suitable boats such as canoes and kayaks. This is no place for row boats or any kind of larger craft. I once heard of two men who unwittingly tried to float a bass boat through the upper Gorge; something it is most assuredly not designed to do. Disaster soon struck at Calaboose Falls. It is also a particularly bad place to take young children for even an advanced canoeist might get a dunking in the "Roughs of the Red" when the water is running well. Don't do a float trip with only one boat, for there are a lot of situations where extra company may be necessary to save your boat or your life.

Don't take anything with you that would suffer from soaking or pounding unless you have such objects in an absolutely waterproof bag securely lashed to your canoe. The sight of Nikons dripping with river water is enough to make a strong man weep. So is the disappearing act that a waterproof bag can quickly perform in the rapids when one upsets and the unsecured bag disappears in the frothing water. When properly prepared, a float through the upper Gorge can give you an excitingly good time, but ruining an $800 canoe or a $500 camera would hardly be classified as a fun experience.

To find Spraddlin Bridge, take the Mountain Parkway and exit at Campton. Take Rt. 191 through the center of Campton and follow it until you hit Rt. 746. Turn left on 746 and you will soon cross over the Mountain Parkway. About four miles from Route 191, Route 746 crosses Stillwater Creek concrete bridge. Just a little over two miles beyond this bridge Route 746 crosses over a second cement bridge. This is Spraddlin Bridge. After crossing the bridge, there is a clearing on the left side of the road where cars may pull off clear of the highway. From this clearing there is a wide path that takes you down to the river.

From the put in where the stream is not much more than 20 feet wide, the first three miles are gentle, flowing through gorgeous country. With a few ledges and ripples at a Class I level, this initial stretch gives you a good chance to limber up for the more exciting water ahead. The river takes you under one enormous rock shelter with ochre colored walls which is breathtaking in its size. When you pass Stillwater Creek on your left you soon will be approaching your first Class II drop at Stillwater Rapids. Although most boats run it successfully (scouting from the left bank recommended), my canoeing friend, Jim Carpenter, calls it "Warm Up Rapids", saying "If you eat this one, you're probably in for a very wet day!"

From here on, the bluffs get higher and the scenery more beautiful with the next challenge at Calaboose Falls. This is a double ledge, each about two feet high. When the water is at a good running level the drop down both levels is best made on river left. At low water levels, the first ledge is still best on river left, but the second drop should be made on river right.

You then have some relatively calm water until the section known as the "Roughs of the Red" or the "Narrows" are reached. Here you have four major rapids rated at Class II+ to Class III with very little recovery space between each one. Although the standing waves are never of the gigantic size, the drop areas are steep and so narrow that they require fast technical manuevering in extremely pushy water. Great gobs of this water is usually pouring over your gunwales, which means having extra flotation in your canoe goes a long way in helping you to keep from swamping. Since rapids change considerably at different water levels, a description here of how to run the drops would accomplish little and each major drop should be scouted from the shore. It is also a good idea to have your more advanced paddlers drop through first, then ready themselves with throw lines for rescue operations at strategic bank locations. If you feel the better part of valor is to portage these drops, you will need painter lines at each end of your canoe to line your boat through for the bank on both sides of the river is made up of huge boulders, making the carrying of a canoe almost impossible.

The most famous, but not the most difficult drop is the second one into "Dog Drowning Hole". It consists of a marvelous, very narrow chute about three feet high on extreme river left that drops you quite suddenly into the pool below. Running this drop to the right can lead to some spectacular boat pinnings, or almost certain upset in the hole below the ledge.

Once through these major drops, you have a real fun ride of Class I+ rapids almost all the way to the cement bridge at Kentucky Route 715. None of these are difficult, but they do require almost constant vigilance in rock dodging to avoid getting stuck or upset. The forest service has a take out point just beyond the bridge on river right where vehicles can be driven down for easier loading.

But there are other problems that should be considered before you begin this otherwise fantastic river run. One of the most important is the rarity of appropriate water for a good run. Add to this that the best water levels almost always occur during the colder months, meaning wet suits should be worn to prevent hypothermia. The upper Gorge can go months at a time when the water is so low that the trip is largely an exhausting drag which becomes a slogging hike. On the other hand, because of the funnel effect of its narrows, the river can rise quite rapidly to a level so severe that the stream is a virtual death trap in high water. If the heavy rain is not followed by a slower fall for any length of time, the river can drop quite rapidly back again to uninteresting low levels.

To determine if you will have enough water for a good float through, the current and predicted river level at downstream Clay City is often reported by River Forecasters. Since Clay City is quite a bit downstream from the upper Gorge, it will not always be accurate for this upstream level, but it usually works out pretty well. If the Clay City prediction is under three feet, that usually translates as a drag through level in the Gorge. ABS boats can still do pretty well at 2½ feet. Between three and six feet of water at Clay City gives you the best running levels. At six to seven feet it becomes very pushy, and beyond that it becomes a suicide run. You can also check the gauge on the Spraddlin Bridge at the put in. If it reads one foot or below and there is still plenty of water to float your canoes, you should have a good run. Between one and two feet, it is dangerous but runnable by experts. If you find the gauge reading is above two feet, the river should not be run. If you cannot get any gauge reading or forecast and you find the water is into the trees along the banks, it again is a kamikaze run. One of my good friends, who today is an advanced white water paddler, was told during his novice days by a macho type who should have kept his mouth shut, that the river was a safe run at any level. My friend miraculously survived a kayak run when the Clay City gauge read 15 feet. His description of the run was "nine miles of sheer white knuckle terror!"

Because of the narrowness of the river, another hazard can be windfall or dead-

One of the few large trees that escaped the extensive logging operations carried out during the late nineteenth and early twentieth centuries

fall trees that block the entire channel. Make sure you have a good lead boat who can do a competent back ferry and scout around blind corners.

I suppose part of the attraction of the upper Gorge is the danger involved, but if you are sensible, knowledgeable and well equipped, the dangers become more seeming than real. On those rare occasions when good running levels and warm sunshiny weather coincided, I have had ideal runs that are remembered as being some of the best parts of my white water days. Going down river with some of the finest paddlers I know, whom I have the privilege to call my personal friends, these trips have become some of the happiest outdoor memories of my life.

XII

OFF TRAIL, PROPOSED TRAIL AND NEW AREA HIKING

Most long time hiker-backpacking gorge visitors have their own off trail esoteric rendezvous somewhere back in the boondocks. One of the facinations of this area for these experienced visitors is to explore and seek out such secret places from the hundreds of possibilities in these back country locations where no official trails exist.

There is no practical way that a guide book of this type can cover the hundreds of such possibilities nor would I want to exposes these private Valhallas to the multitudes. The off trail hikes included in this chapter are really not trailess areas at all. Most have well defined paths that knowledgeable visitors have been following for years. These walks are only classified as "off trail" in the sense that they are not official trails and are not maintained by any government agency.

Because of their proximity to existing official trails, many of the new trails have been added in previous chapters. Other new and proposed trails fit nicely in this final catch-all chapter. It also allows me a handy place to add new trails in future printings.

INDIAN STAIRWAY AND THE SARGENT'S BRANCH-GLADIE CREEK SEGMENT OF THE SHELTOWEE TRACE

Distance: To Indian Stairway 3.5 miles one way
To forest service gravel road 4.6—7 miles
Hike: VERY STRENUOUS
Walking Time: Sheltowee Trace segment 3 hours.
To Indian Stairway from Sheltowee Trace ½ hour

GENERAL REMARKS: Sheltowee is a Shawnee Indian word for big turtle, a name the Shawnee bestowed on Daniel Boone when they held him captive and adopted him into the tribe. The Sheltowee Trace is a National Recreation Trail of approximately 250 miles in length that originates in Tennessee just six miles south of the Kentucky border. It proceeds northward for approximately 250 miles with its terminus at the northern end of the Daniel Boone National Forest about ten miles short of the Ohio River. Since the Trace passes through the middle of the Gorge area, some may wonder why I have not written a complete description of that trail's miles through the vicinity. For the most part, the Trace follows previously established trails both in the state park and national forest already described in the book. Furthermore, the permanent final location of this long trail through the Gorge is anything but settled. It has had two major relocations here since its inception and other reroutings are going to occur within the next few years. I therefore added the only part of the Sheltowee Trace in this area that offers a significant new contribution to the hiking-sightseeing possibilities and the Sargent Branch-Gladie Creek segment is most assuredly that.

In the months when the leaves are off the trees, the walk up the side gorge of Gladie Creek gives excellent views of a series of cliff faces that line the opposite rim. This trail also leads you past one of the more beautiful finished arches (Indian Arch) in the area as well as an easy off trail walk to Indian Stairway and another charming hide-a-way lighthouse arch (Adena Arch). Before this section of the Sheltowee Trace was built, there was no official trail that came anywhere near Indian Stairway, a fascinating archeological remnent of the Indian past which afficinados of the Gorge have known and visited for years.

In the rock surfaces of a rounded cliff almost 100 feet high the ancient Indians

FOREST SERVICE ROAD
SHELTOWEE TRACE
INDIAN STAIRWAY
INDIAN ARCH
ADENA ARCH
GLADIE CREEK
715
SHELTOWEE TRACE
MENIFEE CO
WOLFE CO
RED
Gas Well
Princess Arch
Tower Rock
Cloud Splitter
Powell
Gibson Br
Hale Br
Klaber
Creek

scooped out footholds in the stone wall creating an easier access from the valley of Sargent's Branch to the ridge top and a nearby large recess cave where they lived. There is no positive way of dating the stairway's age, but it was possibly created by the Adena Indians over 1,000 years ago. For those who are not fearful of heights, have proper footwear and are fairly agile, climbing or descending this ancient stone ladder is often a rewarding and long remembered experience. Furthermore, the view from the top of the stairway is downright spectacular. Below is seen a green sea of trees in the valley of Sargent's Branch and the lower gorge of Gladie Creek encased by high cliff-edged ridges in almost every direction with no evidence beyond the stairway of the hand of man. It is a beautiful place to sit alone and let your imagination wander, possibly conjuring up visions of the archaic Indians climbing the stairway with the clothing and implements of their primitive pre-historic culture. I know of one visitor from Spain who was so moved by the atmosphere and the view that he later wrote a poem describing the emotion that encompassed him there.

Less than a quarter mile away is the largest rock shelter I know of in the area. The length of the shelter, which was inhabited by Indians off and on for over a thousand years, is slightly longer than a football field and it recesses over 60 feet from the lip. The first backpacking trip I made in my life included a climb up the stairway and a sheltered night within this cave. Since there is no mention of Indian Stairway or the nearby enormous recess cave in the first edition of this book, it is not surprising that I have been asked the following two question so many times through the ensuing years. "Why didn't you include Indian Stairway in your book?" and "How do you get to it?"

I explained that the first edition of this book dealt almost exclusively with official trails and until the creation of the Sheltowee Trace, the only comparatively easy way to get to Indian Stairway was to follow a vague unofficial path for many miles, much of which traversed privately owned ground. Another reason for its absence from the original edition was that I was asked not to write about it by forest service personnel of the Stanton Ranger District for what was then a very valid reason. At that time, there were no deprecating scars of spray paint can messages or carved names and initials on the easily marred sandstone surfaces of the Stairway. Unfortunately, the easier the access to such natural rock surfaces, the more they become disfigured by mindless humanoids as is painfully visible on the top of both Natural Bridge and Sky Bridge. The forest service was trying to find a way to keep this ancient stairway and its surroundings in this pristine condition and felt that, with time, such protective measures could be introduced. But in the ensuing years too many misguided Michelangelos have already found their way to the stairway and proliferated the upper surfaces with their offensive scratchings.

If you decide that you would like to hike this area, there are a number of variations possible to fit your hiking plans and abilities. Even the easiest of the following variations should be considered only by serious hikers in good physical condition. If you have two cars and can spot one at the end of the forest service gravel road or if you can have someone drive there later to pick you up, you have the option of doing only the Trace section which is entirely on maintained official trails, or you can also include following easy unofficial ridge top trails from the Trace to Adena Arch and the top of Indian Stairway. You can then retrace your steps along the ridge back to the official Trace trail then proceed along the Gladie Creek segment or return the way you came. Any healthy walker who is used to covering several trail miles of up and down terrain will find this version within their capacity. But climbing or descending the stairway is a different matter and isn't for everyone. It is a potentially hazardous and spooky trip up or down for anyone except experienced rock climbers. I once saw a woman who became petrified with fear at about the half way point and froze, clinging to the curving sandstone wall. It took about almost an hour to get her down. On the other hand, my ten-year-old daughter, who had previously climbed nothing more challenging than a jungle gym,

Adena Arch

went up and down the stairway with the grace and speed of a Big Horn Sheep. If you feel you can do the stairway, it makes a loop trip in either direction possible. Since it is much easier and safer to climb the cliff than it is to descend, I suggest you do the loop in that direction by following the Trace down into the valley of Sargent's Branch.

There is some guesswork in the mileage of this section of the Sheltowee Trace. A mileage indication of 4.6 miles for this stretch appears on a brief map of the entire trail issued by the forest service, but I'm sure the distance is much longer than that. By figuring the amount of time it took to walk the trail, I believe that it is about seven miles long. The trail is blazed with white diamond patches and is also frequently distinguished by a white logo of a turtle back.

FINDING THE TRAIL HEADS: By using the road map of the Gorge found on page 164, follow Route 77 from Route 11 and 15 through the village of Nada and through the Nada Tunnel. Shortly after crossing the iron bridge across the North Fork of the Red River, Route 77 turns left at a point where Route 715 begins. If you want to spot a car at the end of the forest service gravel road, you turn left here and follow the directions in the next paragraph. To find the trail head for the southern part of this segment, proceed straight ahead from this point on Route 715. In just about two miles on the right hand side of the road, there is a national trails recreation sign with the Sheltowee Trace turtle logo. The trail begins on the left side of the road across from the sign. At this writing, there is no official parking area here and the space for roadside parking is not very large.

To find the north end of this segment, make the left turn on Route 77 at the junction point with Route 715 and proceed up hill, passing through the small hamlet of Frenchburg. About 7.5 miles from the Route 77 and Route 715 junction there is a narrow paved road that leaves 77 on the right hand side with a tan and white mobile home on the corner. Turn right here and, in about a mile of ridge top driving, the paved road ends. To the right you will see the beginning of the forest service gravel road. You follow it a little over 2.5 miles to its end where there is room to park two or three cars.

TRAIL DESCRIPTION. From its beginning on Route 715, the trail parallels the road briefly before moving back in the forest. The climb up to the finger of the ridge that holds Adena and Indian Arch, although long, is almost never steep. After a few minutes of walking you will come to a place where the trail crosses a tiny branch, and immediately switches back sharply to the right. You now begin a climb up to and over a small ridge finger which should consume a little over a half hours walking time from the trail head.

After dropping off this ridge the trail begins a long more or less level stretch with minor up and down parts which takes you back up and around the head of Greasy Branch. It will take about an hour to go from the crossing of the ridge finger to a point where the trail makes a sharp needle point switch back to the left. From here you have a short, easy uphill section that places you on the top of the ridge.

You are not on the ridge top very long before you come to a V in the trail where the blaze marks indicate taking the right fork. By taking the right fork, it is only a very short distance before you arrive at Indian Arch to the left. But before following the trail to the right, this fork is an important decision point in determining what you wish to see in the vicinity of this ridge and the kind of hike you want to make. If you take the left fork, an easy ridge top walk will take you to Indian Stairway. (see page 155). But before proceeding either to Indian Arch and Sargent's Branch or the ridge top walk to the stairway, you might want to turn around and head back the way you came, for if you follow the top of the ridge in this opposite direction, it will take you about ten minutes to walk to the charming hide-a-way Adena Arch. If you opt to see this lighthouse arch you will find a point on a rock outcropping where the ridge drops rather steeply for a few feet. The arch is just a few yards beyond this point on the left.

If you wish to continue your hike on the Sheltowee Trace, after following the right fork and passing Indian Arch you will go down 40 wooden steps just beyond the arch. This is the beginning of the descent to Sargent's Branch. It is a moderate walk which sometimes follows along the bottom of a cliff wall and will take ten to 15 minutes down to the stream. Although the branch almost always has flowing water, a dry crossing is not difficult.

Not far beyond, you cross a small tributary of Sargent's Branch which is important to remember if you plan to do a loop hike by climbing up Indian Stairway. About 200 paces or about two minutes walking beyond the crossing of this small branch look for a faint trail going off to the left. This is the unofficial trail which will take you to the stairway (for directions on this loop hike see page 156).

Continuing on the Sheltowee Trace, the trail heads in the direction of Gladie Creek. As you near its valley there is a distinct fork in the trail where a blaze mark indicates the following of the left fork. It stays on the side of the ridge while the unofficial trail to the right drops off the ridge heading down towards Gladie Creek. Gradually swinging left, the trail now hangs on the ridge side of the Gladie Creek Gorge and from here to the end of this section there are occasional exquisite views of the high cliffs on the opposite side during the late fall and winter months. Continuing the left swing, the trail curves into the side hollow of Klaber Branch and begins a rather straight diagonal drop to that stream.

This moderately steep, narrow path crosses over one outcopping of shale which gives unsure and slippery footing for a few feet. The point where you cross the stream is not distinct and on my first hike here, my hiking partner and I spent about 20 minutes trying to find the trail on the opposite bank. There is a good landmark to tell you where to cross. Almost at the point where the trail reaches the stream there are a few very large rocks that lie across the stream bed almost

Indian Stairway

like a dam. If you cross at this point, you will find the continuation of the trail just downstream from there.

Then the trail climbs easily up the side of the hollow returning to the side of the Gladie Creek Gorge. Hanging on the side of the gorge for about three quarters of a mile, the trail then swings left into the Garret Branch side hollow. Retreating quite a distance into this beautiful hollow, the forest here has a feeling of being primeval. You do not have a long descent down to the stream as you did at Klaber Branch, but there is one brief uphill section of a few feet just after the crossing. This leads you into a rock garden for a few yards. Walking back towards Gladie Creek Gorge, you have one section that goes rather steeply down to Salt Fork. The trail crosses it just a few feet away from where that stream enters into Gladie Creek. A dry crossing can be difficult if there has been a continued rainy spell.

After the beautiful unspoiled walk, entering this area can often offer an unpleasant contrast, for the surroundings are often trashed up. The end of the gravel road is just across the stream, making this location one of easy access for drinking parties. Once across the stream, go up the little rise to the left where you will find the end of the forest service road.

RIDGETOP HIKE TO INDIAN STAIRWAY

Despite the fact that this off-trail hike is not maintained, the path is distinct and quite easy to follow with little physical demands made on the hiker. It is a little over a mile to the stairway, and you should be able to walk it in roughly a half hour. Most of the way you follow the ridge top as it curves right, going around the head of the hollow cut by Sargent's Branch. In many places the trail is close to the cliff edge and the drop off is severe so don't let children run wild.

After taking the left fork from the junction near Indian Arch, you will find the trail fairly level with beautiful views down into the valley of Sargent's Branch. In about 20 minutes you leave the cliff area and you will find yourself on an old trace road. Look for a trail that leaves the trace road on the right and drops down into a small semi swampy area. There is an old fire ring right at this junction point. If you miss this turnoff, you will eventually walk into a large open field. Retrace your steps, keeping a sharp eye out for this trail turnoff.

After following this trail down to the boggy area, you cross it. The trail then swings right and will soon bring you to a large area with a sandstone floor. Walk across this stone outcropping to its far left edge, then turn right following the edge until you can see a place where you can drop down a couple of feet off the edge. After you are off the rock ledge, continue in the same direction which leads you into the large rock shelter.

To find Indian Stairway, return to the large sandstone area that you encountered before dropping into the recess cave.

There are lots of little paths going in many directions from this point and it is hard to tell which of them leads to Indian Stairway. The direction therefore has to be somewhat vague, but should suffice for anyone with some pathfinding ability. With the valley of Sargent's Branch to your right, keep the cliff edge on your right hand side and walk away from the rock shelter. Don't follow close to the cliff edge but walk, more or less parallel to it. In three or four minutes you should arrive at a small open area blighted by fire rings. Indian Stairway is just to the right of this small area. The stairway is easily seen from above, so if you come up to one of the cliff edges and you can't see the stairway immediately below, you are not at the stairway. Since this is a high cliff area, it is not necessary to get dangerously close to these drop-offs in locating the stairway.

If you are agile enough to negotiate the stairway and wish to return by a different route, you will find at the bottom of the stairs there is another drop which is not near as high as the stairway, but is more of a vertical one. It can be negotiated with hand holds of small trees and roots. Once you are at the bottom, it is an easy short walk on a rather faint path to a junction with the Sheltowee Trace. A right turn here takes you back up to Indian Arch. A left turn takes you into the valley of Gladie Creek.

INDIAN STAIRWAY FROM SARGENT'S BRANCH

Although it is not hard to follow, this is not an official trail and is not maintained so it is classified as an off trail hike. The scramble up Indian Stairway isn't for everyone, but if you think you may be agile enough, you can take this short walk to the bottom of the stairway and decide. If you feel that it is a little too risky, retrace your steps over the short trail back to Sheltowee Trace.

Once you find the narrow faint turnoff trail, you follow it uphill for a few minutes until you arrive at a ledge that is about ten feet above you. By hanging on a various trees and roots, pull yourself up to this ledge. Once up, walk a few feet beyond it and you will see Indian Stairway to the right.

There you can decide whether you want to proceed onto the large recess cave and return by taking the ridge loop trail. In that case, the stairway has to be negotiated to the top. If you have a tendency to panic in high places, you will be better off not going up the stairway.

If you go up and see the magnificent view and wish to see the rock shelter, you will find several little paths going in many directions. Follow one that goes to the left but does not come close to the cliff face. In a couple of minutes you should come to an open area with a large sandstone floor. Follow the left edge of this rock outcropping until you see a place to drop down a few feet. Once down, continue walking in the same direction which will take you into the cave.

To return via the ridge top walk, retrace your steps to the open sandstone area. Once on the sandstone surface, with the cliff area at your back and the direction of the stairway to your right, walk across the sandstone surface and look for a

Large recess cave near Indian Stairway

trail leading directly left away from the area of the cave. In a couple of minutes this trail angles left, dropping down to a small swampy area. Here you cross the little stream which is the one that drops over the lip of the shelter. After going directly across the swampy area, you have an easy short climb up to an old trace road. Turn left on the road which soon takes you out on the ridge with high cliffs on the left. This unofficial trail follows the ridge as it curves to the left and eventually junctions with the Sheltowee Trace near Indian Arch. Once you find the trace road, the walk should take you a little less than a half hour to the junction.

ROAD TRAIL TO RAVEN'S ROCK

Distance: 1.7 miles
Hike: MODERATE to STRENUOUS
Walking Time: 45 minutes to one hour one way

GENERAL REMARKS: For a discussion of the recent history of Raven's Rock, see page 47 . Since this high promotory sits smack in the middle of the lower Gorge of the Red River's North Fork, the views from the top offer the best panoramic scenery in the entire area. Recently acquired by the federal government, this addition, plus the cement bridge-Moonshiner's Arch area are the two most important land acquisitions made by the forest service in the Gorge area since the first publication of this book. At this writing there is no official trail to the top, so it must be rated as an off trail hike, but since a partially paved automobile toll road that goes to the top was used in a commercial venture until a few years ago, your path finding abilities needn't be any sharper than a shopping center adventurer in following the unofficial trail.

The distance too, would also put it in the classification of a possible hike for those whose walking abilities are just slightly above those of a Sunday stroller.

A challenging drop through the Roughs of the Red

But there is one staggering fact that places this walk in the realm of healthy conditioned hikers only—the climb. In just a little over a half mile, the trailroad raises you up approximately 500 feet.

This old road is now closed to all vehicular traffic. Those of you that have F.W.D. type vehicles and would like to drive this illegal trip anyway will find several washouts on the old road that are wide enough to be classified as gullies and are impassible for anything less than a tank. Another problem is the scarcity of adequate parking space. There is precious little of that along Route 77 and the road turnoff from the paved route where limited parking is possible is on private property. Since the available space is small and the home owners there need room for their own autos, one should be careful of possible places to leave autos. There is room enough for a car or two, so I asked the residents there how they felt about hikers leaving their vehicles parked alongside the narrow road adjacent to their property. Their reply was sensible and friendly. Don't park in such a way as to block passage of their lawns and most important, ask permission to park there. If people do not follow these sensible suggestions, I'm sure it will result in the area being restricted for any parking.

For those following Route 77 through Nada, the road turnoff is to the left a little over a mile and a half beyond the Nada Tunnel. For those following Route 77 in the opposite direction, this turnoff is on the right, just under a half mile after crossing the iron bridge.

TRAIL DESCRIPTION. The first mile of this hike is level and very easy, briefly following the left bank of the Red River's North Fork. Since the road itself has not been maintained for several years, the road is full of huge chuck holes, many of them as wide as the entire road. They often fill with water, causing deep puddles that last for days and sometimes weeks after rainy periods. Because of foliage along the road edges, skirting the puddles can sometimes be a problem for those who wish to keep their feet dry.

Just before the climb, the road turns to the left and you can see the beginning of the rise ahead of you. Although part of the old road proceeds straight ahead, the left turn uphill is easy to see. At this writing there are still signs alongside the road. One tells drivers to put their car in low gear. The other gives the fares for the trip. One dollar for adults, and 50 cents for the children.

Since the toll road has been closed for several years, the signs will eventually disappear. With a series of six curving auto switchbacks on the way to the top, the road is often fairly level between them. You might notice, as you catch your breath getting ready for the next uphill section, that the level parts of the road are gravel while the uphill sections are paved.

About two thirds of the way up, you will notice a large metal post in the ground with the road passing on either side of it. This was the location of the old toll booth. The last three switchback sections occur close to one another on the steepest part of the climb, but they are also very close to the top.

When you arrive at the top the view to the right is looking down the lower Gorge where both Auxier Ridge and Courthouse Rock are easily seen. The scene to the left is a view looking up the North Fork's lower gorge where the iron bridge, used in the gorge loop drive, is easily seen below you. There are iron railings at the better viewing locations, but since they are no longer being maintained, it would be best not to test their durability. No loop hike is possible here unless you're an experienced rock climber or happen to have brought along a parachute.

OFF TRAIL RIDGE WALK TO STARGAP ARCH AND BEYOND

Distance: To Stargap Arch: 1/3 mile
To end of ridge: 1½ miles
Hike: EASY
Walking Time: To Stargap Arch—15-20 minutes
To end of ridge—40 minutes to 1 hour

GENERAL REMARKS. Although this is officially an off trail hike, it is so easy to follow that only someone who is incapacitated or blind would experience any difficulty in following the trail. Although visible to visitors from Tunnel Ridge for years and easily accessible by foot, Stargap Arch was on privately owned ground. A recent land acquisition by the forest service included the arch and the right half of the major ridge from which it is appended. So now it is quite legal to walk out the ridge and not be trespassing. Although the trail that follows the ridge makes no great physical demands on any healthy walker, there are three things to consider before hiking out. First, the trail is unofficial so it is not maintained, and there are no signs. Second, if you decided to follow the side finger of the ridge that contains Stargap Arch, there is one testy place where a jump down and a return scramble up a ledge must be negotiated if one wants to go under the arch. This five foot drop isn't for everybody. You don't have to be an advanced rock climber to do it, and if you are used to easy scrambling, you will probably consider this obstacle a minor one. However, some walkers would have no trouble on the easy ridge top walk but might find the side trip down to the arch more than they would like to try. Third, this is a high cliff area. It is not as narrow as Auxier Ridge and no problem for the sensible, but potentially hazardous for the reckless. Several areas along this walk offer superb views down into the valley of the Middle Fork of the Red River, where often interesting rock promontories at the end of side ridges and parts of the Mountain Parkway are visible. The Nada Twin Arches, I'm told, are also visible from one of the ridge fingers, but I have never been able to locate them.

View along the North Fork in the upper Red River Gorge from the Douglas Trail

TRAIL DESCRIPTION. To find this trail head, go out Tunnel Ridge Road until you hit the turnoff that takes you to the parking lot for the Courthouse Rock and Auxier Ridge trails. From that point, check your speedometer. Stay on Tunnel Ridge Road about a half mile and you will see an F.W.D.-type road that goes up an embankment on the left. That is the beginning of this trail. There are no signs since this is an unofficial trail. You may also find it by following Tunnel Ridge Road past the turnoff to the Courthouse Rock parking lot until you arrive at the Stargap Arch View. After viewing the arch, turn around and go a very short distance to a small embankment on the right side of the road. An F.W.D.-type road begins at that point, which is the trail head. There is enough room to park a couple of cars alongside the gravel road. You follow this old F.W.D. road out the ridge.

If you wish to visit Stargap Arch, when you have been walking between eight and ten minutes, look for a well defined trail that goes off from the right side of the F.W.D. road. It leads you out a side ridge where, in another five minutes of walking, you should arrive at the top of the arch. To find the easiest way under the arch, turn around and while retracing your steps back, look for a small trail going to the left. It will soon lead you to a ledge where you must drop down about five feet before continuing on. Once the ledge drop is negotiated, a few yards of walking brings you under the arch.

If you wish to continue the scenic ridge walk, you will find the old F.W.D. road ends in another five minutes of hiking, but the trail beyond is distinct and easy to follow. Except for the crossing of one saddle where you must drop down over a rounded rock outcropping, the walk is relatively level. There are a few trails to the left which take you out on various ridge fingers, often giving you excellent views. But remember that the left side of the ridge is still private property so these side trails are not on government land. Not long after the trail gradually swings right, it ends where the gradient becomes steep on three sides. You should find the walk back to Tunnel Ridge Road as pleasant as the walk out.

THE DOUGLAS TRAIL

Distance: about 2 miles
Hike: MODERATE
Walking Time: 1¼ to 2 hours one way

GENERAL REMARKS. This marvelously scenic off trail route follows the north bank of the North Fork of the Red River upstream about two miles through the lower part of the Red River's upper gorge. Because of its rugged beauty and easy access, it has long been a favorite area for hiking and camping among college age young adults and local fishermen who have been angling along the stream banks for generations. Some of the more attractive sites for camping near the bank have lost their pristine loveliness from over use, abandoned trash and indiscriminate fire rings. None the less, these scars are not so intrusive as to ruin one of the most attractive walks in the entire area. It somewhat resembles the Swift Creek Trail in appearance, but with several distinct differences. Swift Creek is quite a bit smaller stream than the North Fork, and one will find the Swift Creek Trail is usually high above the stream with many strenuous up and down sections, while the Red River walk is mostly quite close to the stream and has no really difficult climbs or descents.

Although most of this two mile stretch of the north bank has been part of the national forest for many years, the entrance corridor to this section of the north bank and the parking lot next to the cement bridge were in private hands. Both the owner and the forest service knew this piece of real estate was a prime location for many outdoor activities and negotiations for purchase of this area went on for many years. For awhile the owner tried to charge a fee for parking and permission to cross his land, which was well within his legal rights to do. But tempers boiled over a few times when people who had used this access free for many years felt that they had a right to park and enter the area without charge. This resulted in a confrontation with firearms on at least one occasion. It was not until the late summer of 1985 that the land was acquired by the federal government, opening up legal access to this unofficial north bank trail. I feel that along with the acquisition of Raven's Rock, these are the two most significant land additions to the gorge area in the last 20 years.

Naming of this trail also was the result of another longer confrontation between opposing groups which reached national attention. During the 1960's a proposed Red River dam, which would have totally inundated the lower gorge, making the scenic drive along the boulder strewn river into a lake, came close to being a reality. In order to arouse public interest, groups opposing the dam got Supreme Court Justice William O. Douglas to visit the area and he hiked this trail, which now unofficially bears his name. When the Governor of Kentucky vetoed the dam project, people wrongly assumed that this ended the possibility of the dam being built forever. Unfortunately, it is still a remote possibility and there have been recent rumblings that the issue may surface again. I am not one who feels that all such dams are bad, and I have seen several, both in Kentucky and Ohio, where the positive factors of building such dams have slightly outweighed the negative. But the negative factors are always there and in the case of the North Fork of the Red River, they far outweigh the limited benefits. In my estimation, such a dam would be an unmitigated ecological disaster, wiping out the Lower Gorge canoe run and one of the prettiest sections of the auto loop trip. High water levels would inundate the slopes with mud slicks and leave deposits of collected trash and human offal along the lovely escarpment of the lower Gorge. Such a dam would be loaded with short term pork barrel political boondoggling, resulting in astronomical construction expenses paid out to annihilate a beautiful Kentucky area. The only long term

Two splash dams on the Red River's North Fork as seen from the Douglas Trail

positive benefit would be to offer some flood protection to Clay City, and this protection could be more easily accomplished at a fraction of the cost by building a flood control dam around the town.

Although there are a few places along the trail where one must scramble a bit, none of them present serious problems for any agile person. If the river level is not too high, you will be able to see one very interesting historical remnent of the old logging days—the foundations of two old splash dams. Since the destruction of a similar dam by natural forces along Swift Camp Creek in 1984, these dams are the only ones in the area that are close to a trail.

TRAIL DESCRIPTION. To find the trail head, follow the directions to Moonshiner's Arch given in the chapter on the Automobile Scenic Loop Drive found on page 45 . Since the trail is unofficial and there are many little side trails along the way, occasionally deciding on the right trail can be momentarily confusing. The best general idea is to follow the trail that is closest to the river. Sometimes a trail will lead to the river and end. When this occurs, just back up to the last trail junction and take the trail in the upstream direction that is not quite so close to the bank. Most of the time the river is frequently in sight, but there are some stretches where the river is not visible and the trail is fairly high above it for a few hundred yards. There are a couple of minor tributary stream crossings which are no trouble to negotiate except after torrential rains, before the trail comes to its end at Clifty Creek.

Federal property ownership ends at Clifty Creek, and the land on its opposite bank is posted with NO TRESPASSING signs. Clifty Creek is not hard to identify for even during extended dry spells, it is wide enough that crossing it without getting in the water is not easy. During periods of heavy rain, it is not crossable except by beavers. But the best part of the walk is before you reach this stream.

Beyond the creek, this shore walk is not near as scenic and is extremely difficult walking since there is no established trail and one is usually forced to trespass on a road used for timber operations. The opposite or south bank of this North Fork of the Red River is on federally owned land from the cement bridge upstream to Calaboose Creek about 1½ miles further upstream beyond Clifty Creek.

At one time, the forest service planned a trail to that point. Since the terrain on the south bank does not lend itself to easy trail construction, there was not enough government money budgeted for its construction. Someday it probably will be built. Eventually too, the private land on the north bank running from Clifty Creek to the Calaboose Falls will probably be acquired by the federal government. That would make possible an approximate six mile trail on either bank of the Red River in the upper gorge. This could occasionally be utilized as a loop trip when the water level of the river at the entrance to Calaboose Creek was low enough for a safe river crossing.

PROPOSED RAVEN'S ROCK TRAIL

GENERAL REMARKS. While having a friendly discussion with Don Fig a few years back about possible trail additions in the gorge area, we both agreed that it would be a very desirable addition if a trail could be built that would link the Double Arch-Courthouse Rock trail system at the extreme northwest corner of the gorge official paths to the Rock Bridge area at the extreme southeast corner. Since the 7.6 mile Swift Camp Creek Trail and the 8.5 mile Rough Trail already tie together, the missing link was between the end of the Martin's Branch section of Rough Trail at Ky. Route 77 and the Courthouse Rock area. Since the trail had to be entirely on federal land and much of the area between Courthouse Rock and the trail head at Highway 77 was in private hands, there was not much acreage to work in. I proposed that a trail be built from the highway up to the top of Tunnel Ridge and utilize Tunnel Ridge Road to the Courthouse Rock Trails. Don told me to scout it out and flag it and the trail could be built.

I discovered that in this vicinity there were extremely high cliffs between the bottom and top of Tunnel Ridge, and I never did find an easy route up that formidible wall. Then a major land acquisition around and including Raven's Rock changed the whole picture. By locating a trail starting at the bottom of Courthouse Rock, heading south through the valley of Fish Trap Branch between Auxier Ridge and Raven's Rock, a linking trail between the two areas could easily be accomplished without climbing any cliffs at all. This routing would also eliminate the road walking on top of Tunnel Ridge, and, with this three to four mile addition, a backpacker wishing to do an extended trip could hike over 20 continuous miles in one direction. In that distance the trail would only cross two paved and one forest service gravel road. Don then laid out and flagged such a trail to be known officially as the Raven's Rock Trail.

Since there were no government funds available for the trail construction, a volunteer group from a local college agreed to do the necessary labor during the early summer of 1985. The trail was then scheduled to open officially late that summer, which would have been plenty of time to include a description of the trail in this book. But, for some unexplained reason, the volunteer group never showed, so at this writing, it remains a proposed trail. If other volunteers should come forth, the trail could be a reality in a year or two. If you have a desire to hike his stretch, you can call the Stanton District Ranger Station during the regular work week to find out the trail's present status.

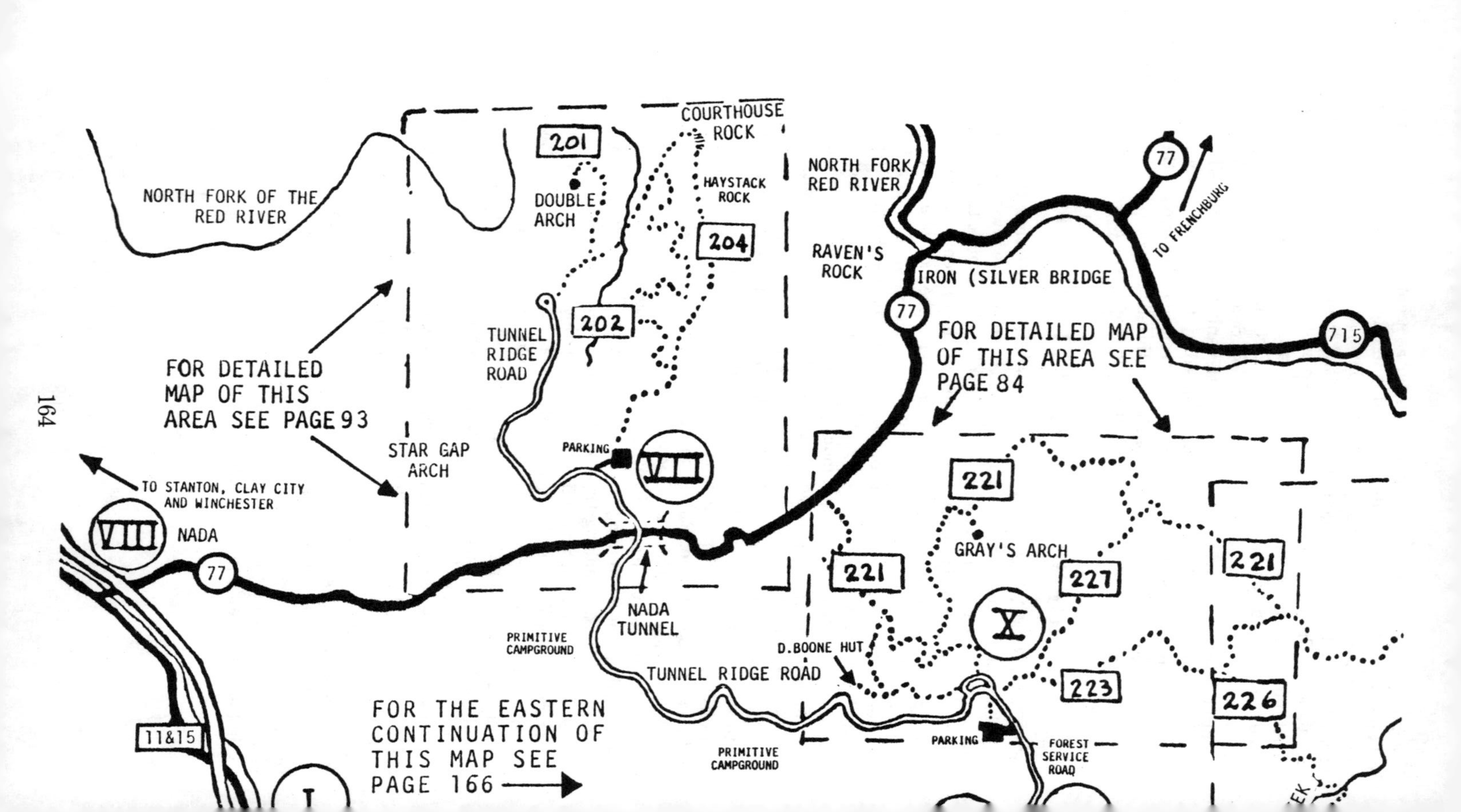

NORTH FORK OF THE
RED RIVER
201
DOUBLE
ARCH
COURTHOUSE
ROCK
HAYSTACK
ROCK
204
NORTH FORK
RED RIVER
77
TO FRENCHBURG
RAVEN'S
ROCK
IRON (SILVER BRIDGE
77
715
202
TUNNEL
RIDGE
ROAD
FOR DETAILED
MAP OF THIS
AREA SEE PAGE 93
FOR DETAILED MAP
OF THIS AREA SEE
PAGE 84
STAR GAP
ARCH
PARKING
VIII
TO STANTON, CLAY CITY
AND WINCHESTER
VIII
NADA
77
221
GRAY'S ARCH
221
227
221
X
NADA
TUNNEL
PRIMITIVE
CAMPGROUND
D.BOONE HUT
TUNNEL RIDGE ROAD
223
226
FOR THE EASTERN
CONTINUATION OF
THIS MAP SEE
PAGE 166
11&15
PARKING
FOREST
SERVICE
ROAD
PRIMITIVE
CAMPGROUND

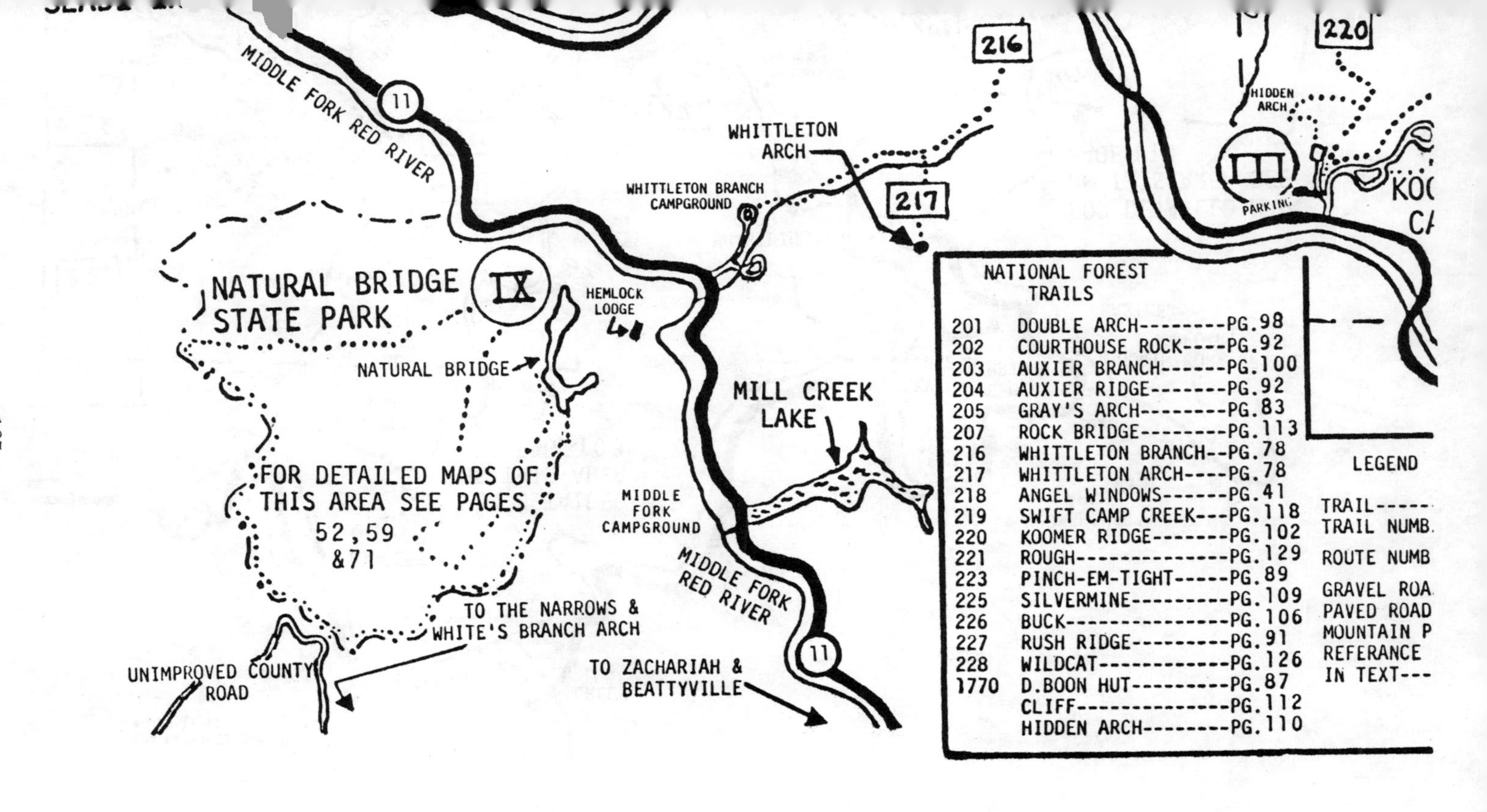

MIDDLE FORK RED RIVER
11
216
WHITTLETON ARCH
WHITTLETON BRANCH CAMPGROUND
217
220
HIDDEN ARCH
III
PARKING
NATURAL BRIDGE STATE PARK
IX
HEMLOCK LODGE
NATURAL BRIDGE
MILL CREEK LAKE
FOR DETAILED MAPS OF THIS AREA SEE PAGES 52,59 &71
MIDDLE FORK CAMPGROUND
MIDDLE FORK RED RIVER
TO THE NARROWS & WHITE'S BRANCH ARCH
UNIMPROVED COUNTY ROAD
TO ZACHARIAH & BEATTYVILLE
NATIONAL FOREST TRAILS
201 DOUBLE ARCH--------PG.98
202 COURTHOUSE ROCK----PG.92
203 AUXIER BRANCH------PG.100
204 AUXIER RIDGE-------PG.92
205 GRAY'S ARCH--------PG.83
207 ROCK BRIDGE--------PG.113
216 WHITTLETON BRANCH--PG.78
217 WHITTLETON ARCH----PG.78
218 ANGEL WINDOWS------PG.41
219 SWIFT CAMP CREEK---PG.118
220 KOOMER RIDGE-------PG.102
221 ROUGH--------------PG.129
223 PINCH-EM-TIGHT-----PG.89
225 SILVERMINE---------PG.109
226 BUCK---------------PG.106
227 RUSH RIDGE---------PG.91
228 WILDCAT------------PG.126
1770 D.BOON HUT---------PG.87
CLIFF--------------PG.112
HIDDEN ARCH--------PG.110
LEGEND
TRAIL-----
TRAIL NUMB.
ROUTE NUMB
GRAVEL ROA
PAVED ROAD
MOUNTAIN P
REFERANCE IN TEXT---

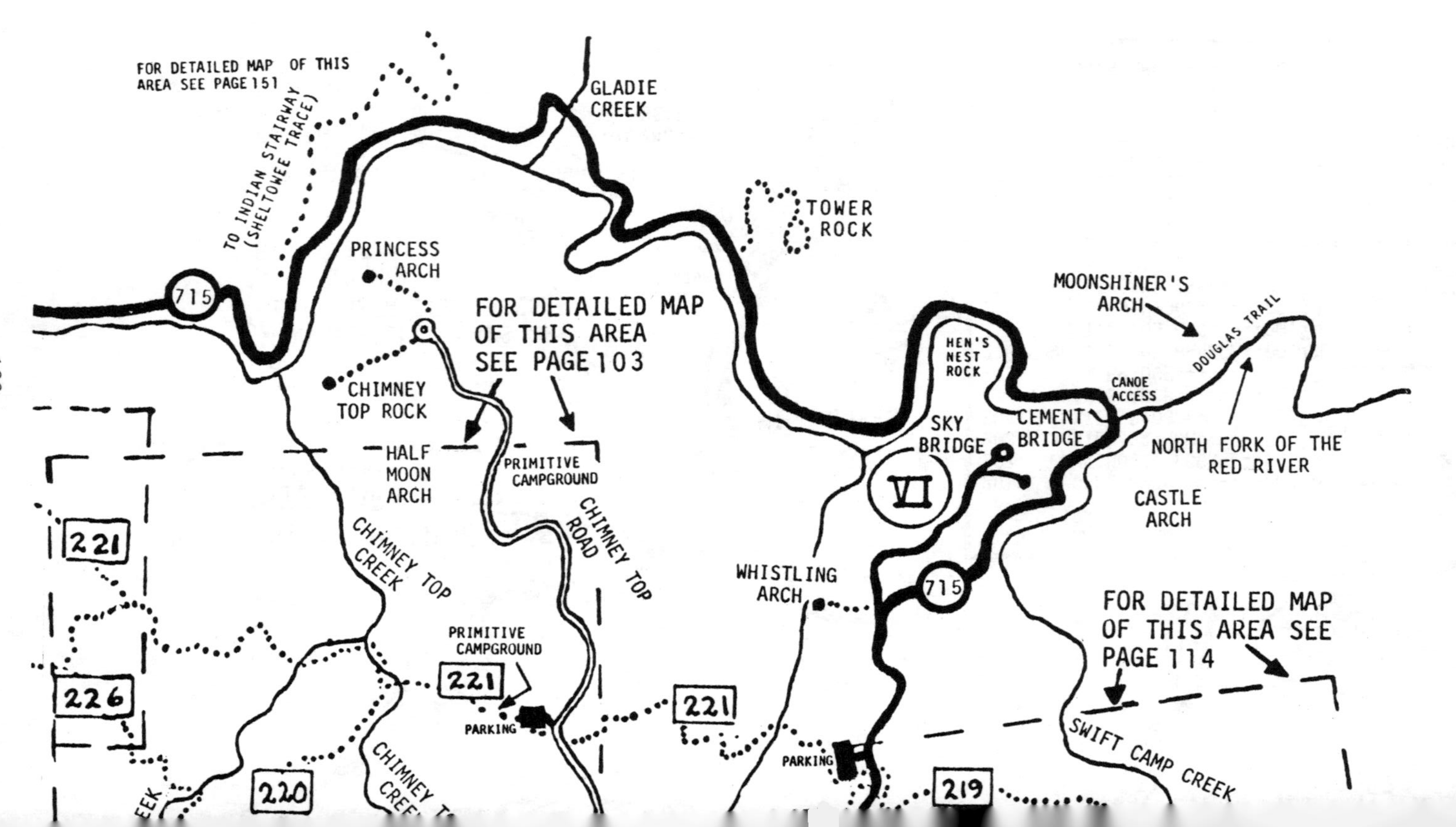
FOR DETAILED MAP OF THIS AREA SEE PAGE 151
TO INDIAN STAIRWAY (SHELTOWEE TRACE)
GLADIE CREEK
TOWER ROCK
715
PRINCESS ARCH
FOR DETAILED MAP OF THIS AREA SEE PAGE 103
CHIMNEY TOP ROCK
HALF MOON ARCH
PRIMITIVE CAMPGROUND
CHIMNEY TOP ROAD
CHIMNEY TOP CREEK
221
226
220
PRIMITIVE CAMPGROUND
221
PARKING
221
MOONSHINER'S ARCH
DOUGLAS TRAIL
HEN'S NEST ROCK
CANOE ACCESS
SKY BRIDGE
CEMENT BRIDGE
NORTH FORK OF THE RED RIVER
VI
CASTLE ARCH
WHISTLING ARCH
715
FOR DETAILED MAP OF THIS AREA SEE PAGE 114
SWIFT CAMP CREEK
PARKING
219

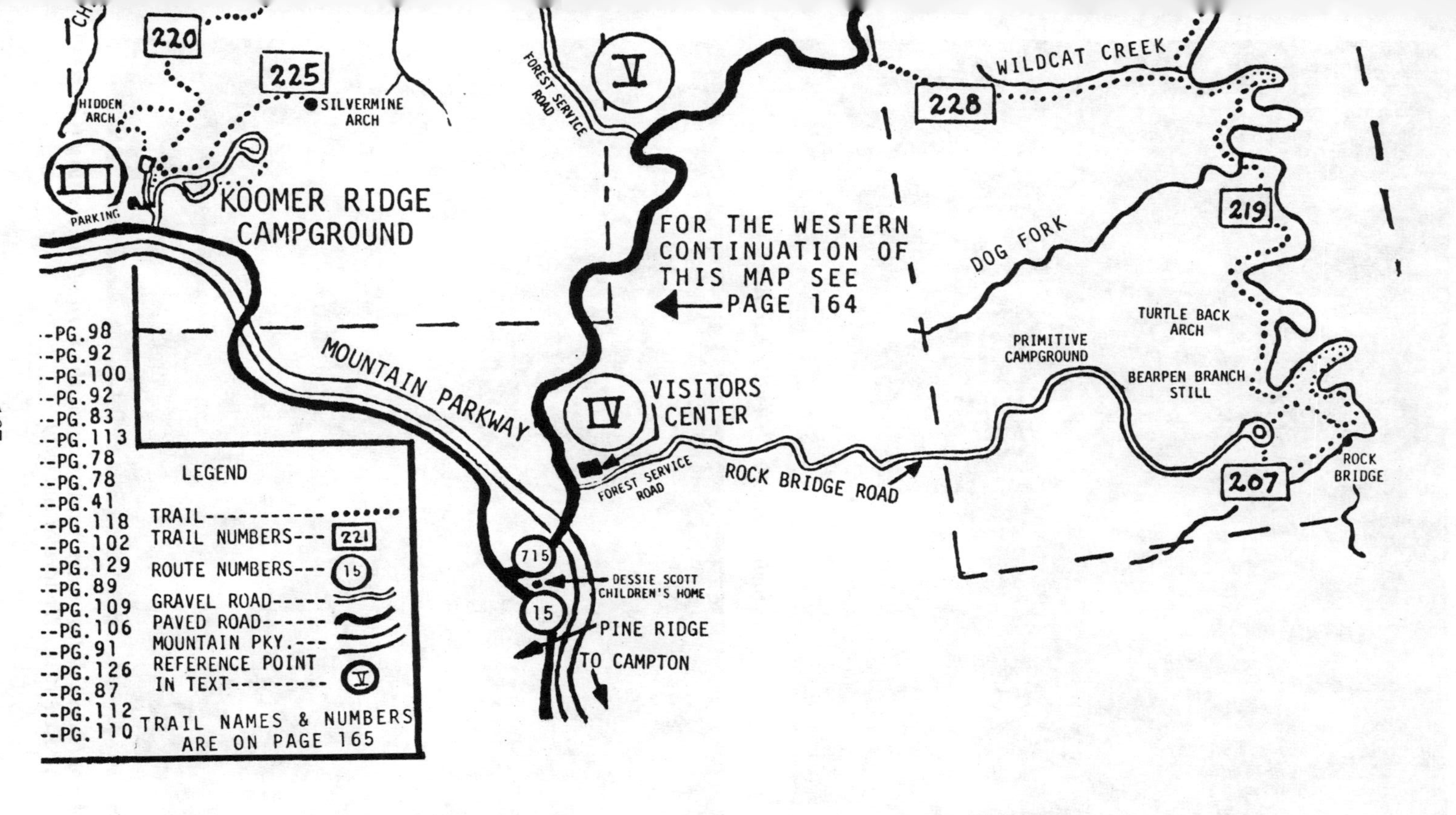
220
225
HIDDEN ARCH
SILVERMINE ARCH
III
PARKING
KOOMER RIDGE CAMPGROUND
FOREST SERVICE ROAD
V
228
WILDCAT CREEK
219
DOG FORK
FOR THE WESTERN CONTINUATION OF THIS MAP SEE PAGE 164
TURTLE BACK ARCH
PRIMITIVE CAMPGROUND
BEARPEN BRANCH STILL
MOUNTAIN PARKWAY
IV
VISITORS CENTER
FOREST SERVICE ROAD
ROCK BRIDGE ROAD
207
ROCK BRIDGE
715
DESSIE SCOTT CHILDREN'S HOME
15
PINE RIDGE
TO CAMPTON
--PG.98
--PG.92
--PG.100
--PG.92
--PG.83
--PG.113
--PG.78
--PG.78
--PG.41
--PG.118
--PG.102
--PG.129
--PG.89
--PG.109
--PG.106
--PG.91
--PG.126
--PG.87
--PG.112
--PG.110
LEGEND
TRAIL
TRAIL NUMBERS 221
ROUTE NUMBERS 15
GRAVEL ROAD
PAVED ROAD
MOUNTAIN PKY.
REFERENCE POINT IN TEXT V
TRAIL NAMES & NUMBERS ARE ON PAGE 165

Swift Creek's "Devil's Kitchen"

An old horse drawn tram railway about the turn of the century (Courtesy of the Red River Historical Society)